DEPARTMENT FOR EDUCATION AND SKILLS
NATIONAL ASSEMBLY FOR WALES
SCOTTISH EXECUTIVE
NORTHERN IRELAND DEPARTMENT OF EDUCATION
HIGHER EDUCATION STATISTICS AGENCY
NORTHERN IRELAND DEPARTMENT FOR EMPLOYMENT AND LEARNING

EDUCATION AND TRAINING STATISTICS FOR THE UNITED KINGDOM

2003 EDITION

Published with the permission of the Department for Education and Skills on behalf of the Controller of Her Majesty's Stationery Office.

© Crown copyright 2003

All rights reserved.

Copyright in the typographical arrangement and design is vested in the Crown. Applications for reproduction should be made in writing to the Copyright Unit, Her Majesty's Stationery Office, St Clements House, 2–16 Colegate, Norwich NR3 1BQ.

First published 2003

ISBN 0 11 271155 3

Contents

Introduction

This is the seventh edition of *Education and Training Statistics for the United Kingdom* and again provides an integrated overview of statistics on education and training in the UK. It largely follows the format of last year's volume; however, there have been a few changes in the 2003 volume:

- In Table 1.1 it is not possible to give education expenditure by function;

- HESA, 2001/02 higher education student data in Tables 3.6, 3.7, 3.9 and 3.12 are based on the July 'standard registration' count and are not directly comparable with previous data using the December 'annual snapshot' count;

- Table 3.10 is new, and gives a time-series of further and higher education students;

- The previous Table 3,15, covering Work-based learning for young people starts by sector, has been dropped, and has been replaced by former Table 3.10 covering participants in Work-based learning for young people programmes;

- It has not been possible to update the Work-based learning for young people data for England in Tables 3.13, 3.14 and 3.15;

- Table 4.4 now includes VCE A/AS and Double Award passes for young people, rather than Advanced GNVQs;

- Table 4.6 now covers success rates in LSC funded Work-based learning programmes;

- Table 4.7 has been updated to show progress towards selected national targets for England and for Wales;

- Table 5.1 now reports school leaver destinations for Wales, however the survey used is not classified as 'National Statistics';

International Chapter
The international chapter (Chapter 7) largely reports data available from the Organisation for Economic Co-operation and Development (OECD) publication *Education at a Glance 2003*.

Regional Analyses
Where regional analyses are given they are on the basis of Government Office Regions (GORs). These have been the primary classification for the presentation of regional statistics since April 1997.

Contributions
The efforts of the statistics teams in DfES, National Assembly for Wales, Scottish Executive, Northern Ireland Department of Education and Northern Ireland Department for Employment and Learning, who have contributed data for the volume, are again greatly appreciated. In DfES the people responsible for bringing all the data together and producing the 2003 volume were the UK and Local Statistics Dissemination Unit within Analytical Services and, in particular, Martin Johnson, Graham Devonshire and Dave Walton.

Chapter 1
Expenditure

CHAPTER 1: EXPENDITURE

Key Facts

- Expenditure on education services by central and local government in the UK in 2001-02 was £49.4 billion, including £2.8 billion directly on under fives, £29.1 billion on schools, £7.3 billion on further education and £6.0 billion on higher education. £32.9 billion was spent by local education authorities and £16.4 billion by central government. **(Table 1.1)**

- Expenditure on education services by central and local government in the UK in 2001-02 represented 4.9 per cent of Gross Domestic Product - the same proportion as in 1995-96. **(Table 1.2)**

- In 2001-02, identifiable expenditure on education services in the UK represented £841 per head of population, compared with £607 per head in 1995-96. Identifiable expenditure ranged from £816 per head in England to £1,048 per head in Northern Ireland. **(Table 1.3)**

CHAPTER 1: EXPENDITURE - LIST OF TABLES

EXPENDITURE

1.1

Education expenditure on services by function[1]

United Kingdom Financial year 1 April 2001-31 March 2002[2] £ million

	Local education authorities	Central government	Total		Local education authorities	Central government	Total
Under fives				**Student support (inc mandatory awards & access funds)**			
Total current[3]	2,707.7	114.7	2,822.4	Total current[3]	127.0	1,374.0	1,501.0
Total capital[4]	-	21.5	21.5	Total capital[4]	.	1.1	1.1
Total under fives	**2,707.7**	**136.2**	**2,843.9**	**Total student support**	**127.0**	**1,375.1**	**1,502.2**
				Miscellaneous educational services, research and administration			
Schools				Total current[3]	1,316.3	1,171.4	2,487.7
Total current[3]	25,573.3	1,472.1	27,045.4	Total capital[4]	179.9	50.6	230.6
Total capital[4]	1,862.0	147.4	2,009.4	**Total miscellaneous etc**	**1,496.3**	**1,222.0**	**2,718.3**
Total schools	**27,435.3**	**1,619.5**	**29,054.8**				
Further Education				**GRAND TOTALS**			
Total current[3]	1,062.6	5,747.9	6,810.4	Total current[3]	30,798.8	15,496.7	46,295.4
Total capital[4]	108.9	346.9	455.7	Total capital[4]	2,150.8	907.7	3,058.5
Total further education	**1,171.4**	**6,094.7**	**7,266.2**	**TOTAL Education Expenditure**	**32,949.6**	**16,404.4**	**49,353.9**
Higher Education							
Total current[3]	11.8	5,616.6	5,628.4				
Total capital[4]	.	340.2	340.2				
Total higher education	**11.8**	**5,956.8**	**5,968.6**				

Source: HM Treasury - Public Expenditure Statistical Analysis

1 Expenditure on services is a definition of aggregate public spending consistent with Total Managed Expenditure (TME), where TME is a measure of public sector expenditure drawn from components in national accounts produced by the Office for National Statistics (ONS). It is the consolidated sum of current and capital expenditure of central and local government, and public corporations, but excludes net public service pension payments in Annually Managed Expenditure (AME), debt interest payments and other accounting adjustments.

2 Provisional.

3 Including general administrative expenses and purchases of goods and services which are not of a capital nature.

4 Comprising expenditure on new construction, the purchase of land, buildings and other physical assets, less the proceeds from sales of similar assets and the value of net changes in the level of stocks. Also includes grants to the private sector, nationalised industries and other public corporations.

1.2

EXPENDITURE
Summary of expenditure on education services[1] - time series

United Kingdom		Financial Year 1 April to 31 March		£ million
	1995-96	1999-00[2]	2000-01[2]	2001-02
Local education authorities				
Current	23,962	26,207	27,997	30,799
Capital	1,202	1,510	1,810	2,151
Total	**25,165**	**27,718**	**29,807**	**32,950**
Central Government				
Current	9,703	12,894	13,770	15,497
Capital	706	283	599	908
Total	**10,408**	**13,177**	**14,369**	**16,404**
All public authorities				
Current	33,665	39,101	41,767	46,295
Capital	1,908	1,793	2,409	3,058
Total	**35,573**	**40,895**	**44,176**	**49,354**
Gross Domestic Product (GDP, cash)[3]	729,389	919,696	963,508	1,006,043
Education expenditure as a percentage of GDP	**4.9**	**4.4**	**4.6**	**4.9**
GDP deflator[3]	86.231	95.852	97.504	100.000
GDP in real terms[4]	845,850	959,495	988,175	1,006,043
Total education expenditure in real terms[4]	**41,253**	**42,664**	**45,307**	**49,354**

Sources: HM Treasury - Public Expenditure Statistical Analysis; Office for National Statistics

1   Expenditure on services is a definition of aggregate public spending consistent with Total Managed Expenditure (TME), where TME is a measure of public sector expenditure drawn from components in national accounts produced by the Office for National Statistics (ONS). It is the consolidated sum of current and capital expenditure of central and local government, and public corporations, but excludes net public service pension payments in Annually Managed Expenditure (AME), debt interest payments and other accounting adjustments.

2   Includes revised data.

3   Source: Office for National Statistics - September 2003 National Accounts release.

4   At 2001-02 prices.

1.3 EXPENDITURE
Identifiable[1] expenditure on education services[2] by country — time series

	Financial Year 1 April to 31 March			cash £ million
	1995-96	1999-00[3]	2000-01[3]	2001-02
By country				
England	28,314	32,975	35,780	40,107
Scotland	4,075	4,293	4,451	4,992
Wales	1,799	2,026	2,215	2,587
Northern Ireland	1,377	1,593	1,716	1,771
United Kingdom	**35,565**	**40,887**	**44,162**	**49,457**
				£ per head[4]
By country				
England	579	663	716	816
Scotland	793	839	880	986
Wales	617	690	752	891
Northern Ireland	832	949	1,019	1,048
United Kingdom	**607**	**687**	**740**	**841**

Sources: HM Treasury - Public Expenditure Statistical Analysis

1 A small amount of expenditure cannot be disaggregated to individual country level. Therefore, the figures in this table are slightly different from those shown in Table 1.2.

2 Expenditure on services is a definition of aggregate public spending consistent with Total Managed Expenditure (TME), where TME is a measure of public sector expenditure drawn from components in national accounts produced by the Office for National Statistics (ONS). It is the consolidated sum of current and capital expenditure of central and local government, and public corporations, but excludes net public service pension payments in Annually Managed Expenditure (AME), debt interest payments and other accounting adjustments.

3 Includes revised data.

4 Comparisons of expenditure per head between countries should be made with caution e.g. different countries have different proportions of young people within their population.

Chapter 2
Schools

CHAPTER 2: SCHOOLS

Key Facts

- There were 10.1 million full-time and part-time pupils in 34.6 thousand schools in 2002/03, compared with 9.3 million pupils in 34.6 thousand schools in 1990/91. **(Tables 2.1, 2.2, 2.3)**

- There were 296.9 thousand full-time and part-time pupils with statements of Special Educational Needs (SEN) in 2002/03, representing 2.9% of all pupils, with 63% of SEN pupils with statements being educated in mainstream schools. **(Table 2.4)**

- There were 507.3 thousand full-time qualified teachers in the United Kingdom in 2001/02, of which over two-thirds were female. Eighty-six per cent of full-time teachers were employed in maintained nursery, primary and secondary schools. **(Table 2.5)**

- There were, on average 43 pupils per maintained mainstream nursery school in 2002/03, 229 pupils per primary school and 933 pupils per secondary school. **(Table 2.6)**

- The average class size in primary schools in the United Kingdom in 2002/03 was 26.0 pupils. The average class size in secondary schools in England and Wales was 21.9 pupils. **(Table 2.7)**

- The average size of one-teacher classes in primary and secondary schools in England in 2002/03 was 26.3 pupils and 21.9 pupils respectively. **(Table 2.7)**

- The average pupil/teacher ratio in nursery schools in 2002/03 was 23.6. In primary schools the ratio was 22.0 and in secondary schools it was 16.4. The average pupil/teacher ratio for all schools was 17.6 compared to 17.3 in 1990/91. **(Table 2.8)**

- 70% of boys and 80% of girls in England achieved Level 4 or above in the 2003 Key Stage 2 English test. 74% of boys and 84% of girls in Wales achieved Level 4 or above. **(Table 2.9)**

- 73% of boys and 72% of girls in England achieved Level 4 or above in the 2003 Key Stage 2 Maths test. 74% of boys and 76% of girls in Wales achieved Level 4 or above. **(Table 2.9)**

- In 2002/03, 14.3% of pupils in maintained nursery & primary schools were taking free school meals, compared with 14.0% in 1990/91. In maintained secondary schools, in 2002/03, 14.9% of pupils were known to be eligible for free school meals, but only 10.8% of pupils were taking free school meals. The proportion of pupils in maintained special schools taking free school meals was 31.4%. **(Table 2.10)**

CHAPTER 2: SCHOOLS - LIST OF TABLES

2.1 SCHOOLS
Number of schools, by type of school – time series

United Kingdom   Numbers

	Academic years				
	1990/91	1995/96	2000/01	2001/02[1]	2002/03
UNITED KINGDOM					
Public sector mainstream					
Nursery[2]	1,364	1,486	3,228	3,227	3,394
Primary	24,135	23,441	22,902	22,800	22,638
Secondary[3]	4,790	4,463	4,337	4,306	4,284
of which					
middle deemed secondary	491	400	316	300	294
modern	171	113	145	130	130
Grammar	222	231	231	232	234
Technical	3	1	3	3	2
Comprehensive	3,696	3,509	3,443	3,450	3,436
of which 6th form colleges	116				
Other	207	209	199	191	188
of which Specialist schools[4]	.	107	536	685	992
Non-maintained mainstream	2,508	2,436	2,414	2,409	2,380
Special - maintained }		1,456	1,401	1,387	1,367
}	1,830				
- non maintained }		109	97	96	104
Pupil referral units	.	315	338	340	389
ALL SCHOOLS	34,627	33,706	34,717	34,565	34,556
ENGLAND					
Public sector mainstream					
Nursery	566	547	506	494	475
Primary	19,047	18,480	18,069	17,985	17,861
Secondary[3]	3,897	3,594	3,481	3,457	3,436
of which					
middle deemed secondary	491	400	316	300	294
modern	171	113	145	130	130
Grammar	152	160	159	161	163
Technical	3	1	3	3	2
Comprehensive	3,042	2,876	2,825	2,836	2,823
of which 6th form colleges	114				
Other	38	44	33	27	24
of which Specialist schools[4]	.	107	536	685	992
Non-maintained mainstream	2,289	2,266	2,205	2,206	2,180
Special - maintained }		1,191	1,113	1,098	1,088
}	1,380				
- non maintained }		72	62	63	72
Pupil referral units	.	291	308	312	360
ALL SCHOOLS	27,179	26,441	25,744	25,615	25,472
WALES					
Public sector mainstream					
Nursery	54	52	41	40	37
Primary	1,717	1,681	1,631	1,624	1,602
Secondary[3,5]	230	228	229	227	227
of which 6th form colleges	2	.	.	.	.
Non-maintained mainstream	71	62	54	56	59
Special (maintained)	61	54	45	44	43
Pupil referral units	.	24	30	28	29
ALL SCHOOLS	2,133	2,101	2,030	2,019	1,997
SCOTLAND					
Public sector mainstream					
Nursery[2]	659	796	2,586	2,597	2,782
Primary	2,372	2,332	2,278	2,271	2,258
Secondary[5]	424	405	389	387	386
Non-maintained mainstream	131	87	129	122	119
Special - maintained	343	164	195	197	189
- non maintained	.	37	35	33	32
ALL SCHOOLS	3,929	3,821	5,612	5,607	5,766
NORTHERN IRELAND					
Grant aided mainstream					
Nursery[6]	85	91	95	96	100
Primary[7]	999	948	924	920	917
Secondary	239	236	238	235	235
of which					
Grammar	70	71	72	71	71
Other (Secondary intermediate)	169	165	166	164	164
Non-maintained mainstream	17	21	26	25	22
Special (maintained)	46	47	48	48	47
ALL SCHOOLS	1,386	1,343	1,331	1,324	1,321

Sources: Department for Education and Skills; National Assembly for Wales; Scottish Executive; Northern Ireland Department of Education

1   Revised to include 2001/02 nursery schools data for Scotland.
2   Nursery schools figures for Scotland prior to 1998/99 only include data for Local Authority pre-schools. Data thereafter include partnership pre-schools.
3   From 1993/94, excludes sixth form colleges in England and Wales which were reclassified as further education colleges on 1 April 1993.
4   Operational from September of the first year shown.
5   All secondary schools are classed as Comprehensive.
6   Excludes voluntary and private pre-school education centres (363 in total in 2002/03).
7   From 1995/96, includes Preparatory Departments in Grammar Schools (20 in total in 2002/03).

SCHOOLS
Full-time and part-time pupils by age[1], gender[2] and school type, 2002/03[3]

United Kingdom   Thousands

| | Maintained schools[4] | | | | | | | | Non-maintained | | | All schools |
	Nursery Schools[5,6]	Nursery Classes	Other Classes[7]	Total Primary Schools	Secondary Schools	Special schools	Pupil Referral Units[8]	All maintained schools	Special schools	Other Schools[9]	All non-maintained schools	
		Primary Schools										
Age at 31 August 2002[10]												
All												
2–4[11]	153.9	323.1	633.2	956.3	0.1	6.4	-	1,116.7	0.1	71.8	71.9	1,188.6
5	-	-	697.3	697.3	.	4.3	-	701.7	0.1	33.4	33.5	735.2
6	-	-	684.4	684.4	.	4.5	0.1	689.1	0.1	33.0	33.1	722.2
7	-	-	693.8	693.8	0.1	5.2	0.1	699.2	0.1	35.2	35.3	734.5
8	-	-	709.1	709.1	0.1	6.1	0.1	715.5	0.2	37.9	38.1	753.5
9	-	-	683.3	683.3	27.7	6.9	0.2	718.1	0.2	38.6	38.9	756.9
10	-	-	703.3	703.3	33.6	7.8	0.3	745.0	0.3	41.3	41.7	786.6
11	-	-	49.5	49.5	678.4	9.9	0.3	738.1	0.5	52.3	52.8	790.9
12	-	-	0.4	0.4	718.9	10.7	0.8	730.8	0.6	52.8	53.5	784.2
13	-	-	-	-	707.9	11.2	1.6	720.7	0.7	52.1	52.8	773.5
14	-	-	-	-	716.4	11.8	2.9	731.1	0.9	52.9	53.8	784.8
15	-	-	-	-	682.0	11.5	5.8	699.4	0.9	50.9	51.8	751.2
16	-	-	-	-	242.7	4.0	0.1	246.8	0.4	43.2	43.6	290.5
17	-	-	-	-	173.5	3.1	-	176.6	0.4	40.1	40.5	217.1
18	-	-	-	-	12.5	2.0	-	14.6	0.2	5.6	5.8	20.3
19 and over	-	-	-	-	1.0	-	-	1.0	0.1	2.3	2.5	3.5
Total[12]	**153.9**	**323.1**	**4,855.1**	**5,178.2**	**3,995.0**	**105.6**	**12.4**	**9,445.2**	**5.9**	**643.5**	**649.5**	**10,094.6**
of which												
England	40.5	291.3	4,017.7	4,309.0	3,308.0	88.9	12.0	7,758.5	4.9	603.3	608.3	8,366.8
Wales	2.1	24.0	254.7	278.7	214.3	3.8	0.4	499.3	.	9.8	9.8	509.2
Scotland[6]	105.1	-	413.7	413.7	316.9	8.0	.	843.7	1.0	29.4	30.4	874.0
Northern Ireland[5]	6.3	7.8	169.0	176.8	155.7	4.9	.	343.7	.	0.9	0.9	344.6
Males[2]												
2–4[11]	25.4	164.6	323.5	488.1	-	4.2	-	517.8	-	35.5	35.5	553.3
5	-	-	356.4	356.4	-	3.0	-	359.5	-	16.8	16.8	376.3
6	-	-	350.7	350.7	-	3.1	-	353.9	0.1	16.7	16.7	370.6
7	-	-	354.7	354.7	0.1	3.6	0.1	358.4	0.1	17.7	17.8	376.2
8	-	-	361.7	361.7	0.1	4.3	0.1	366.2	0.1	19.3	19.4	385.6
9	-	-	348.4	348.4	14.1	4.9	0.2	367.5	0.2	19.7	19.9	387.3
10	-	-	358.5	358.5	17.1	5.5	0.3	381.4	0.3	21.2	21.5	402.9
11	-	-	25.9	25.9	344.4	6.9	0.3	377.5	0.4	26.5	26.9	404.5
12	-	-	0.3	0.3	365.7	7.4	0.7	374.1	0.5	26.9	27.3	401.4
13	-	-	-	-	359.1	7.8	1.3	368.2	0.5	26.5	27.1	395.2
14	-	-	-	-	362.5	8.1	2.2	372.8	0.7	27.1	27.8	400.6
15	-	-	-	-	344.8	7.8	4.1	356.8	0.6	26.2	26.8	383.6
16	-	-	-	-	115.0	2.4	0.1	117.4	0.3	22.3	22.6	140.0
17	-	-	-	-	81.1	1.8	-	82.9	0.3	20.7	20.9	103.9
18	-	-	-	-	6.9	1.2	-	8.1	0.1	3.0	3.1	11.3
19 and over	-	-	-	-	0.5	-	-	0.5	0.1	1.4	1.4	2.0
Total	**25.4**	**164.6**	**2,480.1**	**2,644.7**	**2,011.3**	**72.1**	**9.3**	**4,762.9**	**4.2**	**327.6**	**331.7**	**5,094.6**
Females[2]												
2–4[11]	23.4	158.5	309.7	468.2	-	2.2	-	493.9	-	36.4	36.4	530.2
5	-	-	340.9	340.9	-	1.3	-	342.3	-	16.6	16.6	358.9
6	-	-	333.8	333.8	-	1.4	-	335.2	-	16.3	16.4	351.5
7	-	-	339.2	339.2	-	1.6	-	340.8	-	17.5	17.5	358.3
8	-	-	347.4	347.4	-	1.8	-	349.3	0.1	18.6	18.6	367.9
9	-	-	334.9	334.9	13.7	2.0	-	350.6	0.1	18.9	19.0	369.6
10	-	-	344.8	344.8	16.5	2.3	-	363.5	0.1	20.1	20.2	383.8
11	-	-	23.6	23.6	333.9	3.0	-	360.5	0.2	25.7	25.9	386.4
12	-	-	0.1	0.1	353.2	3.3	0.1	356.7	0.2	25.9	26.1	382.9
13	-	-	-	-	348.8	3.4	0.3	352.5	0.2	25.6	25.8	378.3
14	-	-	-	-	354.0	3.6	0.7	358.3	0.2	25.8	26.0	384.3
15	-	-	-	-	337.2	3.7	1.7	342.7	0.3	24.7	25.0	367.7
16	-	-	-	-	127.7	1.6	0.1	129.4	0.2	20.9	21.1	150.5
17	-	-	-	-	92.4	1.3	-	93.7	0.1	19.4	19.5	113.2
18	-	-	-	-	5.6	0.8	-	6.4	0.1	2.5	2.6	9.1
19 and over	-	-	-	-	0.5	-	-	0.5	0.1	1.0	1.1	1.5
Total	**23.5**	**158.5**	**2,374.3**	**2,532.8**	**1,983.7**	**33.4**	**3.1**	**4,576.4**	**1.8**	**315.9**	**317.7**	**4,894.1**

Sources: Department for Education and Skills; National Assembly for Wales; Scottish Executive; Northern Ireland Department of Education

1 Figures for Scotland are estimates of the stage rolls.
2 In Scotland gender split is not collected by age but has been estimated according to figures collected in September 2002. In Northern Ireland a gender split is not collected by age but is available by year group and so this is used as a proxy. For example pupils in Year 1 are counted as age 4, pupils in Year 2 are counted as age 5 etc.
3 Provisional.
4 Grant-aided schools in Northern Ireland.
5 Excludes 5,340 children at voluntary and private pre-school centres in Northern Ireland in places funded under the Pre-School Expansion Programme which began in 1998/99.
6 Nursery schools figures for Scotland include pre-school education centres. The "All" figures include nursery school pupils which cannot be split by gender.
7 Includes reception pupils in primary classes and, in Northern Ireland, pupils in preparatory departments of grammar schools.
8 England and Wales only. Figures exclude dually registered pupils.
9 Age 2–4 includes pupils less than 2 years of age in England.
10 1 July for Northern Ireland and 31 December for Scotland.
11 Includes the so-called rising five's (i.e. those pupils who became 5 during the autumn term).
12 Includes pupils with unrecorded gender and ages unknown for Wales and Scotland.

SCHOOLS
Full-time and part-time pupils by gender and school type - time series

United Kingdom   Thousands

| | Maintained Schools[1] | | | | | | | | Non-maintained | | | |
| | | Primary Schools | | | | | | | | | | |
	Nursery schools[2,3]	Nursery classes	Other classes[4]	Total Primary Schools	Secondary schools[5]	Special schools	Pupil Referral Units[6]	All maintained schools	Special schools	Other schools	All non-maintained schools	All schools
1990/91												
All	104.9	4,954.5		4,954.5	3,473.3	107.7	.	8,640.4	6.4	613.4	619.7	9,260.2
Males	54.0	2,529.4		2,529.4	1,753.6	70.6	.	4,407.7	4.2	323.8	328.0	4,735.6
Females	50.9	2,425.1		2,425.1	1,719.7	37.1	.	4,232.8	2.2	289.6	291.8	4,524.5
1995/96												
All	84.2	367.1	4,971.2	5,338.4	3,676.8	107.7	..	9,207.0	6.7	602.7	609.4	9,816.5
Males	43.4	188.2	2,536.9	2,725.1	1,853.0	71.6	..	4,693.2	4.6	314.4	319.0	5,012.2
Females	40.8	178.9	2,434.4	2,613.3	1,823.7	36.1	..	4,513.9	2.2	288.3	290.4	4,804.3
2000/01[7]												
All	152.2	30.3	4,413.7	5,297.7	3,916.9	107.7	9.7	9,484.2	5.7	626.1	631.8	10,116.0
Males	79.2	15.5	2,254.5	2,706.6	1,973.7	72.8	7.4	4,839.7	4.0	321.9	325.8	5,165.5
Females	73.1	14.9	2,159.3	2,591.0	1,943.2	34.9	2.4	4,644.6	1.8	304.2	305.9	4,950.5
2001/02[8]												
All[9]	149.5	330.0	4,915.5	5,245.5	3,949.3	106.4	10.4	9,461.1	5.7	635.0	640.7	10,101.8
Males	26.3	168.3	2,510.7	2,678.9	1,990.0	72.4	7.8	4,775.4	4.0	324.6	328.6	5,104.0
Females	24.4	161.8	2,404.8	2,566.6	1,959.3	34.0	2.6	4,586.9	1.7	310.4	312.1	4,899.0
2002/03[10]												
All[9]	153.9	323.1	4,855.1	5,178.2	3,995.0	105.6	12.4	9,445.2	5.9	643.5	649.5	10,094.6
Males	25.4	164.6	2,480.1	2,644.7	2,011.3	72.1	9.3	4,762.9	4.2	327.6	331.7	5,094.6
Females	23.5	158.5	2,374.3	2,532.8	1,983.7	33.4	3.1	4,576.4	1.8	315.9	317.7	4,894.1

Source: Department for Education and Skills; National Assembly for Wales; Scottish Executive; Northern Ireland Department of Education

1 Grant aided schools in Northern Ireland.
2 For 1990/91 and from 1999/00, nursery schools includes some nursery classes in primary schools for Scotland. From 1999/00 nursery schools figures for Scotland include pre-school education centres.
3 Includes children at voluntary and private pre-school centres (5,804 in 2002/03) in Northern Ireland in places funded under the Pre-School Expansion Programme which began in 1998/99.
4 Includes reception pupils in primary schools and, in Northern Ireland, pupils in preparatory departments of grammar schools.
5 From 1993/94 excludes sixth form colleges in England and Wales which were reclassified as Further Education colleges from 1 April 1993.
6 England and Wales only. Figures exclude dually registered pupils.
7 A spilt between nursery classes and other classes in primary schools is not available for 2–4 year olds in England. Figures are included in the Total Primary Schools column only.
8 Revised to include 2001/02 nursery schools data for Scotland.
9 Includes nursery schools figures for Scotland which cannot be split by gender.
10 Provisional.

SCHOOLS
Full-time and part-time pupils with Special Educational Needs (SEN)[1] by type of school, 2002/03[2]

United Kingdom   Thousands and percentages

	UK	England[3]	Wales	Scotland	N Ireland
ALL SCHOOLS					
Total Pupils	10,100.4	8,366.8	509.2	874.0	350.4
SEN pupils with statements	296.9	250.5	16.0	20.0	10.3
Incidence(%)[4]	*2.9*	*3.0*	*3.1*	*2.3*	*3.0*
MAINTAINED SCHOOLS[5]					
Nursery[6]					
Total Pupils	159.7	40.5	2.1	105.1	12.1
SEN pupils with statements	2.6	0.6	-	2.0	0.1
Incidence(%)[4]	*1.6*	*1.4*	*0.6*	*1.9*	*0.5*
Placement(%)[7]	*0.9*	*0.2*	*0.1*	*10.0*	*0.6*
Primary[8]					
Total Pupils	5,178.2	4,309.0	278.7	413.7	176.8
SEN pupils without statements	710.0	685.1	..	..	24.9
SEN pupils with statements	84.2	71.0	5.8	4.2	3.2
Pupils with statements - Incidence(%)[4]	*1.6*	*1.6*	*2.1*	*1.0*	*1.8*
Pupils with statements - Placement(%)[7]	*28.4*	*28.4*	*36.1*	*20.8*	*30.8*
Secondary					
Total Pupils	3,995.0	3,308.0	214.3	316.9	155.7
SEN pupils without statements	440.0	430.1	..	..	10.0
SEN pupils with statements	92.9	79.3	6.1	4.9	2.6
Pupils with statements - Incidence(%)[4]	*2.3*	*2.4*	*2.8*	*1.5*	*1.7*
Pupils with statements - Placement(%)[7]	*31.3*	*31.7*	*38.0*	*24.3*	*25.3*
Special[9,10]					
Total Pupils	105.6	88.9	3.8	8.0	4.9
SEN pupils with statements	101.7	85.8	3.7	7.7	4.5
Incidence(%)[4]	*96.3*	*96.5*	*98.5*	*96.6*	*91.8*
Placement(%)[7]	*34.3*	*34.2*	*23.3*	*38.6*	*43.3*
Pupil Referral Units[9,11]					
Total Pupils	12.4	12.0	0.4	.	.
SEN pupils with statements	2.1	2.0	0.1	.	.
Incidence(%)[4]	*17.0*	*16.8*	*25.5*	.	.
Placement(%)[7]	*0.7*	*0.8*	*0.7*	.	.
OTHER SCHOOLS					
Independent					
Total Pupils	643.5	603.3	9.8	29.4	0.9
SEN pupils with statements	7.6	7.0	0.3	0.3	..
Incidence(%)[4]	*1.2*	*1.2*	*3.0*	*1.0*	*..*
Placement(%)[7]	*2.6*	*2.8*	*1.9*	*1.4*	*..*
Non-maintained Special[9]					
Total Pupils	5.9	4.9	.	1.0	.
SEN pupils with statements	5.8	4.8	.	1.0	.
Incidence(%)[4]	*97.9*	*97.8*	.	*98.7*	.
Placement(%)[7]	*2.0*	*1.9*	.	*4.9*	.

Sources: Department for Education and Skills; National Assembly for Wales; Scottish Executive; Northern Ireland Department of Education

1 For Scotland, pupils with a Record of Needs including some who had an Individualised Educational Programme.
2 Provisional.
3 Includes new codes for recording SEN status following the introduction of a new SEN Code of Practice from January 2002. Data are not therefore directly comparable prior to 2001/02.
4 Incidence of pupils – the number of pupils with statements within each school type expressed as a proportion of the total number of pupils on roll in each school type.
5 Grant-Aided schools in Northern Ireland.
6 Includes pupils in Voluntary and Private Pre-School Centres in Northern Ireland funded under the Pre-School Expansion Programme which began in 1998/99.
7 Placement of pupils – the number of pupils with statements within each school type expressed as a proportion of the number of pupils with statements in all schools.
8 Includes nursery classes (except for Scotland, where they are included with Nursery schools) and reception classes in primary schools.
9 England and Wales figures exclude dually registered pupils.
10 Including general and hospital special schools.
11 England and Wales only.

2.5 SCHOOLS
Qualified teachers by type of school and gender – time series

(i) Full-time teachers
Thousands

	Public sector mainstream schools		Non-maintained mainstream schools	All Special schools	Total All Schools
	Nursery and Primary	Secondary[1]			
All teachers					
Great Britain					
1990/91	200.3	223.2	44.9	18.2	**486.6**
1995/96	203.3	212.2	48.6	16.6	**480.6**
1996/97	202.8	211.4	48.2	16.3	**478.7**
1997/98	201.3	209.8	49.1	16.0	**476.2**
United Kingdom					
1999/00[2]	211.1	223.0	51.2	16.6	**502.0**
2000/01[3,4,5]	211.5	225.3	52.3	16.6	**505.7**
2001/02[6]	211.6	226.6	52.8	16.3	**507.3**
of which:					
England & Wales[7]	181.5	194.2	50.2	13.5	**439.4**
Scotland	21.5	22.7	2.5	2.1	**48.8**
Northern Ireland	8.6	9.7	0.1	0.8	**19.1**
Males					
Great Britain					
1990/91	35.8	116.0	20.6	5.8	**178.2**
1995/96	33.8	103.4	21.1	5.3	**163.5**
1996/97	33.0	101.7	20.6	5.1	**160.4**
1997/98	31.9	99.4	20.7	5.0	**157.1**
United Kingdom					
1999/00[2]	32.6	102.9	21.1	5.0	**161.6**
2000/01[3,4,5]	32.1	102.8	21.3	5.0	**161.2**
2001/02[6]	31.9	102.4	21.5	4.9	**160.7**
of which:					
England & Wales[7]	28.9	87.8	20.5	4.3	**141.5**
Scotland	1.5	10.7	1.0	0.5	**13.6**
Northern Ireland	1.5	3.9	-	0.1	**5.6**
Females					
Great Britain					
1990/91	164.5	107.1	24.3	12.4	**308.4**
1995/96	169.5	108.8	27.4	11.3	**317.0**
1996/97	169.8	109.7	27.6	11.2	**318.3**
1997/98	169.3	110.3	28.5	11.0	**319.1**
United Kingdom					
1999/00[2]	178.5	120.1	30.2	11.6	**340.4**
2000/01[3,4,5]	179.4	122.5	30.9	11.6	**344.5**
2001/02[6]	179.7	124.2	31.2	11.5	**346.6**
of which:					
England & Wales[7]	152.6	106.4	29.7	9.2	**297.9**
Scotland	20.0	12.0	1.5	1.7	**35.2**
Northern Ireland	7.1	5.8	0.1	0.6	**13.6**

(ii) Full-time equivalent (FTE) of part-time teachers
Thousands

	Public sector mainstream schools		Non-maintained mainstream schools	All Special schools	Total All Schools
	Nursery and Primary	Secondary[1]			
All teachers					
Great Britain					
1990/91	..	..	..	..	**30.0**
1995/96	18.7	17.6	8.9	1.5	**46.7**
1996/97	17.8	15.7	9.4	1.4	**44.3**
1997/98	18.0	16.2	10.7	1.4	**46.4**
United Kingdom					
1999/00[2,3]	20.0	17.3	10.3	1.6	**49.2**
2000/01[3,4,5]	21.9	16.7	10.3	1.6	**50.4**
2001/02[6]	23.3	17.4	10.5	1.8	**53.0**

Sources: Department for Education and Skills; National Assembly for Wales; Scottish Executive; Northern Ireland Department of Education

1 From 1993/94 excludes sixth form colleges in England and Wales which were reclassified as further education colleges on 1 April 1993.
2 Includes 1998/99 data for Northern Ireland.
3 Includes revised data.
4 Includes 1999/00 nursery data for Scotland.
5 Includes 2001/02 data for Northern Ireland.
6 Provisional.
7 A gender breakdown of public sector teachers in England and Wales is only available from the Database of Teachers Records (DTR) where some in-service teachers may be shown as not in service because their service details are not recorded. A more complete coverage of teachers in England and Wales is available from the Form 618G survey, and published in "Statistics of Education: School workforce in England (including teachers pay for England and Wales)".

SCHOOLS

2.6

Schools, and pupils by size of school[1] and school type, 2002/03[2]

United Kingdom — (i) Number of schools — Numbers

	25 and under	26 to 50	51 to 100	101 to 200	201 to 300	301 to 400	401 to 600	601 to 800	801 to 1,000	1,001 to 1,500	1,501 and over	Total
United Kingdom												
Public sector mainstream												
Nursery[3,4]	1,527	985	989	254	2	-	-	-	-	-	-	**3,757**
Primary[5]	352	1,084	2,677	5,774	6,841	3,354	2,314	223	18	1	-	**22,638**
Secondary[6]	4	9	14	48	76	159	510	786	923	1,454	301	**4,284**
Pupil referral units	250	68	39	29	2	-	1	-	-	-	-	**389**
Non-maintained mainstream[7]	221	192	320	555	347	239	228	118	85	74	1	**2,380**
Special	161	322	617	342	27	2	-	-	-	-	-	**1,471**
All schools	**2,515**	**2,660**	**4,656**	**7,002**	**7,295**	**3,754**	**3,053**	**1,127**	**1,026**	**1,529**	**302**	**34,919**
England												
Public sector mainstream												
Nursery	4	52	289	129	1	-	-	-	-	-	-	**475**
Primary	80	556	1,875	4,460	5,827	2,847	2,016	186	14	-	-	**17,861**
Secondary	-	-	4	26	49	119	370	621	734	1,243	270	**3,436**
Pupil referral units	227	65	36	29	2	-	1	-	-	-	-	**360**
Non-maintained mainstream[7]	170	170	290	526	329	221	213	109	80	71	1	**2,180**
Special	63	243	532	301	19	2	-	-	-	-	-	**1,160**
All schools	**544**	**1,086**	**3,026**	**5,471**	**6,227**	**3,189**	**2,600**	**916**	**828**	**1,314**	**271**	**25,472**
Wales												
Public sector mainstream												
Nursery	3	13	19	2	-	-	-	-	-	-	-	**37**
Primary	54	165	265	514	403	133	64	4	-	-	-	**1,602**
Secondary	-	-	-	-	-	7	33	51	48	71	17	**227**
Pupil referral units	23	3	3	-	-	-	-	-	-	-	-	**29**
Non-maintained mainstream	19	6	8	9	4	5	4	4	-	-	-	**59**
Special	-	8	22	11	2	-	-	-	-	-	-	**43**
All schools	**99**	**195**	**317**	**536**	**409**	**145**	**101**	**59**	**48**	**71**	**17**	**1,997**
Scotland												
Public sector mainstream												
Nursery[3]	1,184	882	598	117	1	-	-	-	-	-	-	**2,782**
Primary	194	263	316	554	479	286	156	10	-	-	-	**2,258**
Secondary	4	9	9	10	8	12	47	66	98	113	10	**386**
Non-maintained mainstream	20	12	19	18	13	13	11	5	5	3	-	**119**
Special	93	66	46	13	3	-	-	-	-	-	-	**221**
All schools	**1,495**	**1,232**	**988**	**712**	**504**	**311**	**214**	**81**	**103**	**116**	**10**	**5,766**
Northern Ireland												
Grant aided mainstream												
Nursery[4]	336	38	83	6	-	-	-	-	-	-	-	**463**
Primary[5]	24	100	221	246	132	88	78	23	4	1	-	**917**
Secondary[6]	-	-	1	12	19	21	60	48	43	27	4	**235**
Non-maintained mainstream	12	4	3	2	1	-	-	-	-	-	-	**22**
Special	5	5	17	17	3	-	-	-	-	-	-	**47**
All schools	**377**	**147**	**325**	**283**	**155**	**109**	**138**	**71**	**47**	**28**	**4**	**1,684**

Sources: Department for Education and Skills; National Assembly for Wales; Scottish Executive; Northern Ireland Department of Education

1 School size on a pupil headcount basis.
2 Provisional.
3 Nursery schools figures for Scotland include pre-school education centres.
4 Northern Ireland figures include 363 Voluntary and Private Pre-School Centres including 5,804 pupils, funded under the Pre-School Expansion Programme which began in 1998/99.
5 Includes 20 preparatory departments attached to Grammar Schools in Northern Ireland.
6 Includes Voluntary Grammar Schools in Northern Ireland.
7 Includes City Technology Colleges and Academies.
8 Includes pupils in nursery classes in primary schools in Scotland.
9 Includes pupils in nursery classes and reception classes, except for Scotland - see footnote 8.

2.6 SCHOOLS

Schools, and pupils by size of school[1] and school type, 2002/03[2]

United Kingdom (ii) Number of pupils Thousands

	25 and under	26 to 50	51 to 100	101 to 200	201 to 300	301 to 400	401 to 600	601 to 800	801 to 1,000	1,001 to 1,500	1,501 and over	Total
United Kingdom												
Public sector mainstream												
Nursery[3,4,8]	22.6	36.1	69.2	31.4	0.5	-	-	-	-	-	-	**159.7**
Primary[5,9]	6.1	42.4	204.0	891.2	1,652.2	1,156.8	1,060.1	148.5	15.7	1.1	-	**5,178.2**
Secondary[6]	-	0.3	1.0	8.0	19.3	55.9	258.4	556.4	830.2	1,756.0	509.4	**3,995.0**
Pupil referral units	2.4	2.4	2.7	3.9	0.5	-	0.5	-	-	-	-	**12.4**
Non-maintained mainstream[7]	3.0	7.2	23.8	82.3	85.5	82.5	109.8	82.1	76.1	88.0	3.1	**643.5**
Special	2.1	12.5	45.3	44.9	6.0	0.7	-	-	-	-	-	**111.5**
All schools	**36.2**	**101.1**	**346.0**	**1,061.8**	**1,764.0**	**1,296.0**	**1,428.7**	**787.0**	**922.0**	**1,845.1**	**512.4**	**10,100.4**
England												
Public sector mainstream												
Nursery	0.1	2.1	21.8	16.2	0.2	-	-	-	-	-	-	**40.5**
Primary[9]	1.5	22.4	144.2	694.2	1,404.9	981.6	924.1	123.9	12.2	-	-	**4,309.0**
Secondary	-	-	0.3	4.5	12.2	41.8	188.3	439.2	661.2	1,504.4	456.2	**3,308.0**
Pupil referral units	2.3	2.3	2.5	3.9	0.5	-	0.5	-	-	-	-	**12.0**
Non-maintained mainstream[7]	2.3	6.4	21.7	78.1	81.2	76.3	102.5	75.8	71.6	84.4	3.1	**603.3**
Special	1.0	9.7	39.1	39.1	4.3	0.7	-	-	-	-	-	**93.9**
All schools	**7.2**	**43.0**	**229.7**	**836.0**	**1,503.3**	**1,100.4**	**1,215.3**	**638.8**	**745.0**	**1,588.7**	**459.3**	**8,366.8**
Wales												
Public sector mainstream												
Nursery	0.1	0.5	1.3	0.2	-	-	-	-	-	-	-	**2.1**
Primary[9]	1.0	6.3	19.9	77.3	96.9	45.5	29.0	2.7	-	-	-	**278.7**
Secondary	-	-	-	-	-	2.3	16.4	36.7	43.5	86.6	28.9	**214.3**
Pupil referral units	0.1	0.1	0.2	-	-	-	-	-	-	-	-	**0.4**
Non-maintained mainstream	0.3	0.2	0.5	1.3	1.0	1.7	2.0	2.8	-	-	-	**9.8**
Special	-	0.3	1.5	1.5	0.4	-	-	-	-	-	-	**3.8**
All schools	**1.5**	**7.4**	**23.5**	**80.3**	**98.4**	**49.6**	**47.4**	**42.2**	**43.5**	**86.6**	**28.9**	**509.2**
Scotland												
Public sector mainstream												
Nursery[3,8]	17.5	32.3	40.8	14.2	0.2	-	-	-	-	-	-	**105.1**
Primary	3.1	9.8	23.3	83.8	118.1	99.1	69.8	6.7	-	-	-	**413.7**
Secondary	-	0.3	0.7	1.5	2.0	4.4	24.0	46.5	87.0	133.4	17.2	**316.9**
Non-maintained mainstream	0.3	0.5	1.4	2.7	3.1	4.6	5.3	3.5	4.4	3.6	-	**29.4**
Special	1.0	2.3	3.3	1.8	0.6	-	-	-	-	-	-	**9.0**
All schools	**21.9**	**45.3**	**69.4**	**103.9**	**124.0**	**108.1**	**99.1**	**56.7**	**91.4**	**137.1**	**17.2**	**874.0**
Northern Ireland												
Grant aided mainstream												
Nursery[4]	5.0	1.2	5.2	0.8	-	-	-	-	-	-	-	**12.1**
Primary[5,9]	0.4	4.0	16.6	35.9	32.3	30.5	37.2	15.2	3.5	1.1	-	**176.8**
Secondary[6]	-	-	0.1	2.1	5.1	7.4	29.7	34.1	38.6	31.6	7.1	**155.7**
Non-maintained mainstream	0.2	0.1	0.2	0.3	0.2	-	-	-	-	-	-	**0.9**
Special	0.1	0.2	1.4	2.5	0.7	-	-	-	-	-	-	**4.9**
All schools	**5.7**	**5.5**	**23.3**	**41.6**	**38.3**	**38.0**	**66.9**	**49.3**	**42.1**	**32.7**	**7.1**	**350.4**

Sources: Department for Education and Skills; National Assembly for Wales; Scottish Executive; Northern Ireland Department of Education

See previous page for footnotes.

SCHOOLS
2.7
Average class size[1], by Government Office Region[2] - time series

United Kingdom

	One teacher classes		All classes[3]	
	Primary	Secondary[4]	Primary	Secondary[4]
1990/91				
Great Britain	..	..	26.4	21.0
North East	26.0	20.6	26.5	21.6
North West	27.1	20.4	27.5	21.1
Yorkshire and the Humber	25.9	20.5	26.4	21.2
East Midlands	26.1	20.1	26.5	20.9
West Midlands	26.3	20.6	26.8	21.1
Eastern	26.0	20.9	26.4	21.7
London	25.8	20.7	26.2	21.4
South East	26.7	20.7	27.1	21.4
South West	26.4	20.9	26.7	21.4
England	26.3	20.6	26.8	21.3
Wales	..	19.5	24.8	21.0
Scotland	..	..	24.7	18.5
1995/96				
Great Britain	..	..	27.1	21.6
North East	27.1	22.0	27.2	22.5
North West	27.7	21.8	28.0	22.0
Yorkshire and the Humber	27.6	21.9	27.9	22.1
East Midlands	27.6	21.6	27.8	21.9
West Midlands	27.3	21.8	27.6	22.0
Eastern	26.6	21.3	26.8	21.6
London	27.0	21.7	27.3	22.0
South East	27.3	21.4	27.4	21.6
South West	27.3	21.8	27.4	22.0
England	27.3	21.7	27.5	21.9
Wales	..	..	25.9	20.2
Scotland	..	..	24.8	19.5
2000/01				
United Kingdom	..	..	26.4	22.1 [5]
North East	25.8	22.1	25.9	22.2
North West	26.7	22.0	26.8	22.1
Yorkshire and the Humber	26.6	22.1	26.8	22.3
East Midlands	26.7	22.1	26.8	22.2
West Midlands	26.5	21.9	26.6	22.1
Eastern	26.4	21.8	26.5	22.0
London	27.0	22.1	27.2	22.2
South East	27.0	22.0	27.1	22.0
South West	26.7	22.2	26.8	22.3
England	26.7	22.0	26.8	22.1
Wales	..	..	24.8	21.3
Scotland	24.3	..	24.4	..
Northern Ireland	..	..	23.9 [6]	..

Source: Department for Education and Skills; National Assembly for Wales; Scottish Executive; Northern Ireland Department of Education

1 Maintained schools only.
2 Government Office Regions in England and each UK country.
3 Includes classes where more than one teacher may be present.
4 Figures throughout the table exclude sixth form colleges in England and Wales, which were reclassified as further education colleges from 1 April 1993.
5 England and Wales.
6 Excludes preparatory departments attached to Grammar schools, but includes reception pupils integrated into P1.
7 Provisional.

CONTINUED
SCHOOLS
Average class size[1], by Government Office Region[2] – time series

United Kingdom   Numbers

	One teacher classes		All classes[3]		
	Primary	Secondary[4]	Primary	Secondary[4]	
2001/02					
United Kingdom	..	..	26.0	21.9 [5]	
North East	25.3	21.8	25.4	22.0	
North West	26.1	21.8	26.3	21.9	
Yorkshire and the Humber	26.4	22.0	26.6	22.1	
East Midlands	26.3	22.1	26.4	22.1	
West Midlands	26.1	21.9	26.3	22.0	
Eastern	26.1	21.6	26.2	21.7	
London	26.9	22.1	27.1	22.2	
South East	26.4	21.8	26.5	21.8	
South West	26.2	22.1	26.3	22.2	
England	26.3	21.9	26.4	22.0	
Wales	..	..	24.4	21.2	
Scotland	24.2	..	24.3	..	
Northern Ireland	..	..	23.6 [6]	..	
2002/03[7]					
United Kingdom	..	..	26.0	21.9 [5]	
North East	25.2	21.8	25.4	21.8	
North West	26.1	21.8	26.2	21.8	
Yorkshire and the Humber	26.3	22.0	26.5	22.1	
East Midlands	26.3	21.9	26.4	22.0	
West Midlands	26.2	21.9	26.4	21.9	
Eastern	26.1	21.6	26.2	21.6	
London	26.9	21.9	27.0	22.1	
South East	26.4	21.8	26.5	21.8	
South West	26.2	22.3	26.2	22.3	
England	26.3	21.9	26.4	21.9	
Wales	..	..	24.4	20.5	
Scotland	24.0	..	24.0	..	
Northern Ireland	..	..	23.3 [6]	..	

Source: Department for Education and Skills; National Assembly for Wales; Scottish Executive; Northern Ireland Department of Education

See previous page for footnotes.

2.8 SCHOOLS
Pupil/teacher[1] ratios[2] by type of school and Government Office Region[3] – time series

United Kingdom

Numbers

	Public sector mainstream			Non-maintained mainstream schools	Pupil Referral Units	Special schools		All schools
	Nursery Schools	Primary Schools[4]	Secondary Schools[5]			Maintained	Non-maintained	
1990/91								
United Kingdom	21.6	22.0	15.2	10.7	.	5.9	..	17.3
North East	19.3	22.3	15.6	12.5	.	6.1	4.7	18.0
North West	19.3	22.8	15.4	12.6	.	5.7	5.0	18.1
Yorkshire and the Humber	18.1	21.9	15.5	11.6	.	5.8	4.7	17.6
East Midlands	19.1	22.4	15.2	10.5	.	5.7	5.4	17.5
West Midlands	24.0	22.4	15.5	10.6	.	6.3	3.9	17.7
Eastern	18.7	22.4	16.2	10.7	.	5.8	5.0	17.6
London	16.9	20.6	15.3	11.6	.	5.1	4.8	16.6
South East	18.1	22.8	16.2	9.9	.	7.0	4.8	17.0
South West	19.2	22.4	16.0	9.8	.	6.5	4.9	17.2
England	19.1	22.2	15.7	10.8	.	6.0	4.8	17.4
Wales	20.6	22.3	15.4	9.8	.	6.3	.	18.2
Scotland	25.7	19.5	12.2	10.5	.	4.5	..	15.2
Northern Ireland	24.7	22.9	14.7	11.0	.	6.9	.	18.1
1995/96[5]								
United Kingdom	21.3	22.7	16.1	10.3	..	6.3	.	18.0 [6]
North East	21.3	23.7	17.1	11.9	5.7	7.1	5.0	19.3
North West	20.0	23.7	16.6	11./	4.1	5.8	4.5	18.9
Yorkshire and the Humber	18.7	23.8	17.0	11.3	4.6	6.5	3.8	19.2
East Midlands	19.2	24.1	16.8	10.1	2.9	6.2	5.2	18.9
West Midlands	23.3	23.5	16.7	10.4	3.1	7.1	3.6	18.7
Eastern	19.3	22.7	16.5	10.1	4.3	6.6	4.1	17.9
London	16.4	21.6	15.8	10.8	5.2	5.5	5.5	17.0
South East	17.0	23.0	16.7	9.4	3.9	7.1	4.7	17.2
South West	20.4	23.6	17.1	9.4	4.1	6.9	4.9	18.2
England	19.2	23.2	16.6	10.2	4.3	6.7	4.6	18.2
Wales	19.5	22.5	16.0	10.1	..	6.7	.	18.7 [6]
Scotland	24.3	19.5	12.9	11.0	.	4.8	3.7	15.5
Northern Ireland	24.1	20.7	14.8	10.9	.	6.7	.	17.2
2000/01[5,7]								
United Kingdom	23.1	22.3	16.5	9.7	..	6.3	.	17.9 [6]
North East	19.9	22.6	17.0	11.4	4.4	7.1	5.0	18.6
North West	18.1	22.9	16.6	10.7	6.8	6.4	4.9	18.4
Yorkshire and the Humber	16.9	23.1	17.3	10.9	5.5	6.3	4.3	19.1
East Midlands	16.7	23.5	17.3	9.9	4.1	6.2	5.3	18.9
West Midlands	21.2	23.1	17.0	9.9	3.4	7.0	3.5	18.5
Eastern	17.0	22.8	17.4	9.3	2.8	6.9	5.2	18.1
London	16.4	22.5	16.6	10.4	4.7	6.0	5.5	17.5
South East	15.9	22.9	17.4	8.9	4.0	6.9	4.8	17.2
South West	17.5	23.0	17.5	9.0	4.6	6.4	5.3	18.0
England	17.7	22.9	17.1	9.7	4.4	6.6	4.8	18.1
Wales	17.3	21.5	16.6	9.6	..	6.8	.	18.4 [6]
Scotland[8]	28.5	19.0	13.0	10.1	.	4.2	3.3	15.4
Northern Ireland	24.4	20.1	14.5	9.3	.	5.9	.	16.6

Sources: Department for Education and Skills; National Assembly for Wales; Scottish Executive; Northern Ireland Department of Education

1 Qualified teachers only for all countries.
2 Includes full-time equivalents of part-time pupils and teachers.
3 Government Office Regions in England and each UK country.
4 Includes preparatory departments attached to grammar schools in Northern Ireland.
5 From 1993/94 excludes sixth form colleges in England and Wales which were reclassified as further education colleges from 1 April 1993.
6 Excludes Pupil Referral Units as information on teachers is not collected for Wales.
7 Includes revised data.
8 Nursery schools figures for Scotland include pre-school education centres and are not therefore directly comparable with figures prior to 1999/00.
9 Provisional. Includes 2001/02 primary and secondary schools data for Wales.

2.8

SCHOOLS

Pupil/teacher[1] ratios[2] by type of school and Government Office Region[3] – time series

United Kingdom

Numbers

	Public sector mainstream			Non-maintained mainstream schools	Pupil Referral Units	Special schools		All schools
	Nursery Schools	Primary Schools[4]	Secondary Schools[5]			Maintained	Non-maintained	
2001/02[5,7]								
United Kingdom	23.6	22.0	16.4	10.1	..	6.2	.	17.7 [6]
North East	18.7	22.0	16.6	11.8	5.1	7.1	5.1	18.2
North West	17.1	22.3	16.3	11.3	6.6	6.3	4.5	18.1
Yorkshire and the Humber	15.4	22.7	16.9	11.1	6.1	6.5	4.7	18.7
East Midlands	15.5	23.2	17.2	10.3	3.9	6.6	5.3	18.8
West Midlands	18.9	22.5	16.9	10.2	3.4	6.7	3.2	18.2
Eastern	15.8	22.7	17.5	10.1	2.5	6.9	5.6	18.2
London	15.6	22.4	16.6	10.7	4.8	6.0	5.4	17.5
South East	15.7	22.3	17.2	9.2	3.7	6.8	4.8	17.0
South West	17.0	22.4	17.3	9.4	4.0	6.3	5.3	17.8
England	16.6	22.5	16.9	10.1	4.4	6.5	4.8	18.0
Wales	16.4	21.0	16.4	9.7	..	6.7	.	18.1 [6]
Scotland[8]	29.8	18.9	12.9	10.0	.	4.0	3.2	15.4
Northern Ireland	24.4	19.8	14.4	8.2	.	5.9	.	16.4
2002/03[5,9]								
United Kingdom	23.6	22.0	16.4	9.7	..	6.1	.	17.6 [6]
North East	18.3	21.9	16.7	11.5	5.2	6.8	5.0	18.1
North West	16.2	22.3	16.4	10.8	6.4	6.2	4.7	18.0
Yorkshire and the Humber	16.7	22.7	16.9	10.7	4.9	6.4	4.4	18.6
East Midlands	16.0	23.1	17.2	10.2	4.4	6.6	5.2	18.6
West Midlands	18.8	22.5	17.0	9.7	3.4	6.6	3.7	18.1
Eastern	15.6	22.8	17.5	9.5	2.3	6.8	6.3	18.1
London	16.0	23.3	16.9	10.2	4.6	5.9	5.6	17.7
South East	14.6	22.4	17.3	8.8	3.5	6.8	4.9	16.9
South West	15.5	22.4	17.2	9.1	4.3	6.3	5.1	17.6
England	16.4	22.6	17.0	9.7	4.2	6.5	4.9	17.9
Wales	16.7	21.0	16.4	9.7	..	6.6	.	18.1 [6]
Scotland[8]	29.8	18.0	12.7	10.0	.	3.9	3.3	14.9
Northern Ireland	24.1	19.6	14.4	8.5	.	6.0	.	16.3

Sources: Department for Education and Skills; National Assembly for Wales; Scottish Executive; Northern Ireland Department of Education

See previous page for footnotes.

2.9 SCHOOLS
Proportion of pupils reaching or exceeding expected standards, by key stage, subject and gender – time series

England, Wales and Northern Ireland   Percentages

| | England | | | | Wales | | | | Northern Ireland | | | |
| | Tests | | Teacher assessment | | Tests | | Teacher assessment | | Tests | | Teacher assessment | |
	Boys	Girls	Boys	Girls	Boys	Girls	Boys	Girls	Boys	Girls	Boys	Girls
1996												
Key Stage 1[1]												
English	.	.	74	84	.	.	73	84	..	..	..	..
Reading	73	83	73	83	72	83	72	84	..	..	..	..
Writing	74	85	71	82	72	84	70	82	..	..	..	..
Maths	81	84	80	83	80	84	78	84	..	..	..	..
Science	.	.	83	85	.	.	81	85	..	..	..	..
Key Stage 2[2]												
English	50	65	53	68	48	65	53	68	..	..	..	..
Maths	54	54	58	62	56	56	60	64	..	..	..	..
Science	61	63	64	67	64	66	66	70	..	..	..	..
Key Stage 3[3]												
English	48	66	51	70	47	65	48	68	..	..	..	..
Maths	56	58	60	64	53	56	58	62	..	..	..	..
Science	57	56	59	61	55	55	57	60	..	..	..	..
1999												
Key Stage 1[1]												
English	.	.	78	87	.	.	76	87	.	.	92	96
Reading	78	86	78	86	75	86	76	86	..	..	..	..
Writing	78	88	75	85	76	87	73	85	..	..	..	..
Welsh	.	.	.	.	84	91	83	91	.	.	.	.
Reading	.	.	.	.	77	87	76	87	.	.	.	.
Writing	.	.	.	.	71	84	69	83	.	.	.	.
Maths	85	88	84	88	84	88	83	88	.	.	93	95
Science	.	.	85	88	.	.	84	88	.	.	.	.
Key Stage 2[2]												
English	65	76	62	74	63	74	61	73	.	.	64	75
Welsh	.	.	.	.	59	72	57	70	.	.	.	.
Maths	69	69	69	70	67	67	68	70	.	.	71	77
Science	79	78	75	76	77	77	75	76	.	.	.	.
Key Stage 3[3]												
English	55	73	55	73	54	70	54	71	58	77	65	80
Welsh	.	.	.	.	63	79	64	79	.	.	.	.
Maths	62	62	63	66	60	60	62	64	68	72	68	75
Science	55	55	59	62	55	55	59	60	63	68	67	73
2000												
Key Stage 1[1]												
English	.	.	80	88	.	.	77	88	.	.	92	97
Reading	79	88	80	88	77	87	77	87	..	..	..	..
Writing	80	89	77	87	78	88	75	87	..	..	..	..
Welsh	.	.	.	.	84	91	82	91	.	.	.	.
Reading	.	.	.	.	76	88	76	87	.	.	.	.
Writing	.	.	.	.	68	83	67	83	.	.	.	.
Maths	89	91	87	89	88	92	85	90	.	.	94	96
Science	.	.	87	89	.	.	86	90	.	.	.	.
Key Stage 2[2]												
English	70	79	65	76	67	80	63	76	.	.	66	77
Welsh	.	.	.	.	61	75	60	74	.	.	.	.
Maths	72	71	71	73	67	71	69	73	.	.	73	78
Science	84	85	78	80	79	82	76	80	.	.	.	.
Key Stage 3[3]												
English	55	73	56	73	51	68	54	72	59	79	65	81
Welsh	.	.	.	.	61	78	62	81	.	.	.	.
Maths	64	65	65	68	60	61	63	66	64	70	69	75
Science	61	58	60	63	60	58	60	62	64	69	67	74

Sources: Department for Education and Skills; National Assembly for Wales; Northern Ireland Department of Education

1 Percentage of pupils achieving level 2 or above.
2 Percentage of pupils achieving level 4 or above.
3 Percentage of pupils achieving level 5 or above.
4 Includes revised figures.
5 Key Stage 1, Key Stage 2 and Key Stage 3 Assessment results in Northern Ireland were affected by industrial action in that some schools did not submit their results.
6 From 2002, statutory assessment at the end of Key Stage 1 in Wales is by means of teacher assessment only, following the discontinuation of the National Curriculum tests/tasks.
7 Figures for England are provisional.

CONTINUED
SCHOOLS
Proportion of pupils reaching or exceeding expected standards, by key stage, subject and gender – time series

England, Wales and Northern Ireland   Percentages

	England				Wales				Northern Ireland			
	Tests		Teacher assessment		Tests		Teacher assessment		Tests		Teacher assessment	
	Boys	Girls	Boys	Girls	Boys	Girls	Boys	Girls	Boys	Girls	Boys	Girls
2001												
Key Stage 1[1]												
English	.	.	81	89	.	.	79	89	.	.	93	97
Reading	80	88	80	88	79	88	79	88	..	..	..	..
Writing	82	90	79	88	79	89	76	88	..	..	..	..
Welsh	.	.	.	.	82	91	82	91	.	.	.	.
Reading	.	.	.	.	75	85	74	85	.	.	.	.
Writing	.	.	.	.	69	83	68	82	.	.	.	.
Maths	90	92	87	90	90	93	87	91	.	.	94	96
Science	.	.	88	90	.	.	87	91	.	.	.	.
Key Stage 2[2]												
English	70	80	67	78	72	82	67	79	.	.	67	79
Welsh	.	.	.	.	65	78	63	77	.	.	.	.
Maths	71	70	73	74	73	76	73	77	.	.	73	79
Science	87	88	81	83	81	83	80	83	.	.	.	.
Key Stage 3[3]												
English	57	73	57	73	53	71	54	72	64	80	64	81
Welsh	.	.	.	.	63	79	63	78	.	.	.	.
Maths	65	67	67	70	60	63	63	67	67	71	68	75
Science	66	66	63	66	63	64	62	64	66	69	67	74
2002[4,5,6]												
Key Stage 1[1,6]												
English	.	.	81	89	.	.	79	88	.	.	92	97
Reading	81	88	81	88	.	.	78	86	..	..	..	..
Writing	82	90	79	88	.	.	76	86	..	..	..	..
Welsh	.	.	.	.	.	.	83	91	.	.	.	.
Reading	.	.	.	.	.	.	74	85	.	.	.	.
Writing	.	.	.	.	.	.	68	83	.	.	.	.
Maths	89	92	87	90	.	.	86	89	.	.	94	96
Science	.	.	88	91	.	.	87	90	.	.	.	.
Key Stage 2[2]												
English	70	79	67	78	75	84	71	81	.	.	68	80
Welsh	.	.	.	.	68	82	66	81	.	.	.	.
Maths	73	73	74	75	72	74	73	76	.	.	74	80
Science	86	87	82	83	85	87	82	85	.	.	.	.
Key Stage 3[3]												
English	59	76	59	75	53	70	56	73	65	80	67	81
Welsh	.	.	.	.	63	79	63	80	.	.	.	.
Maths	67	68	69	72	62	62	65	67	71	75	69	74
Science	67	67	66	69	67	67	65	68	67	69	69	74
2003[6]												
Key Stage 1[1,7]												
English	.	.	81	89	.	.	78	87	..	..	..	..
Reading	80	88	81	89	.	.	77	86	..	..	..	..
Writing	76	87	78	87	.	.	75	85	..	..	..	..
Welsh	.	.	.	.	.	.	82	91	.	.	.	.
Reading	.	.	.	.	.	.	75	85	.	.	.	.
Writing	.	.	.	.	.	.	70	82	.	.	.	.
Maths	89	91	87	90	.	.	85	89	.	.	.	.
Science	.	.	88	91	.	.	86	90	.	.	.	.
Key Stage 2[2]												
English	70	80	67	78	74	84	71	82	.	.	..	..
Welsh	.	.	.	.	72	83	70	81	.	.	.	.
Maths	73	72	74	75	74	76	75	78	.	.	..	..
Science	86	87	81	83	87	88	83	86	.	.	.	.
Key Stage 3[3]												
English	61	75	60	75	55	72	56	74	..	..	..	..
Welsh	.	.	.	.	66	81	65	81	.	.	.	.
Maths	69	72	70	74	67	69	67	71	..	..	..	..
Science	68	68	68	70	70	69	68	70	..	..	..	..

Sources: Department for Education and Skills; National Assembly for Wales; Northern Ireland Department of Education

See previous page for footnotes

2.10

SCHOOLS
School meal arrangements: time series

United Kingdom

Numbers and Percentages

	Maintained Nursery and Primary schools[1,2]			Maintained Secondary schools[1]			All Special schools[3]		
	Number on roll (thousands)	Percentage known to be eligible for free meals	Percentage taking free school meals[4]	Number on roll (thousands)	Percentage known to be eligible for free meals	Percentage taking free school meals[4]	Number on roll (thousands)	Percentage known to be eligible for free meals	Percentage taking free school meals[4]
1990/91									
United Kingdom[3]	**4,838.8**	..	**14.0**	**3,316.7**	..	**8.3**	**94.6**	..	**30.7**
England	4,099.6	..	13.7	2,848.2	..	8.3	83.0	..	28.1
Wales	280.6	17.6	17.1	185.2	13.4	9.8	3.7	44.1	45.1
Scotland	458.7	19.6	17.6	283.3	13.6	9.6	8.0	63.1	62.7
Northern Ireland	..	..	..	..	..	..	..	..	..
1995/96									
United Kingdom	**5,349.1**	..	**19.2**	**3,663.6**	..	**13.3**	**101.1**	..	**39.3**
England	4,441.6	..	18.7	3,006.9	..	13.3	89.8	..	37.2
Wales	285.0	25.9	24.0	198.5	20.0	16.1	3.6	55.1	52.5
Scotland	437.1	23.7	20.5	306.6	16.9	11.5	7.8	68.2	67.0
Northern Ireland	185.4	29.4	26.8	151.6	25.0	19.3	..	..	..
2000/01									
United Kingdom	**5,336.4**	**18.2**	**14.7**	**3,899.9**	**16.2**	**11.2**	**102.8**	**40.7**	**32.9**
North East	239.5	24.0	19.8	181.7	21.1	12.9	6.0	50.9	37.1
North West	663.6	21.7	17.6	461.8	20.3	14.5	15.2	46.4	36.7
Yorkshire and the Humber	485.2	18.3	14.9	339.3	17.2	11.1	7.8	41.3	34.4
East Midlands	382.2	13.6	11.0	289.6	12.6	8.6	5.9	35.6	30.0
West Midlands	507.1	19.1	15.6	369.3	17.4	11.9	12.6	38.9	32.8
East of England	464.0	12.4	9.7	372.0	10.5	7.4	8.6	28.6	21.6
London	647.7	25.9	20.8	406.2	25.8	18.6	12.5	45.7	35.0
South East	660.0	10.8	8.3	493.0	9.1	6.3	15.1	29.4	23.5
South West	401.9	12.0	9.8	314.1	9.7	7.1	7.3	30.3	24.5
England	4,451.2	17.6	14.2	3,227.0	15.8	11.0	91.1	38.6	30.7
Wales	288.2	20.5	19.3	210.4	17.7	14.2	3.8	49.3	46.9
Scotland	424.5	20.8	17.5	307.0	17.2	11.5	8.0	60.3	62.1
Northern Ireland	172.5	23.1	20.0	155.6	22.0	17.0	..	..	..

Sources: Department for Education and Skills; National Assembly for Wales; Scottish Executive; Northern Ireland Department of Education

1 Includes middle schools as deemed.
2 Figures for Northern Ireland include reception pupils and pupils in preparatory departments of grammar schools.
3 Great Britain only.
4 Figures shown for Wales and Scotland are calculated as the percentage of the day pupils present on the census day, therefore the percentage taking free school meals may exceed the percentage known to be eligible. Figures for England, Northern Ireland and the UK, however, are percentages of the numbers of pupils on the school roll.
5 Provisional. Figures for Wales refer to 2001/02.
6 For 2002/03, figures for England and its GORs include boarding pupils as well as solely and dually registered pupils.

United Kingdom

Numbers and Percentages

	Maintained Nursery and Primary schools[1,2]			Maintained Secondary schools[1]			All Special schools[3]		
	Number on roll (thousands)	Percentage known to be eligible for free meals	Percentage taking free school meals[4]	Number on roll (thousands)	Percentage known to be eligible for free meals	Percentage taking free school meals[4]	Number on roll (thousands)	Percentage known to be eligible for free meals	Percentage taking free school meals[4]
2001/02									
United Kingdom	**5,296.7**	**17.7**	**14.4**	**3,933.2**	**15.3**	**11.0**	**99.4**	**40.4**	**34.1**
North East	235.3	22.5	19.5	180.9	19.0	12.5	5.8	50.6	43.3
North West	650.8	21.0	17.3	464.6	19.3	14.2	14.6	46.1	39.1
Yorkshire and the Humber	478.8	17.9	14.4	343.0	16.4	10.6	7.6	41.3	34.6
East Midlands	380.6	13.2	10.9	291.9	11.8	8.5	5.7	34.8	29.4
West Midlands	499.9	18.9	15.7	372.7	16.3	11.4	12.0	40.1	33.2
East of England	463.0	11.9	9.5	377.2	9.8	7.0	8.6	27.8	24.4
London	644.0	25.5	21.1	412.4	24.5	18.7	11.8	45.2	38.1
South East	654.0	10.4	8.0	499.6	8.7	7.2	14.8	28.3	23.2
South West	399.0	11.7	9.4	318.8	9.3	6.9	7.0	31.1	25.5
England	4,405.6	17.1	14.0	3,260.9	14.9	10.9	87.9	38.3	32.2
Wales	284.8	19.4	17.7	212.0	16.8	13.4	3.7	47.3	44.8
Scotland	421.2	20.1	16.9	304.7	15.9	10.9	7.8	59.9	59.2
Northern Ireland	185.1	22.1	18.0	155.5	21.4	16.7	..	..	..
2002/03[5,6]									
United Kingdom	**5,232.8**	**17.4**	**14.3**	**3,984.3**	**14.9**	**10.8**	**106.0**	**37.4**	**31.4**
North East	230.1	22.1	19.1	180.4	18.1	12.6	6.0	49.8	42.6
North West	636.4	20.6	17.2	470.9	18.8	13.9	15.0	43.5	36.1
Yorkshire and the Humber	470.5	17.4	14.3	347.6	16.0	10.9	8.1	36.8	30.6
East Midlands	375.9	12.7	10.5	297.5	11.2	8.3	6.1	32.9	27.6
West Midlands	493.0	18.5	15.5	378.6	15.9	11.4	12.9	36.8	31.8
East of England	459.0	11.7	9.5	383.9	9.6	7.0	9.2	26.3	21.6
London	640.7	25.7	21.3	417.9	24.0	18.5	12.0	43.9	36.0
South East	649.7	10.1	7.9	507.3	8.4	6.0	17.7	24.4	19.2
South West	395.0	11.3	9.2	324.3	8.9	6.6	7.6	28.4	24.5
England	4,350.3	16.8	13.9	3,308.5	14.5	10.6	94.7	35.3	29.4
Wales	284.8	19.4	17.7	212.0	16.8	13.4	3.7	47.3	44.8
Scotland	414.7	20.2	16.8	308.1	16.0	10.5	7.6	58.1	59.9
Northern Ireland	183.1	21.0	17.3	155.7	20.4	16.5	..	..	..

Sources: Department for Education and Skills; National Assembly for Wales; Scottish Executive; Northern Ireland Department of Education

For footnotes see previous page.

Chapter 3
Post Compulsory Education and Training
(a) Institutions and Staff
(b) Participation Rates
(c) Students and Starters
(d) Job Related Training

CHAPTER 3: POST-COMPULSORY EDUCATION AND TRAINING

Key Facts

(a) INSTITUTIONS AND STAFF

- There were 89 universities, 60 other higher education institutions and 467 further education colleges (of which 103 were 6th form colleges) in the UK in 2002/03. **(Table 3.1)**

- There were 78,000 full-time higher education academic staff and 57,000 full-time further education academic staff in the United Kingdom in 2001/02. **(Table 3.1)**

(b) PARTICIPATION RATES

- 73% of 16 year olds and 58% of 17 year olds were in post-compulsory education either at school or in full-time further education in 2000/01. **(Table 3.2)**

- In Spring 2003, 14% of people of working age had received job-related training in the last four weeks. Employees were more likely to receive job-related training than the self-employed, the unemployed or the economically inactive. **(Table 3.3)**

(c) STUDENTS AND STARTERS

- There were 5.4 million further education students in the United Kingdom during the academic year 2001/02, compared with 2.2 million in 1990/91. Four-fifths of these students in 2001/02 were part time, a similar proportion as in 1990/91. **(Tables 3.5, 3.10)**

- There were 2.3 million [961,700 part-time] higher education students in the United Kingdom in the academic year 2001/02, compared with 1.1 million in 1990/91. Of the students in 2001/02, 472,400 were known to be postgraduate students, 1.1 million were first degree students and 747,800 were on other undergraduate courses. **(Tables 3.6, 3.10)**

- Amongst popular subjects studied were business & financial studies, and social sciences, each with over 110,000 full-time first degree students enrolled. **(Table 3.6)**

- In 2001/02, there were 188,400 students from overseas in total in full-time higher education in the UK. 23,300 of these students were from Greece, the highest of any overseas country. **(Table 3.7)**

- There were 5.1 million further education students in the first year of their course of study in 2001/02 of which 4.1 million were part-time. **(Table 3.11)**

- There were 1.1 million new entrants to higher education in 2001/02, of which just under half were part-time. **(Table 3.12)**

Work-Based Learning for Young People (WBLYP)

Advanced Modern Apprenticeships (AMAs)/ Modern Apprenticeships (MAs)

- There were 66,100 new starts on Advanced Modern Apprenticeship schemes (AMAs) in England & Wales in 2001/02. In 2002-03, there were 6,400 new starts on Modern Apprenticeships in Wales. **(Table 3.13)**

- The overall number of participants in AMAs in March 2002 was 125,100, and represented over 40% of work-based learning for young people participants. The proportion for Modern Apprenticeships in Wales in March 2003 was similar. **(Table 3.15)**

Foundation Modern Apprenticeships (FMAs)/ National Traineeships (NTrs)

- There were 120,200 new starts on Foundation Modern Apprenticeships (FMAs) in England & Wales in 2001/02. In 2002-03, there were 11,200 new starts on National Traineeships in Wales. **(Table 3.13)**

- Male starts on FMAs in the period August - October 2002 (55% of total) outnumbered Female starts (45%). **(Table 3.14)**

- FMA participants accounted for two-fifths of work-based learning for young people participants in March 2002. The proportion for National Traineeships in Wales in March 2003 was similar. **(Table 3.15)**

Other Training (OT)

- As a result of increases in other schemes for young people, the number of new starts on Other Training (OT) programmes in England & Wales in 2001/02, at 48,600, was under a fifth of new starts on WBLYP. **(Table 3.13)**

- The proportion of Ethnic minority OT starts, however, remained at 13% in 2001/02, an increase of four percentage points since 1998/99. In the period August - October 2002, the Ethnic minority proportion was 20%. **(Table 3.14)**

(d) JOB RELATED TRAINING

- In Spring 2003, people in Wales (15.2%) were more likely to have received job-related training in the last four weeks than people in any other region. People in Northern Ireland (11.5%) were least likely to receive training. **(Table 3.16)**

- 21.6% of Black or Black British employees, 18.0% of Chinese employees, and 14.1% of those of Asian or Asian British origin, had received job-related training compared with 15.5% of White employees. **(Table 3.17)**

- People with high levels of qualifications were much more likely than those with low or no qualifications to have received job-related training. **(Table 3.17)**

- In Spring 2003, 7.5% of employees had received off-the-job training in the last four weeks, 4.9% had received only on-the-job training and 3.1% had received both types of training. **(Table 3.17)**

- Employees in public administration, education & health were more likely than employees in other industries to have received job-related training. Those employed in agriculture, forestry & fishing were least likely to have received training. **(Table 3.18)**

- Much of the job-related training received by employees is of short duration; in Spring 2003, over a third of the training received by employees and by the self-employed lasted for less than a week. **(Table 3.21)**

- The economically inactive tend to receive job-related training of a longer duration than that received by employees. **(Table 3.21)**

- A Further Education college or university is the most common location for off-the-job training. The employer's premises are another common location for employees' off-the-job training. **(Table 3.22)**

- In Spring 2003, young employees receiving training *in the last week* spent more hours in job-related training than older employees. Males spent more hours in training than females. **(Table 3.23)**

- In Spring 2003, 33.2% of employees in temporary employment had undertaken job-related training *in the last thirteen weeks* compared to 30.1% of permanent employees. 31.4% of full-time employees had undertaken job-related training compared with 26.4% of part-time employees. **(Table 3.24)**

- In Spring 2003, 30.1% of employees had received job-related training *in the last thirteen weeks*, 15.6% had received job-related training *in the last four weeks*, and 8.4% had received job-related training *in the last week*. 28.8% of employees had never been offered training by their current employer. **(Table 3.25)**

- In Spring 2003, 24.4% of employees who were classed as both DDA disabled and work-limiting disabled had received job-related training *in the last thirteen weeks*, compared with 30.1% of all employees. **(Table 3.26)**

CHAPTER 3: POST-COMPULSORY EDUCATION AND TRAINING – LIST OF TABLES

(a) INSTITUTIONS AND STAFF

3.1 Number of establishments of further and higher education by type, and full-time academic staff by gender - time series

(b) PARTICIPATION RATES

3.2 16 and 17 year olds participating in post-compulsory education and Government supported training - time series

3.3 Participation in job-related training in the last four weeks - time series

3.4 Participation in job-related training in the last four weeks by economic activity and age, 2003

(c) STUDENTS AND STARTERS

3.5 Students in further education by country of study, mode of study, gender and subject group, during 2001/02

3.6 Students in higher education by level, mode of study, gender and subject group, 2001/02

3.7 Full-time students from overseas in higher education, by type of course, gender and country, 2001/02 and time series

3.8 Students in further education by country of study, mode of study, gender and age, during 2001/02

3.9 Students in higher education by level, mode of study, gender and age, 2001/02

3.10 Students in further and higher education - time series

3.11 Further education students in the first year of their course of study by country of study, mode of study, gender and age, 2001/02

3.12 New entrants to higher education by level, mode of study, gender and age, 2001/02

3.13 Starts in Government-Supported Work-Based Learning for Young People programmes by region - time series

3.14 Work-Based Learning for Young People: characteristics of starts - time series

3.15 Participants in Government-Supported Work-Based Learning for Young People programmes by region - time series

(d) JOB RELATED TRAINING

3.16 Participation in job-related training in the last four weeks by economic activity and region, 2003

3.17 Participation by employees in job-related training in the last four weeks by type of training and a range of personal characteristics, 2003

3.18 Participation by employees in job-related training in the last four weeks by a range of economic characteristics, 2003

3.19 Participation by employees in job-related training in the last four weeks by type of training and a range of economic characteristics, 2003

3.20 Participation by employees in job-related training in the last four weeks by region and a range of personal and economic characteristics, 2003

3.21 Length of job-related training, 2003

3.22 Location of off-the-job training, 2003

3.23 Hours spent on job-related training in the last week, 2003

3.24 Participation by employees in job-related training in the last thirteen weeks by a range of personal and economic characteristics - time series

3.25 Employees of working age in the UK – summary of job-related training received, 2003

3.26 Participation by employees in job-related training in the last thirteen weeks by disability status and a range of personal characteristics, 2003

POST-COMPULSORY EDUCATION AND TRAINING – INSTITUTIONS AND STAFF
Number of establishments of further and higher education by type, and full-time academic staff by gender - time series

United Kingdom	(i) Number of establishments of further and higher education				Numbers
	Academic years				
	1990/91	1995/96	2000/01[1]	2001/02[1]	2002/03[2,3]
UNITED KINGDOM					
Universities (including Open University)[4]	48	89	89	89	89
Other higher education institutions	}	66	60	60	60
	} 588				
Further education colleges	}	543	491	483	467
of which 6th form colleges	.	110	103	101	103
ENGLAND					
Universities (including Open University)[4]	37	72	72	72	72
Other higher education institutions	}	50	46	46	46
	} 460				
Further education colleges	}	453	403	396	381
of which 6th form colleges	.	110	103	101	103
WALES					
Universities[4]	1	2	2	2	2
Other higher education institutions	}	5	5	5	5
	} 38				
Further education colleges	}	26	24	24	24
SCOTLAND					
Universities[4]	8	13	13	13	13
Other higher education institutions	}	9	7	7	7
	} 64				
Further education colleges	}	47	47	46	46
NORTHERN IRELAND					
Universities	2	2	2	2	2
Colleges of Education	2	2	2	2	2
Further education colleges	24	17	17	17	16

United Kingdom	(ii) Number of full-time academic staff				Thousands
	Academic years				
	1990/91	1995/96	2000/01[1]	2001/02[2]	2002/03
All					
Further and Higher Education Institutions	122	139	134	135	..
of which					
Further Education Institutions (FEIs)[5,6]	..	63 [6]	56	57	..
Higher Education Institutions (HEIs)[4,8,9]	..	76	78	78	..
Males					
Further and Higher Education Institutions	89	91	84	83	..
of which					
Further Education Institutions (FEIs)[5,6]	..	36 [6]	30	30	..
Higher Education Institutions (HEIs)[4,8,9]	..	55	54	54	..
Females					
Further and Higher Education Institutions	33	48	50	52	..
of which					
Further Education Institutions (FEIs)[5,6]	..	27 [6]	26	27	..
Higher Education Institutions (HEIs)[4,8,9]	..	21	24	25	..

Sources: Department for Education and Skills; National Assembly for Wales; Scottish Executive; Northern Ireland Department for Employment and Learning

1 Includes revised data.
2 Provisional.
3 Includes 2001/02 UK higher education institution data and further education institution data for Wales.
4 From 1993/94 includes former polytechnics and colleges which became universities as a result of the Further and Higher Education Act 1992.
5 Figures for England relate to staff whose primary role is teaching, and do not include other staff whose primary role is supporting teaching and learning or other.
6 Scotland figures include full-time equivalent (rather than headcount) staff in academic departments only. Cross-college staff are excluded.
7 Includes 1996/97 data for Wales.
8 Excludes the Open University.
9 Non-clinical academic staff paid wholly by the institution.

United Kingdom   Percentages[2]

1995/96

| | 16 year olds | | | | | 17 year olds | | | | |
	At school	In further education[3] Full-time	Part-time	Government-supported training (GST)	All in full-time education and GST[4]	At school	In further education[3] Full-time	Part-time	Government-supported training (GST)	All in full-time education and GST[4]
Region of study										
United Kingdom	37	34	8	11 [5]	81 [5]	28	29	10	12 [5]	69 [5]
North East	24	38	8	19	80	18	31	11	19	66
North West	24	42	9	15	79	19	35	11	15	68
Yorkshire and the Humber	30	36	9	14	77	22	29	11	15	65
East Midlands	36	31	8	12	78	27	27	10	15	68
West Midlands	30	38	9	13	80	24	33	10	13	69
Eastern	40	35	6	9	83	31	31	8	11	72
London	39	37	4	5	81	29	34	6	7	68
South East	39	37	5	6	82	31	32	7	9	71
South West	39	37	7	10	84	31	32	8	12	73
England	34	37	7	11	80	26	32	9	12	69
Wales	37	33	10	12	82	28	28	8	15	70
Scotland [6,7]	67	9	19	10	86	40	10	20	14	63
Northern Ireland	46	30	11	..	..	35	29	14	..	..

1998/99[8]

| | 16 year olds | | | | | 17 year olds | | | | |
	At school	In further education[3] Full-time	Part-time	Government-supported training (GST)	All in full-time education and GST[4]	At school	In further education[3] Full-time	Part-time	Government-supported training (GST)	All in full-time education and GST[4]
Region of study										
United Kingdom	38	33	7	9 [5]	79 [5]	29	28	9	12 [5]	67 [5]
North East	26	35	8	15	75	20	29	9	18	66
North West	25	40	8	12	76	20	33	10	14	67
Yorkshire and the Humber	30	34	10	13	75	24	28	12	14	65
East Midlands	37	30	7	10	77	30	26	9	13	67
West Midlands	31	36	8	10	76	25	30	10	12	66
East	41	33	5	6	80	33	28	7	9	68
London	39	34	4	5	78	30	32	6	6	67
South East	39	35	4	6	80	32	30	6	8	69
South West	39	34	6	8	80	31	29	8	11	71
England	35	35	7	9	78	27	30	8	11	67
Wales	38	31	8	16	85	28	26	9	16	70
Scotland [6]	67	11	11	9	88	38	11	13	15	63
Northern Ireland [9]	46	28	13	..	..	37	26	14	..	..

Source: Department for Education and Skills; National Assembly for Wales; Scottish Executive; Northern Ireland Department of Education

1 Excluding higher education.

2 As a percentage of the estimated 16 year old and 17 year old population respectively. Population data does not include post-Census revisions.

3 Including sixth form colleges in England, and a small element of further education in higher education institutions in England, Scotland (from 1998/99) and Wales (from 2000/01).

4 Figures for England exclude overlap between full-time education and Government-supported training.

5 Great Britain only up to 1999/00. For 2000/01, England & Wales.

6 The estimates of 16 year olds at school exclude those pupils who leave school in the Winter term at the minimum statutory school-leaving age.

7 Figures shown for Government-supported training are not directly comparable with later years.

8 Includes revised data.

9 Participation in part-time FE should not be aggregated with full-time FE or schools activity due to the unquantifiable overlap with these activities.

10 Provisional.

3.2 POST-COMPULSORY EDUCATION AND TRAINING – PARTICIPATION RATES

16 and 17 year olds participating in post-compulsory education[1] and government supported training – time series

United Kingdom   Percentages[2]

1999/00[8]

| | 16 year olds | | | | | 17 year olds | | | | |
| | At school | In further education[3] | | Government-supported training (GST) | All in full-time education and GST[4] | At school | In further education[3] | | Government-supported training (GST) | All in full-time education and GST[4] |
		Full-time	Part-time				Full-time	Part-time		
Region of study										
United Kingdom	38	34	7	8 [5]	80 [5]	29	28	8	11 [5]	68 [5]
North East	26	38	8	15	78	21	30	10	17	67
North West	25	42	7	11	77	20	34	9	14	68
Yorkshire and the Humber	31	35	10	12	77	24	29	12	14	65
East Midlands	38	32	7	9	78	30	26	9	12	68
West Midlands	32	37	8	9	77	25	31	10	11	67
East	41	34	5	6	80	33	28	7	8	70
London	40	35	4	4	79	31	32	6	6	68
South East	40	35	4	5	80	32	30	6	8	69
South West	39	35	6	7	81	32	29	8	11	71
England	35	36	6	8	79	28	30	8	11	68
Wales	38	33	6	7	78	29	28	9	12	69
Scotland [6]	69	12	9	9	90	38	11	11	14	63
Northern Ireland [9]	48	29	9	..	..	38	27	8	..	..

2000/01[10]

| | 16 year olds | | | | | 17 year olds | | | | |
| | At school | In further education[3] | | Government-supported training (GST) | All in full-time education and GST[4] | At school | In further education[3] | | Government-supported training (GST) | All in full-time education and GST[4] |
		Full-time	Part-time				Full-time	Part-time		
Region of study										
United Kingdom	39	34	6	8 [5]	79 [5]	30	28	8	10 [5]	68 [5]
North East	27	38	9	15	79	20	31	9	16	67
North West	25	43	6	11	78	20	34	8	14	68
Yorkshire and the Humber	31	36	9	11	77	24	29	10	13	66
East Midlands	38	31	7	9	77	31	26	9	11	68
West Midlands	32	37	7	10	78	26	31	9	11	67
East	42	33	5	7	81	33	27	7	8	68
London	41	36	4	4	81	32	32	6	6	69
South East	39	35	4	6	79	33	29	6	8	69
South West	39	34	5	7	80	32	29	7	11	71
England	35	36	6	8	79	28	30	8	10	68
Wales	39	34	6	8	81	29	28	8	11	68
Scotland [6]	71	14	8	..	..	41	12	11	..	..
Northern Ireland [9]	47	29	10	..	..	40	28	7	..	..
Of which by gender and country										
Males										
United Kingdom	37	32	7	10 [5]	76 [5]	28	27	9	12 [5]	66 [5]
England	33	34	7	10	76	27	28	9	12	66
Wales	36	32	6	9	78	26	27	10	13	67
Scotland [6]	65	15	8	..	..	39	12	13	..	..
Northern Ireland [9]	38	32	10	..	..	33	30	8	..	..
Females										
United Kingdom	41	35	6	7 [5]	82 [5]	32	30	7	9 [5]	71 [5]
England	37	38	5	7	82	30	32	6	9	71
Wales	42	35	6	7	83	32	29	6	9	70
Scotland [6]	74	11	8	..	..	43	12	9	..	..
Northern Ireland [9]	58	25	9	..	..	47	26	6	..	..

Source: Department for Education and Skills; National Assembly for Wales; Scottish Executive; Northern Ireland Department of Education

See previous page for footnotes.

POST COMPULSORY EDUCATION AND TRAINING: PARTICIPATION RATES

3.3

Participation in job-related training[1] in the last four weeks — time series

United Kingdom: People of working age[2]

Thousands and percentages[3]

	1991[4]	1996	2001	2002	2003
Numbers (thousands)					
All People					
All	4,471	4,656	5,365	5,393	5,141
Males	2,385	2,353	2,562	2,588	2,445
Females	2,086	2,303	2,803	2,805	2,696
Employees [5,6]					
All	3,268	3,271	3,961	4,033	3,809
Males	1,745	1,643	1,872	1,930	1,810
Females	1,522	1,628	2,089	2,103	1,999
Self-employed [6,7]					
All	185	199	240	234	244
Males	128	126	147	151	143
Females	57	73	93	84	101
ILO unemployed [8]					
All	142	196	154	173	137
Males	78	117	81	93	72
Females	64	80	73	80	64
Economically inactive [9]					
All	561	811	895	873	882
Males	251	361	390	371	379
Females	310	449	505	502	503
Percentages [3]					
All People					
All	12.7	13.1	14.6	14.6	13.8
Males	13.0	12.6	13.3	13.3	12.5
Females	12.5	13.5	16.0	15.9	15.3
Employees [5,6]					
All	14.9	14.8	16.4	16.6	15.6
Males	14.7	14.1	14.5	14.9	13.9
Females	15.1	15.6	18.5	18.5	17.5
Self-employed [6,7]					
All	5.7	6.4	8.0	7.7	7.6
Males	5.1	5.4	6.6	6.6	6.0
Females	7.5	9.7	12.4	11.2	12.2
ILO unemployed [8]					
All	5.7	8.5	11.0	11.6	9.5
Males	4.9	7.6	9.4	10.1	8.0
Females	7.0	10.2	13.5	13.9	11.9
Economically inactive [9]					
All	8.0	10.4	11.3	11.0	11.1
Males	11.6	12.6	12.5	11.7	12.1
Females	6.4	9.1	10.5	10.5	10.4

Source: Labour Force Survey, Spring of each year[10]

1　Job-related training includes both on and off-the-job training.

2　Working age is defined as males aged 16-64 and females aged 16-59.

3　Expressed as a percentage of the total number of people in each group.

4　Due to a change in the LFS questionnaire, data from Summer 1994 onwards are not comparable with earlier figures.

5　Employees are those in employment excluding the self-employed, unpaid family workers and those on government employment and training programmes.

6　The split into employees and self-employed is based on respondents' own assessment of their employment status.

7　Self-employed are those in employment excluding employees, unpaid family workers and those on government employment and training programmes.

8　Unemployed according to the International Labour Organization (ILO) definition.

9　Economically inactive are those who are neither in employment nor ILO unemployed.

10　Users of these data should read the LFS entry in Annex A, as it contains important information about the LFS and the concepts and definitions used.

POST COMPULSORY EDUCATION AND TRAINING: PARTICIPATION RATES

3.4

Participation in job-related training[1] in the last four weeks by economic activity and age, 2003

United Kingdom: People of working age[2]   Thousands and percentages[3]

	Thousands			Percentages[3]		
	All	Males	Females	All	Males	Females
All people						
All	5,141	2,445	2,696	13.8	12.5	15.3
16-19	633	326	307	21.0	21.2	20.9
20-24	919	456	462	24.7	24.1	25.4
25-29	621	302	319	16.8	16.0	17.7
30-39	1,247	591	657	13.3	12.3	14.3
40-49	1,096	478	618	13.0	11.3	14.8
50-64	625	292	333	7.0	5.7	8.7
Employees [4,5]						
All	3,809	1,810	1,999	15.6	13.9	17.5
16-19	323	163	160	23.1	23.4	22.7
20-24	527	263	264	21.9	20.7	23.2
25-29	497	242	255	18.2	16.4	20.4
30-39	1,019	505	514	15.2	13.9	16.8
40-49	919	401	518	15.4	13.1	17.7
50-64	525	235	289	10.1	8.2	12.4
Self-employed [5,6]						
All	244	143	101	7.6	6.0	12.2
16-19	*	*	*	*	*	*
20-24	12	*	*	11.4	*	*
25-29	20	10	*	10.1	7.2	*
30-39	68	38	30	7.7	5.9	12.8
40-49	84	47	37	8.8	6.9	13.1
50-64	57	39	18	5.5	4.8	8.1
ILO unemployed [7]						
All	137	72	64	9.5	8.0	11.9
16-19	34	19	15	12.1	11.6	12.7
20-24	30	15	16	12.7	9.5	18.5
25-29	12	*	*	7.9	*	*
30-39	25	11	13	7.8	6.0	10.5
40-49	20	12	*	8.5	8.4	*
50-64	16	*	*	7.1	*	*
Economically inactive [8]						
All	882	379	503	11.1	12.1	10.4
16-19	235	119	116	18.9	19.1	18.8
20-24	335	162	173	35.8	44.1	30.4
25-29	87	41	46	14.6	24.6	10.7
30-39	130	33	97	8.8	9.8	8.4
40-49	70	16	54	5.7	4.4	6.2
50-64	26	*	17	1.0	*	1.5

Source: Labour Force Survey, Spring 2003 [9]

1   Job-related training includes both on and off-the-job training.

2   Working age is defined as males aged 16-64 and females aged 16-59.

3   Expressed as a percentage of the total number of people in each group.

4   Employees are those in employment excluding the self-employed, unpaid family workers and those on government employment and training programmes.

5   The split into employees and self-employed is based on respondents' own assessment of their employment status.

6   Self-employed are those in employment excluding employees, unpaid family workers and those on government employment and training programmes.

7   Unemployed according to the International Labour Organization (ILO) definition.

8   Economically inactive are those who are neither in employment nor ILO unemployed.

9   Users of these data should read the LFS entry in Annex A, as it contains important information about the LFS and the concepts and definitions used.

3.5

Students in further education[1] by country of study, mode of study[2], gender and subject group, during 2001/02[3,4,5]

United Kingdom (i) Home and Overseas Students Thousands

	United Kingdom		England[4]		Wales		Scotland[5]		Northern Ireland[3]	
	Full-time	Part-time	Full-time	Part-time	Full-time	Part-time	Full-time	Part-time	Full-time	Part-time
All										
Medicine & Dentistry	-	-	-	-	-	-	-	-	-	-
Subjects Allied to Medicine	144.0	325.9	141.0	309.7	-	-	1.5	14.3	1.6	1.9
Biological Sciences	9.3	11.5	9.2	6.8	-	-	0.2	4.7	-	-
Vet. Science, Agriculture & related	22.5	64.2	21.0	51.4	-	-	1.4	12.4	0.1	0.4
Physical Sciences	9.3	5.1	9.3	3.6	-	-	-	1.3	-	0.2
Mathematical and Computing Sciences	23.3	132.5	18.0	27.0	-	-	3.4	90.0	1.8	15.5
Engineering & Technology	72.9	175.8	64.4	152.3	-	0.1	6.1	19.6	2.5	3.8
Architecture, Building & Planning	43.6	128.0	36.3	115.5	-	-	3.5	10.2	3.8	2.2
Social Sciences	66.7	389.8	59.3	356.4	-	-	6.6	30.7	0.8	2.7
Business & Financial Studies	100.9	457.1	90.4	404.1	-	-	6.8	42.4	3.8	10.6
Librarianship & Info Science	99.3	699.6	98.0	690.3	-	-	0.6	9.0	0.7	0.3
Languages	49.9	168.0	49.1	144.4	-	0.2	0.9	21.4	-	2.1
Humanities	25.8	109.2	25.4	108.3	-	-	0.3	0.9	-	-
Creative Arts & Design	117.8	265.4	108.7	237.1	0.1	-	6.5	25.0	2.5	3.3
Education[6]	3.5	26.2	-	1.9	-	0.2	2.8	20.2	0.6	3.9
Other Subjects[7]	206.5	816.3	198.2	755.4	0.4	6.3	4.5	43.0	3.4	11.5
Unknown	132.9	452.5	88.5	249.3	44.4	203.2	-	-	-	-
All subjects	**1,128.2**	**4,227.1**	**1,016.7**	**3,613.6**	**45.0**	**210.0**	**45.1**	**345.0**	**21.4**	**58.4**
Males										
Medicine & Dentistry	-	-	-	-	-	-	-	-	-	-
Subjects Allied to Medicine	56.1	102.2	55.8	95.5	-	-	0.2	6.5	0.1	0.2
Biological Sciences	3.5	4.4	3.4	1.6	-	-	0.1	2.8	-	-
Vet. Science, Agriculture & related	11.1	30.2	10.3	24.1	-	-	0.8	5.9	-	0.2
Physical Sciences	5.8	2.4	5.8	1.7	-	-	-	0.6	-	0.1
Mathematical and Computing Sciences	14.1	48.2	10.1	9.8	-	-	2.5	33.4	1.4	5.1
Engineering & Technology	65.9	153.2	58.0	134.0	-	0.1	5.6	15.7	2.4	3.5
Architecture, Building & Planning	41.6	116.0	34.5	105.3	-	-	3.4	8.5	3.7	2.2
Social Sciences	27.4	114.6	26.3	108.2	-	-	1.0	6.2	0.1	0.3
Business & Financial Studies	46.9	161.7	43.6	142.0	-	-	2.2	16.9	1.2	2.8
Librarianship & Info Science	63.5	274.9	62.7	271.3	-	-	0.3	3.5	0.4	0.1
Languages	19.9	60.3	19.5	50.6	-	0.1	0.4	8.8	-	0.8
Humanities	10.3	34.2	10.2	33.8	-	-	0.1	0.4	-	-
Creative Arts & Design	50.5	72.0	48.0	65.3	-	-	1.9	6.4	0.6	0.4
Education[6]	2.1	10.9	-	0.5	-	0.1	1.6	8.9	0.4	1.3
Other Subjects[7]	84.3	306.1	80.4	280.7	0.2	2.3	2.0	18.7	1.8	4.5
Unknown	65.9	174.1	44.5	91.1	21.3	83.0	-	-	-	-
All subjects	**569.0**	**1,665.5**	**513.2**	**1,415.6**	**21.6**	**85.5**	**22.1**	**143.1**	**12.1**	**21.4**
Females										
Medicine & Dentistry	-	-	-	-	-	-	-	-	-	-
Subjects Allied to Medicine	87.9	223.7	85.2	214.2	-	-	1.2	7.7	1.5	1.7
Biological Sciences	5.8	7.1	5.8	5.2	-	-	0.1	1.9	-	-
Vet. Science, Agriculture & related	11.3	34.0	10.7	27.2	-	-	0.6	6.6	0.1	0.2
Physical Sciences	3.5	2.7	3.5	1.9	-	-	-	0.7	-	0.1
Mathematical and Computing Sciences	9.2	84.3	7.9	17.3	-	-	0.9	56.6	0.4	10.4
Engineering & Technology	7.0	22.6	6.4	18.3	-	-	0.5	4.0	0.1	0.4
Architecture, Building & Planning	2.0	12.0	1.8	10.2	-	-	0.1	1.7	0.1	0.1
Social Sciences	39.3	275.2	33.0	248.3	-	-	5.6	24.6	0.7	2.4
Business & Financial Studies	54.0	295.3	46.8	262.1	-	-	4.6	25.4	2.6	7.8
Librarianship & Info Science	35.8	424.7	35.3	419.0	-	-	0.3	5.5	0.3	0.2
Languages	30.0	107.7	29.6	93.8	-	0.1	0.5	12.6	-	1.3
Humanities	15.4	75.0	15.2	74.5	-	-	0.2	0.5	-	-
Creative Arts & Design	67.3	193.4	60.7	171.8	-	-	4.6	18.6	1.9	2.9
Education[6]	1.4	15.3	-	1.4	-	0.2	1.2	11.3	0.2	2.5
Other Subjects[7]	122.1	510.2	117.8	474.7	0.2	4.1	2.5	24.3	1.6	7.0
Unknown	67.1	278.4	44.0	158.3	23.1	120.2	-	-	-	-
All subjects	**559.2**	**2,561.6**	**503.5**	**2,198.1**	**23.4**	**124.5**	**22.9**	**202.0**	**9.3**	**37.0**

Sources: Department for Education and Skills; National Assembly for Wales; Scottish Executive; Northern Ireland Department for Employment and Learning

1   Further education (FE) institution figures are whole year counts except for Northern Ireland, which are collected on a snapshot basis. Higher education (HE) institution figures are based on the HESA July 'standard registration' count and are not directly comparable with previous years.
2   Full-time includes sandwich. Part-time comprises both day and evening, including block release.
3   Provisional.
4   Further education institution figures for England include colleges and LSC funded external institutions, but exclude Specialist designated colleges. Figures for 2001/02 are not therefore directly comparable with those shown for 2000/01.
5   Figures for Scotland further education colleges are enrolments rather than headcounts. Due to a reclassification of subject groupings, subject categories for Scotland cannot be directly compared with previous years prior to 1999/00.
6   Including ITT and INSET.
7   Includes Combined and general categories, plus, for England further education institutions, Hotel and Catering and Basic Education.
8   Includes estimated breakdowns for further education students in UK higher education institutions, and in further education institutions in England.

POST COMPULSORY EDUCATION AND TRAINING: STUDENTS AND STARTERS

Students in further education[1] by country of study, mode of study[2], gender and subject group, during 2001/02[3,4,5]

United Kingdom   (ii) of which Overseas Students   Thousands

	United Kingdom		England[4]		Wales		Scotland[5]		Northern Ireland[3]	
	Full-time	Part-time	Full-time	Part-time	Full-time	Part-time	Full-time	Part-time	Full-time	Part-time
All										
Medicine & Dentistry	-	-	-	-					-	-
Subjects Allied to Medicine	1.0	1.8	0.9	1.6				0.2	0.1	-
Biological Sciences	0.1	0.1	0.1	-						
Vet. Science, Agriculture & related	0.2	0.4	0.2	0.3				0.2		-
Physical Sciences	0.2	0.1	0.2	0.1						
Mathematical and Computing Sciences	0.5	0.8	0.4	0.3				0.3		0.2
Engineering & Technology	3.1	3.5	3.1	3.2				0.1		0.2
Architecture, Building & Planning	0.3	1.1	0.3	1.0						0.1
Social Sciences	0.8	2.3	0.8	2.0				0.1		0.2
Business & Financial Studies	2.3	5.7	2.2	5.2				0.3	0.1	0.2
Librarianship & Info Science	1.4	4.5	1.3	4.4				0.1		-
Languages	5.6	14.9	5.2	12.6			0.4	2.3		
Humanities	0.5	0.6	0.5	0.6					-	-
Creative Arts & Design	1.5	2.5	1.4	2.2				0.1	0.1	0.1
Education[6]	-	0.2	-	-						0.1
Other Subjects[7]	10.0	20.6	9.9	20.4						0.2
Unknown	4.7	6.6	4.6	5.7	0.1	0.9				
All subjects	**32.2**	**65.7**	**31.1**	**59.8**	**0.1**	**0.9**	**0.6**	**3.8**	**0.4**	**1.3**
of which European Union[8]	10.5	14.2	9.7	9.8		0.9	0.3	2.3	0.4	1.3
Other Europe[8]	1.3	3.5	1.3	3.2				0.3		-
Commonwealth[8]	3.8	3.1	3.7	2.5	-			0.6		-
Other Countries[8]	16.6	44.9	16.3	44.3	0.1	-	0.2	0.6		-
Males										
Medicine & Dentistry	-	-	-	-						
Subjects Allied to Medicine	0.3	0.6	0.3	0.5				0.2		
Biological Sciences	-	-								
Vet. Science, Agriculture & related	0.1	0.2	0.1	0.1				0.1		-
Physical Sciences	0.2	-	0.2	-						
Mathematical and Computing Sciences	0.3	0.4	0.3	0.1				0.3		0.1
Engineering & Technology	3.0	3.1	3.0	2.9				0.1		0.2
Architecture, Building & Planning	0.3	1.0	0.3	0.9						0.1
Social Sciences	0.4	0.7	0.4	0.6						
Business & Financial Studies	1.1	2.5	1.0	2.2				0.3		0.1
Librarianship & Info Science	0.8	1.9	0.8	1.8						
Languages	2.6	4.2	2.4	3.2			0.2	0.9		
Humanities	0.2	0.2	0.2	0.2						
Creative Arts & Design	0.6	0.5	0.6	0.5						
Education[6]	-	-								
Other Subjects[7]	4.8	9.7	4.8	9.7						
Unknown	2.2	2.4	2.2	1.8	0.1	0.6				
All subjects	**16.9**	**27.5**	**16.4**	**24.6**	**0.1**	**0.6**	**0.3**	**1.9**	**0.1**	**0.4**
of which European Union[8]	4.7	5.4	4.4	3.4		0.5	0.1	1.0	0.1	0.4
Other Europe[8]	0.5	0.8	0.5	0.7				0.1		-
Commonwealth[8]	2.3	2.0	2.3	1.5	-			0.5		-
Other Countries[8]	9.4	19.3	9.2	18.9	0.1		0.1	0.3		-
Females										
Medicine & Dentistry	-	-	-	-						
Subjects Allied to Medicine	0.6	1.2	0.6	1.2					0.1	-
Biological Sciences	-	-								
Vet. Science, Agriculture & related	0.1	0.2	0.1	0.2				0.1		-
Physical Sciences	0.1	-	0.1	-						
Mathematical and Computing Sciences	0.2	0.4	0.2	0.2				0.1		0.1
Engineering & Technology	0.1	0.3	0.1	0.3						-
Architecture, Building & Planning	-	0.1	-	0.1						
Social Sciences	0.4	1.6	0.4	1.4				0.1		0.2
Business & Financial Studies	1.3	3.2	1.2	3.1				0.1	0.1	0.1
Librarianship & Info Science	0.6	2.6	0.5	2.5				0.1		
Languages	3.1	10.8	2.9	9.4			0.2	1.4		
Humanities	0.3	0.4	0.3	0.4						-
Creative Arts & Design	0.9	1.9	0.8	1.7				0.1	0.1	0.1
Education[6]	-	0.1	-	-						0.1
Other Subjects[7]	5.2	10.9	5.1	10.8						0.1
Unknown	2.4	4.3	2.4	3.9	-	0.4				
All subjects	**15.3**	**38.2**	**14.7**	**35.2**	**-**	**0.4**	**0.3**	**1.9**	**0.3**	**0.8**
of which European Union[8]	5.8	8.8	5.3	6.3		0.3	0.2	1.3	0.3	0.8
Other Europe[8]	0.8	2.7	0.8	2.5				0.2		-
Commonwealth[8]	1.4	1.1	1.4	1.1				0.1		-
Other Countries[8]	7.2	25.7	7.1	25.3			0.1	0.3		-

Sources: Department for Education and Skills; National Assembly for Wales; Scottish Executive; Northern Ireland Department for Employment and Learning

See previous page for footnotes.

3.6

Students in higher[1] education by level, mode of study,[2] gender and subject group, 2001/02[3,4]

United Kingdom   (i) Home and Overseas Students   Thousands

| | Postgraduate level | | | | | | First degree | | Other Undergraduate | | Total higher education students[5] | |
| | PhD & equivalent | | Masters and Others | | Total Postgraduate | | | | | | | |
	Full-time	Part-time	Full-time	Part-time	Full-time	Part-time	Full-time	Part-time	Full-time	Part-time	Full-time[5]	Part-time[5]
All												
Medicine & Dentistry	2.8	3.9	2.9	6.2	5.7	10.2	31.3	0.1	0.2	0.1	37.3	10.4
Subjects Allied to Medicine	2.0	2.4	3.9	22.7	5.9	25.0	58.3	32.0	67.8	66.8	132.0	123.9
Biological Sciences	6.6	4.4	4.5	5.5	11.1	9.9	66.3	3.5	1.9	2.6	79.3	16.0
Vet. Science, Agriculture & related	1.0	0.8	1.2	1.1	2.2	1.9	10.5	0.4	4.5	3.2	17.3	5.5
Physical Sciences	6.8	3.2	4.6	3.2	11.4	6.3	43.1	1.8	1.0	3.5	55.6	11.6
Mathematical and Computing Sciences	2.9	1.9	13.1	10.0	15.9	12.0	79.2	6.6	15.1	20.7	110.2	39.2
Engineering & Technology	6.4	4.5	10.9	12.8	17.3	17.2	73.4	7.9	12.1	28.0	102.9	53.1
Architecture, Building & Planning	0.6	0.7	4.2	7.1	4.7	7.9	19.8	6.5	3.1	11.6	27.6	25.9
Social Sciences	4.4	5.3	24.6	24.5	29.0	29.8	114.1	12.6	10.5	34.3	153.6	76.8
Business & Financial Studies	1.6	2.7	24.5	53.6	26.0	56.3	112.0	15.0	29.4	78.6	167.5	149.9
Librarianship & Info Science	0.2	0.3	3.8	4.0	4.0	4.3	21.0	1.0	4.8	6.5	29.8	11.8
Languages	2.5	2.8	5.0	4.9	7.4	7.8	55.6	3.2	2.9	24.7	66.0	35.6
Humanities	2.5	3.2	4.0	7.4	6.4	10.6	33.1	3.9	0.9	22.2	40.5	36.7
Creative Arts & Design	0.8	1.1	6.4	4.3	7.2	5.4	86.9	4.5	22.0	13.3	116.1	23.3
Education[6]	0.9	4.4	27.5	54.5	28.5	58.9	44.7	6.3	2.8	22.9	76.0	88.1
Other subjects[7]	0.7	0.7	3.0	21.4	3.7	22.2	98.7	11.1	10.5	216.5	112.9	249.7
Unknown[5]	-	-	-	0.1	-	0.1	0.6	0.4	0.3	2.2	1.6	4.0
All subjects	**42.6**	**42.4**	**144.0**	**243.4**	**186.6**	**285.8**	**948.7**	**117.0**	**190.2**	**557.6**	**1,326.2**	**961.7**
Males												
Medicine & Dentistry	1.2	2.2	1.2	3.0	2.4	5.1	13.8	0.1	0.1	-	16.3	5.2
Subjects Allied to Medicine	0.9	1.0	1.2	5.9	2.1	6.8	13.2	3.8	9.4	6.8	24.7	17.5
Biological Sciences	2.7	2.0	1.7	1.8	4.4	3.7	24.3	1.3	1.0	1.1	29.7	6.1
Vet. Science, Agriculture & related	0.5	0.4	0.6	0.5	1.1	0.9	3.9	0.2	1.9	1.5	6.9	2.6
Physical Sciences	4.5	2.1	2.6	1.8	7.2	4.0	26.2	1.0	0.7	2.0	34.0	7.0
Mathematical and Computing Sciences	2.2	1.5	9.4	6.6	11.6	8.1	60.5	5.0	12.1	11.1	84.2	24.1
Engineering & Technology	5.0	3.8	8.7	10.9	13.7	14.6	61.9	7.3	10.6	25.8	86.2	47.7
Architecture, Building & Planning	0.4	0.5	2.5	4.7	2.9	5.2	14.2	5.1	2.5	9.3	19.6	19.7
Social Sciences	2.4	2.8	10.7	9.5	13.1	12.3	45.1	4.7	2.6	8.8	60.8	25.8
Business & Financial Studies	1.0	1.8	13.5	28.9	14.4	30.7	53.0	6.6	12.9	29.6	80.3	66.9
Librarianship & Info Science	0.1	0.2	1.3	1.5	1.4	1.6	8.1	0.4	3.3	3.9	12.9	5.9
Languages	1.0	1.2	1.5	1.6	2.6	2.8	15.5	0.9	1.3	9.2	19.3	12.9
Humanities	1.4	1.9	1.9	3.4	3.3	5.3	15.4	1.5	0.3	7.5	19.1	14.3
Creative Arts & Design	0.4	0.6	2.7	1.8	3.1	2.4	34.8	1.6	10.5	4.7	48.4	8.7
Education[6]	0.4	2.0	8.3	15.3	8.6	17.3	10.5	1.5	1.4	5.9	20.6	24.6
Other subjects[7]	0.4	0.4	1.5	11.8	1.9	12.2	42.2	4.0	5.0	89.6	49.1	105.8
Unknown[5]	-	-	-	0.1	-	0.1	0.2	0.2	0.1	0.6	0.7	1.5
All subjects	**24.4**	**24.1**	**69.4**	**108.9**	**93.8**	**133.0**	**442.8**	**45.1**	**75.7**	**217.4**	**612.7**	**396.2**
Females												
Medicine & Dentistry	1.6	1.8	1.7	3.3	3.3	5.1	17.5	0.1	0.2	-	21.0	5.2
Subjects Allied to Medicine	1.1	1.4	2.7	16.8	3.8	18.2	45.1	28.2	58.4	60.0	107.3	106.4
Biological Sciences	3.9	2.4	2.8	3.7	6.6	6.2	42.1	2.1	0.9	1.6	49.6	9.9
Vet. Science, Agriculture & related	0.5	0.3	0.6	0.7	1.1	1.0	6.7	0.3	2.6	1.6	10.4	2.9
Physical Sciences	2.3	1.1	2.0	1.3	4.3	2.4	16.9	0.7	0.4	1.4	21.6	4.6
Mathematical and Computing Sciences	0.7	0.5	3.7	3.4	4.3	3.9	18.7	1.7	3.0	9.6	26.0	15.2
Engineering & Technology	1.4	0.7	2.2	1.9	3.6	2.6	11.5	0.6	1.5	2.2	16.6	5.4
Architecture, Building & Planning	0.2	0.2	1.7	2.4	1.9	2.7	5.6	1.4	0.5	2.2	8.0	6.3
Social Sciences	2.0	2.5	13.9	15.0	15.9	17.5	69.0	7.9	7.9	25.5	92.8	51.0
Business & Financial Studies	0.6	1.0	11.0	24.7	11.6	25.6	59.0	8.5	16.5	49.0	87.2	83.1
Librarianship & Info Science	0.1	0.2	2.4	2.5	2.6	2.7	12.9	0.6	1.5	2.6	16.9	5.9
Languages	1.4	1.6	3.4	3.4	4.9	5.0	40.2	2.3	1.6	15.5	46.7	22.8
Humanities	1.1	1.3	2.1	4.0	3.2	5.3	17.7	2.4	0.6	14.7	21.5	22.4
Creative Arts & Design	0.4	0.6	3.7	2.5	4.1	3.1	52.0	2.9	11.6	8.6	67.7	14.6
Education[6]	0.6	2.4	19.3	39.2	19.8	41.6	34.2	4.8	1.4	17.0	55.4	63.5
Other subjects[7]	0.3	0.4	1.5	9.6	1.8	10.0	56.5	7.1	5.5	126.9	63.8	144.0
Unknown[5]	-	-	-	0.1	-	0.1	0.4	0.2	0.2	1.6	1.0	2.5
All subjects	**18.2**	**18.3**	**74.6**	**134.5**	**92.8**	**152.9**	**505.9**	**71.8**	**114.5**	**340.2**	**713.5**	**565.5**

Sources: Department for Education and Skills; National Assembly for Wales; Scottish Executive; Northern Ireland Department for Employment and Learning

1 Higher Education Statistics Agency (HESA) higher education institutions include Open University students. Part-time figures include dormant modes, those writing up at home and on sabbaticals.
2 Full-time includes sandwich. Part-time comprises both day and evening, including block release and open/distance learning.
3 Revised to include HESA July 'standard registration' count data, and 2001/02 figures for HE students in FE institutions in Wales and Northern Ireland, and FE colleges in Scotland. FE institution figures for England also now exclude Specialist designated colleges.
4 Figures for higher education (HE) institutions are based on the HESA July 'standard registration' count and are not directly comparable with previous years. Figures for further education (FE) institutions (other than in Scotland FE colleges) are snapshots counted at a particular point in the year [November for FE institutions in England and Northern Ireland, and December for FE institutions in Wales]. Students starting courses after these dates will not therefore be counted. Figures for Scotland, however, are whole year (not snapshot) enrolments (rather than headcounts).
5 Includes data for higher education students in further education institutions in Wales which cannot be split by level. Figures for home, part-time UK higher education institution dormant modes, those writing up at home, and on sabbaticals, which cannot be identified by subject are also included in the 'Unknown' row, throughout the levels.
6 Including ITT and INSET.
7 Includes Combined and general categories, plus, for England further education institutions, Hotel and Catering and Basic Education.
8 Numbers in grouped countries do not sum to overall student numbers due to overlaps.

3.6 POST COMPULSORY EDUCATION AND TRAINING: STUDENTS AND STARTERS

Students in higher[1] education by level, mode of study,[2] gender and subject group, 2001/02[3,4]

United Kingdom   (ii) of which Overseas Students   Thousands

| | Postgraduate level | | | | | | First degree | | Other Undergraduate | | Total higher education students[5] | |
| | PhD & equivalent | | Masters and Others | | Total Postgraduate | | | | | | | |
	Full-time	Part-time	Full-time	Part-time	Full-time	Part-time	Full-time	Part-time	Full-time	Part-time	Full-time[5]	Part-time[5]
All												
Medicine & Dentistry	0.8	0.5	1.4	0.8	2.2	1.3	2.7	-	-	-	**4.9**	**1.3**
Subjects Allied to Medicine	0.6	0.4	1.2	2.0	1.8	2.4	3.5	1.2	4.4	1.2	**9.7**	**4.8**
Biological Sciences	1.6	0.9	1.4	0.6	3.0	1.6	4.2	0.1	0.1	0.1	**7.3**	**1.8**
Vet. Science, Agriculture & related	0.4	0.3	0.6	0.1	1.0	0.4	0.9	-	0.2	0.1	**2.0**	**0.5**
Physical Sciences	2.0	0.8	1.6	0.5	3.7	1.4	2.1	-	0.2	0.1	**6.0**	**1.5**
Mathematical and Computing Sciences	1.4	0.7	6.1	1.7	7.5	2.5	7.7	0.4	0.6	0.5	**15.8**	**3.4**
Engineering & Technology	3.7	1.9	7.2	2.7	10.8	4.6	15.3	0.6	1.3	1.0	**27.5**	**6.2**
Architecture, Building & Planning	0.3	0.3	1.8	0.9	2.1	1.2	2.8	0.2	0.3	0.1	**5.2**	**1.5**
Social Sciences	2.5	2.0	10.7	3.0	13.2	5.1	11.7	0.6	0.4	0.3	**25.3**	**5.9**
Business & Financial Studies	1.1	1.0	17.3	7.8	18.4	8.8	17.2	1.1	2.0	1.1	**37.6**	**11.1**
Librarianship & Info Science	0.1	0.1	1.5	0.5	1.6	0.6	1.8	0.1	0.2	0.1	**3.5**	**0.8**
Languages	1.2	1.1	2.5	1.3	3.7	2.4	3.4	0.1	2.4	4.0	**9.5**	**6.4**
Humanities	1.1	0.9	1.5	0.5	2.6	1.4	1.1	0.1	0.1	0.4	**3.8**	**2.0**
Creative Arts & Design	0.3	0.3	2.7	0.5	3.0	0.8	8.0	0.2	0.9	0.2	**11.9**	**1.1**
Education[6]	0.6	1.3	2.7	3.8	3.3	5.2	1.1	0.7	0.1	0.6	**4.5**	**6.5**
Other subjects[7]	0.3	0.2	1.8	0.8	2.1	1.0	8.3	0.4	3.3	2.4	**13.7**	**3.8**
Unknown[5]	-	-	-	-	-	-	-	-	0.3	0.2	**0.3**	**0.3**
All subjects	**17.9**	**12.8**	**62.1**	**27.7**	**80.0**	**40.5**	**91.8**	**5.9**	**16.7**	**12.6**	**188.4**	**59.0**
of which European Union[8]	5.4	4.0	19.2	10.0	24.6	14.1	40.8	2.3	4.6	5.3	**70.0**	**21.7**
Other Europe[8]	1.3	1.0	3.8	2.3	5.1	3.3	7.9	0.3	0.5	0.7	**13.5**	**4.3**
Commonwealth[8]	3.9	2.4	15.0	6.4	18.9	8.8	23.6	1.5	4.7	2.1	**47.3**	**12.4**
Other Countries[8]	7.5	5.6	24.9	9.7	32.4	15.3	22.2	1.9	6.9	4.6	**61.6**	**21.8**
Males												
Medicine & Dentistry	0.4	0.3	0.7	0.4	1.1	0.7	1.2	-	-	-	**2.3**	**0.8**
Subjects Allied to Medicine	0.3	0.2	0.5	0.8	0.8	1.0	1.0	0.3	1.1	0.2	**2.9**	**1.5**
Biological Sciences	0.8	0.5	0.6	0.2	1.4	0.7	1.3	0.1	-	0.1	**2.7**	**0.8**
Vet. Science, Agriculture & related	0.2	0.2	0.3	0.1	0.5	0.3	0.4	-	0.1	0.1	**1.0**	**0.3**
Physical Sciences	1.3	0.5	0.9	0.3	2.3	0.9	1.1	-	0.1	0.1	**3.5**	**1.0**
Mathematical and Computing Sciences	1.0	0.6	4.4	1.2	5.4	1.8	5.6	0.3	0.5	0.4	**11.5**	**2.5**
Engineering & Technology	2.9	1.6	5.9	2.3	8.7	3.9	12.8	0.5	1.2	1.0	**22.8**	**5.4**
Architecture, Building & Planning	0.2	0.2	1.0	0.7	1.2	0.9	1.6	0.1	0.2	0.1	**3.0**	**1.1**
Social Sciences	1.4	1.2	5.3	1.5	6.7	2.7	5.5	0.3	0.2	0.1	**12.3**	**3.1**
Business & Financial Studies	0.7	0.7	9.5	4.8	10.2	5.5	8.5	0.6	1.0	0.7	**19.8**	**6.8**
Librarianship & Info Science	-	0.1	0.5	0.2	0.6	0.2	0.5	-	0.1	-	**1.2**	**0.3**
Languages	0.5	0.5	0.7	0.4	1.1	0.9	0.8	-	1.1	1.7	**3.0**	**2.6**
Humanities	0.7	0.6	0.7	0.3	1.3	0.9	0.5	0.1	0.1	0.2	**1.8**	**1.1**
Creative Arts & Design	0.2	0.1	1.0	0.2	1.2	0.3	2.7	0.1	0.3	0.1	**4.1**	**0.4**
Education[6]	0.3	0.7	0.8	1.3	1.0	2.0	0.3	0.4	-	0.2	**1.3**	**2.6**
Other subjects[7]	0.2	0.1	0.9	0.5	1.1	0.6	3.8	0.2	1.4	0.8	**6.3**	**1.6**
Unknown[5]	-	-	-	-	-	-	-	-	0.1	0.1	**0.1**	**0.1**
All subjects	**11.1**	**7.8**	**33.6**	**15.3**	**44.7**	**23.2**	**47.5**	**3.0**	**7.6**	**5.7**	**99.7**	**31.9**
of which European Union[8]	3.1	2.3	10.2	5.5	13.3	7.7	20.9	1.2	1.8	2.3	**36.0**	**11.2**
Other Europe[8]	0.7	0.6	1.9	1.1	2.6	1.7	3.7	0.1	0.2	0.3	**6.5**	**2.1**
Commonwealth[8]	2.6	1.5	9.6	4.0	12.2	5.5	13.3	0.8	2.3	1.2	**27.8**	**7.5**
Other Countries[8]	4.8	3.6	12.3	5.2	17.1	8.7	11.1	1.0	3.3	2.0	**31.6**	**11.7**
Females												
Medicine & Dentistry	0.4	0.2	0.7	0.3	1.1	0.5	1.5	-	-	-	**2.6**	**0.5**
Subjects Allied to Medicine	0.3	0.2	0.7	1.2	1.0	1.4	2.6	0.9	3.3	1.0	**6.8**	**3.3**
Biological Sciences	0.8	0.5	0.8	0.4	1.7	0.9	2.9	0.1	-	0.1	**4.6**	**1.0**
Vet. Science, Agriculture & related	0.2	0.1	0.2	0.1	0.4	0.2	0.5	-	0.1	-	**1.0**	**0.2**
Physical Sciences	0.7	0.3	0.7	0.2	1.4	0.5	0.9	-	0.1	-	**2.4**	**0.6**
Mathematical and Computing Sciences	0.4	0.2	1.7	0.5	2.0	0.7	2.1	0.1	0.1	0.2	**4.3**	**1.0**
Engineering & Technology	0.8	0.3	1.3	0.4	2.1	0.7	2.5	0.1	0.1	0.1	**4.7**	**0.8**
Architecture, Building & Planning	0.1	0.1	0.8	0.2	0.9	0.3	1.1	0.1	0.1	-	**2.1**	**0.4**
Social Sciences	1.0	0.9	5.5	1.5	6.5	2.4	6.2	0.2	0.3	0.2	**12.9**	**2.8**
Business & Financial Studies	0.4	0.3	7.8	3.0	8.2	3.3	8.8	0.5	0.9	0.5	**17.9**	**4.3**
Librarianship & Info Science	0.1	-	1.0	0.3	1.1	0.4	1.2	0.1	0.1	-	**2.4**	**0.5**
Languages	0.7	0.7	1.9	0.9	2.6	1.5	2.6	0.1	1.3	2.3	**6.5**	**3.9**
Humanities	0.5	0.4	0.8	0.2	1.3	0.6	0.7	0.1	0.1	0.2	**2.0**	**0.9**
Creative Arts & Design	0.2	0.1	1.7	0.3	1.9	0.5	5.3	0.1	0.5	0.1	**7.7**	**0.7**
Education[6]	0.3	0.7	2.0	2.5	2.3	3.2	0.9	0.4	0.1	0.4	**3.2**	**3.9**
Other subjects[7]	0.1	0.1	0.9	0.3	1.0	0.4	4.5	0.2	1.9	1.6	**7.5**	**2.2**
Unknown[5]	-	-	-	-	-	-	-	-	0.2	0.1	**0.2**	**0.2**
All subjects	**6.9**	**5.0**	**28.5**	**12.3**	**35.4**	**17.3**	**44.3**	**2.9**	**9.1**	**6.9**	**88.7**	**27.1**
of which European Union[8]	2.3	1.8	9.0	4.6	11.3	6.3	19.9	1.1	2.8	3.0	**34.1**	**10.4**
Other Europe[8]	0.6	0.4	2.0	1.3	2.6	1.6	4.2	0.2	0.3	0.4	**7.1**	**2.2**
Commonwealth[8]	1.3	0.9	5.4	2.4	6.7	3.3	10.4	0.7	2.4	0.9	**19.5**	**4.9**
Other Countries[8]	2.7	2.0	12.6	4.6	15.3	6.6	11.1	0.9	3.6	2.7	**30.0**	**10.2**

Sources: Department for Education and Skills; National Assembly for Wales; Scottish Executive; Northern Ireland Department for Employment and Learning

See previous page for footnotes.

3.7 POST COMPULSORY EDUCATION: STUDENTS AND STARTERS

Full-time students from overseas in higher education, by level, gender and country, 2001/02[1,2] and time series

United Kingdom   Thousands

2001/02 RANK	2000/01 RANK	TOP FIFTY NAMED COUNTRIES	1980/81 All	2000/01[2] All	Males	Females	2001/02[1,2] All	Males	Females	PhD	Masters	Total post-graduate	First degree	Other under-graduate	Total Full-time Higher Education
1	(1)	Greece	2.5	24.6	14.8	9.8	23.3	14.1	9.1	1.3	9.2	10.5	12.3	0.5	23.3
2	(5)	China	0.2	9.0	4.6	4.5	17.9	8.7	9.2	1.1	7.9	9.0	6.2	2.6	17.9
3	(7)	Malaysia	13.3	7.9	4.5	3.4	9.3	5.3	4.0	0.9	1.7	2.7	6.4	0.2	9.3
4	(4)	Irish Republic	0.5	9.3	3.6	5.7	9.2	3.6	5.6	0.4	1.4	1.9	5.6	1.7	9.2
5	(2)	Germany	1.3	11.3	5.4	5.9	8.4	4.0	4.3	0.9	1.8	2.7	5.1	0.6	8.4
6	(3)	France	0.7	11.0	5.4	5.6	7.9	4.2	3.7	0.7	2.2	2.9	4.5	0.5	7.9
7	(12)	India	0.9	3.5	2.4	1.1	6.6	4.9	1.7	0.5	4.1	4.6	1.6	0.4	6.6
8	(6)	USA	2.9	8.8	3.7	5.1	6.6	2.8	3.8	1.0	2.9	3.9	1.6	1.1	6.6
9	(9)	Hong Kong	7.2	5.5	2.8	2.6	6.4	3.2	3.2	0.1	1.1	1.2	4.8	0.3	6.4
10	(10)	Japan	0.3	4.9	1.8	3.1	4.9	1.7	3.1	0.4	1.8	2.1	1.9	0.9	4.9
11	(8)	Spain	0.2	6.2	2.9	3.3	4.4	2.3	2.1	0.4	1.0	1.4	2.5	0.5	4.4
12	(16)	Taiwan	..	3.3	1.3	2.0	3.8	1.5	2.3	0.4	2.4	2.8	0.8	0.2	3.8
13	(11)	Italy	0.1	4.8	2.3	2.6	3.8	1.9	1.9	0.7	1.1	1.8	1.7	0.2	3.8
14	(13)	Singapore	1.6	3.7	2.2	1.5	3.4	2.0	1.4	0.2	0.6	0.8	2.5	0.1	3.4
15	(14)	Norway	0.5	3.5	1.5	2.0	3.3	1.4	1.8	0.1	0.6	0.7	2.5	-	3.3
16	(17)	Cyprus	1.5	3.2	1.7	1.5	3.2	1.7	1.5	0.1	0.8	0.9	2.2	0.1	3.2
17	(15)	Sweden	0.1	3.4	1.2	2.2	3.0	1.1	1.9	0.1	0.4	0.5	2.4	0.1	3.0
18	(24)	Nigeria	5.2	2.0	1.1	0.9	2.8	1.6	1.2	0.1	1.1	1.2	1.4	0.2	2.8
19	(20)	Zimbabwe	0.9	2.1	0.9	1.2	2.6	1.1	1.5	0.1	0.2	0.3	0.5	1.8	2.6
20	(19)	Thailand	0.2	2.2	1.0	1.2	2.5	1.0	1.4	0.4	1.4	1.8	0.6	0.1	2.5
21	(21)	Kenya	1.1	2.1	1.0	1.0	2.3	1.1	1.1	0.1	0.5	0.6	1.6	0.1	2.3
22	(-)	Korea[3]	0.1	1.9	1.1	0.8	2.3	1.2	1.1	0.4	0.8	1.2	0.9	0.1	2.3
23	(28)	Pakistan	0.8	1.5	1.2	0.3	2.2	1.8	0.3	0.2	1.1	1.2	0.8	0.1	2.2
24	(22)	Canada	0.7	2.1	0.9	1.2	2.1	0.9	1.2	0.4	1.0	1.5	0.5	0.1	2.1
25	(18)	Finland	-	2.3	0.8	1.5	1.8	0.6	1.2	0.1	0.2	0.3	1.4	0.1	1.8
26	(25)	Portugal	0.2	1.8	0.9	0.9	1.8	0.9	0.9	0.4	0.4	0.7	1.0	0.1	1.8
27	(23)	Belgium	0.1	2.0	1.0	1.0	1.8	0.9	0.9	0.1	0.3	0.5	1.2	0.1	1.8
28	(27)	Netherlands	0.1	1.7	0.8	1.0	1.4	0.7	0.7	0.1	0.4	0.6	0.8	0.1	1.4
29	(31)	Sri Lanka	1.2	1.1	0.7	0.4	1.4	0.9	0.5	0.1	0.3	0.5	0.8	0.1	1.4
30	(30)	Turkey	0.7	1.3	0.8	0.6	1.3	0.8	0.6	0.2	0.6	0.8	0.5	0.1	1.3
31	(35)	Mauritius	0.4[4]	1.0	0.6	0.5	1.3	0.7	0.6	-	0.2	0.3	0.7	0.4	1.3
32	(33)	Mexico	0.4	1.1	0.7	0.4	1.3	0.8	0.5	0.5	0.7	1.2	0.1	-	1.3
33	(29)	Denmark	-	1.5	0.6	0.9	1.3	0.5	0.8	0.1	0.4	0.4	0.8	0.1	1.3
34	(32)	Russia	..	1.1	0.5	0.6	1.3	0.6	0.7	0.2	0.4	0.6	0.7	-	1.3
35	(40)	Ghana	0.7	0.8	0.6	0.3	1.3	0.9	0.4	0.1	0.6	0.7	0.4	0.2	1.3
36	(37)	Saudi Arabia	0.4	1.0	0.7	0.2	1.1	0.9	0.3	0.4	0.3	0.7	0.3	0.1	1.1
37	(-)	Libya	0.3	0.5	0.5	-	1.1	1.0	0.1	0.2	0.7	0.9	0.1	0.1	1.1
38	(38)	Oman	-	0.9	0.7	0.2	1.0	0.8	0.2	0.1	0.2	0.3	0.6	0.1	1.0
39	(42)	Brazil	0.5	0.8	0.4	0.4	0.9	0.5	0.4	0.2	0.5	0.7	0.2	-	0.9
40	(39)	Indonesia	0.3	0.9	0.5	0.3	0.9	0.5	0.4	0.1	0.5	0.6	0.3	-	0.9
41	(36)	Switzerland	0.2	1.0	0.5	0.5	0.9	0.4	0.5	0.1	0.2	0.3	0.6	-	0.9
42	(34)	Austria	..	1.1	0.5	0.6	0.9	0.4	0.4	0.1	0.2	0.3	0.6	-	0.9
43	(-)	Bangladesh	0.2	0.6	0.4	0.1	0.9	0.7	0.2	0.1	0.3	0.5	0.3	0.1	0.9
44	(41)	Australia	0.5	0.8	0.4	0.4	0.8	0.4	0.4	0.2	0.3	0.6	0.2	-	0.8
45	(50)	Iran	6.6	0.6	0.5	0.1	0.7	0.5	0.2	0.3	0.2	0.6	0.2	-	0.7
46	(48)	United Arab Emirates	0.1	0.6	0.4	0.2	0.7	0.5	0.2	0.1	0.2	0.2	0.4	0.1	0.7
47	(47)	Jordan	1.2	0.6	0.4	0.2	0.7	0.5	0.2	0.2	0.3	0.5	0.2	-	0.7
48	(46)	South Africa	0.4	0.7	0.4	0.3	0.7	0.4	0.3	0.2	0.2	0.4	0.2	0.1	0.7
49	(44)	Brunei	1.0	0.7	0.4	0.4	0.7	0.4	0.3	-	0.1	0.1	0.5	0.1	0.7
50	(43)	Israel	0.2	0.7	0.5	0.3	0.7	0.4	0.3	0.1	0.2	0.4	0.3	-	0.7
		Other/unknown	18.0	16.0	8.8	7.2	18.1	9.8	8.3	2.5	5.9	8.4	7.4	2.3	18.1
		TOTAL	75.6	181.3	93.3	88.0	188.4	99.7	88.7	17.9	62.1	80.0	91.8	16.7	188.4

Full-time students from overseas of which

			1980/81 All	2000/01 All	Males	Females	All	Males	Females	PhD	Masters	Total post-graduate	First degree	Other under-graduate	Total Full-time Higher Education
		European Union[5]	6.3[6]	82.3	40.9	41.4	70.0	36.0	34.1	5.4	19.2	24.6	40.8	4.6	70.0
		Other Europe[5]	2.6[6]	13.4	6.4	6.9	13.5	6.5	7.1	1.3	3.8	5.1	7.9	0.5	13.5
		Commonwealth[5]	39.7[6]	39.1	22.1	17.0	47.3	27.8	19.5	3.9	15.0	18.9	23.6	4.7	47.3
		Other Countries[7]	27.4[6]	50.4	25.9	24.5	61.6	31.6	30.0	7.5	24.9	32.4	22.2	6.9	61.6

Sources: Department for Education and Skills; National Assembly for Wales; Scottish Executive; Northern Ireland Department for Employment and Learning

1 Revised to include HESA July 'standard registration' count data, and 2001/02 figures for HE students in FE institutions in Wales and Northern Ireland, and FE colleges in Scotland. FE institution figures for England also now exclude Specialist designated colleges.
2 Figures for higher education (HE) institutions are based on the HESA July 'standard registration' count and are not directly comparable with previous years. Figures for further education (FE) institutions (other than in Scotland FE colleges) are snapshots counted at a particular point in the year [November for FE institutions in England and Northern Ireland, and December for FE institutions in Wales]. Students starting courses after these dates will not therefore be counted. Figures for Scotland, however, are whole year (not snapshot) enrolments (rather than headcounts).
3 Includes North Korea and South Korea [South Korea was ranked 26 in 2000/01].
4 Data are for 1981/82.
5 Except for 1980/81 Gibraltar is included in both EU and Commonwealth figures, and Cyprus and Malta are included in Other Europe and Commonwealth figures. Numbers in grouped countries do not sum to overall student numbers due to overlaps.
6 Estimated.
7 Includes those students whose country of domicile is not known.

3.8

Students in further education[1] by country of study, mode of study[2], gender and age[3], during 2001/02[4,5]

United Kingdom　　　　　　　　Home and Overseas Students　　　　　　　　　　　Thousands

	United Kingdom		England[4]		Wales		Scotland[5]		Northern Ireland	
	Full-time	Part-time	Full-time	Part-time	Full-time	Part-time	Full-time	Part-time	Full-time	Part-time
All										
Age[3] <16	15.7	95.0	12.8	52.8	1.1	5.2	1.8	33.3	0.1	3.7
16	272.7	91.8	240.7	66.6	14.5	4.0	9.8	16.2	7.7	5.0
17	221.3	100.1	194.6	76.3	11.2	4.5	8.6	15.4	6.9	4.0
18	110.7	103.5	95.4	85.5	5.4	4.9	6.0	10.4	3.9	2.6
19	53.4	90.9	47.1	75.8	2.2	4.7	2.9	8.6	1.2	1.8
20	34.5	84.6	31.0	71.7	1.3	4.3	1.8	7.1	0.4	1.5
21	27.5	86.8	25.1	74.5	0.8	4.4	1.3	6.5	0.2	1.4
22	22.3	84.7	20.5	72.9	0.6	4.2	1.0	6.3	0.1	1.3
23	18.8	80.0	17.3	69.2	0.5	3.9	0.9	5.6	0.1	1.3
24	16.8	78.0	15.6	67.8	0.4	3.7	0.7	5.3	0.1	1.2
25	15.9	81.7	14.8	71.2	0.4	3.9	0.6	5.5	0.1	1.2
26	15.3	83.5	14.4	73.0	0.3	3.8	0.6	5.6	-	1.1
27	15.0	85.5	14.0	74.8	0.4	4.1	0.6	5.6	-	1.1
28	14.6	88.6	13.7	77.4	0.4	4.1	0.5	5.9	-	1.1
29	14.4	92.2	13.6	80.7	0.3	4.4	0.5	5.9	-	1.2
30+	255.6	2,852.9	242.5	2,479.8	5.1	142.8	7.6	201.9	0.4	28.3
Unknown	3.7	47.5	3.6	43.6	0.1	3.1	-	-	-	0.7
All ages	1,128.2	4,227.1	1,016.7	3,613.6	45.0	210.0	45.1	345.0	21.4	58.4
Males										
Age[3] <16	8.7	50.5	6.9	28.7	0.7	3.1	1.1	16.4	0.1	2.4
16	135.3	47.3	118.1	35.9	7.3	1.9	5.5	7.2	4.4	2.3
17	108.4	53.0	94.8	41.2	5.3	2.5	4.4	7.5	3.9	1.8
18	58.3	55.4	50.2	45.1	2.8	2.8	3.0	6.2	2.4	1.4
19	29.7	45.6	26.4	37.3	1.2	2.6	1.5	4.8	0.7	0.9
20	18.9	39.7	17.0	33.1	0.7	2.2	1.0	3.8	0.2	0.6
21	14.5	37.9	13.3	32.2	0.4	2.0	0.7	3.2	0.1	0.5
22	11.5	35.2	10.6	30.1	0.3	1.8	0.5	2.8	0.1	0.4
23	9.5	32.1	8.8	27.7	0.2	1.6	0.4	2.4	0.1	0.4
24	8.5	31.2	7.9	27.2	0.2	1.6	0.3	2.1	-	0.4
25	7.9	32.8	7.4	28.6	0.2	1.7	0.3	2.2	-	0.4
26	7.7	33.6	7.3	29.4	0.1	1.5	0.2	2.3	-	0.4
27	7.5	34.1	7.1	29.9	0.1	1.6	0.3	2.2	-	0.3
28	7.3	34.9	6.9	30.5	0.1	1.6	0.2	2.4	-	0.3
29	7.1	36.2	6.8	31.7	0.1	1.7	0.2	2.4	-	0.4
30+	125.9	1,047.5	121.5	910.1	1.7	53.9	2.6	75.1	0.1	8.4
Unknown	2.2	18.4	2.2	16.7	-	1.4	-	-	-	0.3
All ages	569.0	1,665.5	513.2	1,415.6	21.6	85.5	22.1	143.1	12.1	21.4
Females										
Age[3] <16	7.1	44.4	5.9	24.1	0.4	2.1	0.7	16.9	0.1	1.3
16	137.4	44.5	122.6	30.7	7.2	2.1	4.3	9.0	3.3	2.7
17	112.9	47.1	99.8	35.0	5.8	2.0	4.2	7.9	3.1	2.2
18	52.3	48.0	45.2	40.4	2.7	2.1	2.9	4.3	1.5	1.3
19	23.6	45.3	20.8	38.5	1.0	2.1	1.4	3.8	0.5	0.9
20	15.6	44.9	14.0	38.6	0.6	2.1	0.8	3.3	0.2	0.9
21	13.0	48.9	11.8	42.3	0.4	2.4	0.6	3.3	0.1	0.9
22	10.8	49.6	9.9	42.9	0.3	2.4	0.5	3.4	0.1	0.9
23	9.4	47.9	8.5	41.6	0.3	2.3	0.5	3.2	0.1	0.8
24	8.4	46.8	7.7	40.6	0.2	2.1	0.4	3.2	-	0.8
25	8.0	48.8	7.4	42.6	0.2	2.2	0.3	3.2	-	0.8
26	7.6	49.9	7.0	43.6	0.2	2.3	0.3	3.3	-	0.8
27	7.4	51.4	6.9	44.8	0.2	2.5	0.3	3.3	-	0.8
28	7.3	53.7	6.7	46.9	0.2	2.5	0.3	3.5	-	0.8
29	7.3	56.0	6.8	49.0	0.2	2.7	0.3	3.5	-	0.8
30+	129.7	1,805.4	121.1	1,569.7	3.4	88.9	4.9	126.9	0.3	19.9
Unknown	1.5	29.1	1.4	26.9	-	1.7	-	-	-	0.4
All ages	559.2	2,561.6	503.5	2,198.1	23.4	124.5	22.9	202.0	9.3	37.0

Sources: Department for Education and Skills; National Assembly for Wales; Scottish Executive; Northern Ireland Department for Employment and Learning

1 Further education (FE) institution figures are whole year counts except for Northern Ireland, which are collected on a snapshot basis. Higher education (HE) institution figures are based on the HESA July 'standard registration' count and are not directly comparable with previous years.
2 Full-time includes sandwich. Part-time comprises both day and evening, including block release and open/distance learning.
3 Ages as at 31 August 2001 (1 July for Northern Ireland and 31 December for Scotland).
4 Further education institution figures for England include colleges and LSC funded external institutions, but exclude Specialist designated colleges. Figures for 2001/02 are not therefore directly comparable with those shown for 2000/01.
5 Figures for Scotland further education colleges are enrolments rather than headcounts.

POST COMPULSORY EDUCATION AND TRAINING: STUDENTS AND STARTERS

3.9 Students in higher[1] education by level, mode of study[2], gender and age[3], 2001/02[4,5]

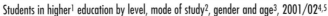

| United Kingdom | | | | | | | | | | | | Home and Overseas Students | | Thousands |

| | Postgraduate level | | | | | | First degree | | Other Undergraduate | | Total higher education students[6] | |
| | PhD & equivalent | | Masters and Others | | Total Postgraduate | | | | | | | |
Age[3]	Full-time	Part-time	Full-time	Part-time	Full-time	Part-time	Full-time	Part-time	Full-time	Part-time	Full-time[6]	Part-time[6]
All												
<16	-	-	-	-	-	-	-	-	-	0.4	-	0.4
16	-	-	-	-	-	-	0.4	-	0.8	1.0	1.2	1.1
17	-	-	-	-	-	-	10.1	0.1	5.0	1.8	15.1	1.9
18	-	-	-	-	-	-	152.9	1.0	23.8	7.2	176.9	8.2
19	-	-	0.1	0.1	0.1	0.1	205.4	2.9	30.2	11.7	235.9	14.7
20	0.1	-	1.2	0.2	1.3	0.2	213.3	4.6	24.0	13.9	238.6	18.8
21	0.9	-	14.5	1.6	15.4	1.7	145.0	6.3	15.9	14.6	176.3	22.6
22	3.1	0.2	21.6	5.2	24.8	5.3	66.2	6.2	10.8	14.4	101.8	26.1
23	4.8	0.3	18.5	7.6	23.4	7.9	32.0	5.0	7.8	14.1	63.1	27.1
24	5.2	1.2	14.3	8.3	19.5	9.5	18.5	4.4	6.1	14.1	44.2	28.0
25	4.1	2.4	10.9	8.9	15.0	11.2	12.8	4.0	5.4	14.5	33.1	29.8
26	3.4	2.4	8.6	9.0	12.0	11.4	9.8	3.9	4.8	14.6	26.6	29.9
27	2.9	2.2	7.2	9.5	10.0	11.7	8.0	3.7	4.3	14.7	22.3	30.1
28	2.4	2.2	5.9	9.7	8.3	11.9	7.0	3.8	3.8	15.7	19.1	31.3
29	2.1	2.1	5.2	10.0	7.2	12.1	6.2	3.7	3.8	15.9	17.2	31.8
30+	13.6	29.4	35.8	171.3	49.4	200.7	60.9	67.1	43.5	375.2	153.9	643.6
Unknown	-	0.1	0.2	2.1	0.2	2.2	0.3	0.3	0.2	13.8	0.6	16.2
All ages	**42.6**	**42.4**	**144.0**	**243.4**	**186.6**	**285.8**	**948.7**	**117.0**	**190.2**	**557.6**	**1,326.2**	**961.7**
Males												
<16	-	-	-	-	-	-	-	-	-	0.1	-	0.1
16	-	-	-	-	-	-	0.2	-	0.3	0.5	0.4	0.5
17	-	-	-	-	-	-	4.5	0.1	2.0	0.8	6.5	0.9
18	-	-	-	-	-	-	68.9	0.5	11.0	4.0	80.0	4.6
19	-	-	-	-	-	-	94.5	1.6	14.1	6.7	108.7	8.4
20	-	-	0.5	0.1	0.6	0.1	98.5	2.6	10.9	7.5	110.1	10.2
21	0.5	-	6.0	0.6	6.4	0.6	71.1	3.4	7.2	7.2	84.8	11.1
22	1.9	0.1	9.8	2.1	11.7	2.2	34.9	3.3	4.7	6.2	51.3	11.7
23	2.8	0.2	8.6	3.1	11.4	3.2	17.1	2.6	3.2	5.6	31.6	11.4
24	3.0	0.7	6.8	3.3	9.8	3.9	9.9	2.0	2.4	5.5	22.1	11.5
25	2.2	1.4	5.4	3.7	7.6	5.1	6.6	1.7	2.0	5.6	16.2	12.3
26	1.8	1.4	4.1	3.7	6.0	5.0	4.8	1.5	1.7	5.6	12.5	12.2
27	1.5	1.2	3.5	3.9	5.1	5.1	3.9	1.4	1.5	5.8	10.4	12.4
28	1.4	1.2	3.0	4.3	4.4	5.5	3.2	1.5	1.3	6.1	8.9	13.1
29	1.2	1.2	2.7	4.6	3.9	5.7	2.9	1.5	1.3	6.3	8.1	13.5
30+	8.0	16.8	18.9	78.7	26.9	95.5	21.7	21.4	11.9	139.3	60.6	256.5
Unknown	-	-	0.1	0.9	0.1	1.0	0.1	0.1	0.1	4.7	0.4	5.8
All ages	**24.4**	**24.1**	**69.4**	**108.9**	**93.8**	**133.0**	**442.8**	**45.1**	**75.7**	**217.4**	**612.7**	**396.2**
Females												
<16	-	-	-	-	-	-	-	-	-	0.2	-	0.2
16	-	-	-	-	-	-	0.2	-	0.5	0.5	0.7	0.6
17	-	-	-	-	-	-	5.6	0.1	3.0	1.0	8.6	1.0
18	-	-	-	-	-	-	84.0	0.5	12.8	3.1	96.9	3.6
19	-	-	0.1	-	0.1	-	111.0	1.2	16.1	5.0	127.2	6.3
20	-	-	0.7	0.1	0.7	0.1	114.7	2.0	13.0	6.4	128.5	8.6
21	0.4	-	8.5	1.1	8.9	1.1	73.9	2.9	8.7	7.5	91.5	11.5
22	1.2	0.1	11.9	3.1	13.1	3.2	31.3	3.0	6.1	8.2	50.5	14.4
23	2.1	0.2	9.9	4.5	12.0	4.7	14.9	2.5	4.6	8.5	31.4	15.7
24	2.2	0.5	7.5	5.0	9.7	5.5	8.6	2.4	3.8	8.6	22.1	16.6
25	1.8	1.0	5.5	5.2	7.4	6.2	6.2	2.4	3.3	8.9	16.9	17.5
26	1.6	1.1	4.5	5.3	6.1	6.4	5.0	2.3	3.1	9.0	14.1	17.8
27	1.3	1.0	3.6	5.6	5.0	6.6	4.1	2.2	2.8	8.9	11.9	17.8
28	1.0	1.0	2.9	5.4	3.9	6.4	3.8	2.3	2.5	9.6	10.2	18.3
29	0.9	0.9	2.5	5.5	3.4	6.4	3.3	2.2	2.5	9.6	9.2	18.2
30+	5.5	12.5	16.9	92.6	22.5	105.1	39.2	45.7	31.6	235.9	93.3	387.1
Unknown	-	-	0.1	1.1	0.1	1.2	0.1	0.1	0.1	9.1	0.3	10.4
All ages	**18.2**	**18.3**	**74.6**	**134.5**	**92.8**	**152.9**	**505.9**	**71.8**	**114.5**	**340.2**	**713.5**	**565.5**

Sources: Department for Education and Skills; National Assembly for Wales; Scottish Executive; Northern Ireland Department for Employment and Learning

1 Higher Education Statistics Agency (HESA) higher education institutions include Open University students. Part-time figures include dormant modes, those writing up at home and on sabbaticals.
2 Full-time includes sandwich. Part-time comprises both day and evening, including block release and open/distance learning.
3 Ages as at 31 August 2001 (1 July for Northern Ireland and 31 December for Scotland).
4 Figures for higher education (HE) institutions are based on the HESA July 'standard registration' count and are not directly comparable with previous years. Figures for further education (FE) institutions (other than in Scotland FE colleges) are snapshots counted at a particular point in the year [November for FE institutions in England and Northern Ireland, and December for FE institutions in Wales]. Students starting courses after these dates will not therefore be counted. Figures for Scotland, however, are whole year (not snapshot) enrolments (rather than headcounts).
5 Revised to include HESA July 'standard registration' count data, and 2001/02 figures for HE students in FE institutions in Wales and Northern Ireland, and FE colleges in Scotland.
6 Includes data for HE students in FE institutions in Wales which cannot be split by level.

POST COMPULSORY EDUCATION AND TRAINING: STUDENTS AND STARTERS

3.10

Students[1] in further and higher[2] education - time series

United Kingdom   (i) Further education students   Thousands

	United Kingdom		England		Wales		Scotland		Northern Ireland	
	Full-time[3]	Part-time[3]	Full-time[3]	Part-time[3]	Full-time[3]	Part-time[3]	Full-time[3]	Part-time[3]	Full-time[3]	Part-time[3]
1990/91[4]										
All[5]	**480.4**	**1,758.5**	..	..	..	..	..	..	..	..
Males	218.8	767.5	..	..	..	..	..	..	..	..
Females	260.9	986.1	..	..	..	..	..	..	..	..
1995/96[4,6]										
All	**815.1**	**1,710.3**	..	..	..	..	..	..	..	..
Males	394.8	686.4	..	..	..	..	..	..	..	..
Females	419.0	1,020.8	..	..	..	..	..	..	..	..
1999/00[7]										
All	**1,036.3**	**3,015.2**	**932.0**	**2,502.7**	**45.3**	**181.5**	**38.2**	**273.7**	**20.7**	**57.3**
Males	518.2	1,251.1	466.9	1,038.2	21.1	74.3	19.5	117.8	10.8	20.7
Females	518.1	1,764.1	465.1	1,464.5	24.2	107.1	18.8	155.9	10.0	36.5
2000/01[7]										
All	**1,081.3**	**3,765.7**	**974.4**	**3,207.3**	**44.6**	**186.2**	**41.3**	**313.8**	**21.0**	**58.3**
Males	542.4	1,489.1	489.2	1,260.9	20.8	75.2	20.6	132.1	11.8	20.8
Females	538.9	2,276.6	485.2	1,946.4	23.8	111.0	20.7	181.8	9.2	37.5
2001/02[7]										
All	**1,128.2**	**4,227.1**	**1,016.7**	**3,613.6**	**45.0**	**210.0**	**45.1**	**345.0**	**21.4**	**58.4**
Males	569.0	1,665.5	513.2	1,415.6	21.6	85.5	22.1	143.1	12.1	21.4
Females	559.2	2,561.6	503.5	2,198.1	23.4	124.5	22.9	202.0	9.3	37.0

United Kingdom   (ii) Higher education students   Thousands

	Postgraduate level						First degree		Other Undergraduate		Total higher education students[3,8]	
	PhD & equivalent		Masters and Others		Total Postgraduate							
	Full-time[3]	Part-time[3]	Full-time[3]	Part-time[3]	Full-time[3]	Part-time[3]	Full-time[3]	Part-time[3]	Full-time[3]	Part-time[3]	Full-time[3,8]	Part-time[3,8]
1990/91												
All	..	..	..	..	**83.9**	**78.6**	**553.2**	**45.2**	**111.5**	**209.1**	**748.6**	**332.9**
Males	..	..	..	..	50.1	45.9	286.1	23.8	58.5	123.8	394.7	193.4
Females	..	..	..	..	33.8	32.8	266.9	21.4	52.1	84.2	352.8	138.4
1995/96[9]												
All	..	..	..	..	**135.4**	**186.2**	**872.1**	**177.8**	**175.1**	**353.1**	**1,182.6**	**717.1**
Males	..	..	..	..	75.6	97.7	432.8	83.9	85.7	137.2	594.0	318.7
Females	..	..	..	..	59.8	88.6	439.3	94.0	89.4	215.8	588.6	398.4
1999/00[10]												
All	**36.9**	**37.4**	**116.2**	**205.8**	**153.1**	**243.2**	**921.3**	**94.2**	**186.0**	**425.5**	**1,260.4**	**762.9**
Males	21.8	22.1	56.4	99.2	78.3	121.3	435.7	38.0	77.9	179.3	591.9	338.6
Females	15.0	15.3	59.8	106.6	74.8	121.9	485.7	56.3	108.1	246.1	668.6	424.3
2000/01[10]												
All	**38.1**	**37.2**	**124.4**	**203.4**	**162.5**	**240.6**	**920.1**	**100.2**	**191.7**	**443.4**	**1,275.0**	**785.5**
Males	22.1	21.6	59.7	95.9	81.9	117.5	431.2	40.0	78.7	183.6	592.1	341.6
Females	15.9	15.6	64.7	107.5	80.6	123.1	488.9	60.2	113.0	259.9	682.8	443.9
2001/02[11]												
All	**42.6**	**42.4**	**144.0**	**243.4**	**186.6**	**285.8**	**948.7**	**117.0**	**190.2**	**557.6**	**1,326.2**	**961.7**
Males	24.4	24.1	69.4	108.9	93.8	133.0	442.8	45.1	75.7	217.4	612.7	396.2
Females	18.2	18.3	74.6	134.5	92.8	152.9	505.9	71.8	114.5	340.2	713.5	565.5

Sources: Department for Education and Skills; National Assembly for Wales; Scottish Executive; Northern Ireland Department for Employment and Learning

1 Home and overseas students.
2 Higher education (HE) figures include Open University students. Part-time figures include dormant modes, those writing up at home and on sabbaticals.
3 Full-time includes sandwich. Part-time comprises both day and evening, including block release and open/distance learning.
4 Further education (FE) figures are enrolments and are not comparable with later figures (other than for Scotland further education colleges) which are headcounts.
5 Includes students in Scotland whose gender is not recorded.
6 Estimated.
7 FE institution figures are whole year counts except for Northern Ireland, which are collected on a snapshot basis.
8 Figures for 2000/01 and 2001/02 include data for FE institutions in Wales which cannot be split by level.
9 Includes 1994/95 higher education in further education institution data for England and for Wales.
10 Figures for students (other than in Scotland further education colleges) are snapshots counted at a particular point in the year [December for UK HE institutions and FE institutions in Wales, November for FE institutions in England and Northern Ireland]. Students starting courses after these dates will not therefore be counted. Figures for Scotland, however, are whole year (not snapshot) enrolments (rather than headcounts).
11 Figures for higher education (HE) institutions are based on the HESA July 'standard registration' count and are not directly comparable with previous years.

3.11

POST COMPULSORY EDUCATION AND TRAINING: STUDENTS AND STARTERS

Further education[1] students in the first year of their course of study, by country of study, mode of study[2], gender and age[3], 2001/02[4,5]

United Kingdom   Home and Overseas Students   Thousands

		United Kingdom		England[4]		Wales		Scotland[5]		Northern Ireland	
		Full-time	Part-time	Full-time	Part-time	Full-time	Part-time	Full-time	Part-time	Full-time	Part-time
All											
Age[3]	<16	15.4	92.2	12.6	51.1	0.9	4.6	1.7	33.3	0.1	3.2
	16	271.1	90.7	240.4	66.5	13.3	3.6	9.7	16.1	7.7	4.5
	17	166.2	84.5	147.8	63.9	6.4	3.3	8.3	14.3	3.8	3.0
	18	88.4	90.3	77.2	76.1	3.2	3.5	5.8	8.8	2.2	2.0
	19	42.2	79.3	37.4	67.2	1.4	3.3	2.7	7.5	0.6	1.3
	20	27.9	75.7	25.1	65.0	0.8	3.1	1.7	6.5	0.3	1.1
	21	23.7	80.3	21.6	69.7	0.6	3.3	1.3	6.2	0.2	1.1
	22	20.1	80.0	18.5	69.5	0.5	3.3	1.0	6.1	0.1	1.0
	23	17.5	76.5	16.1	67.0	0.4	3.1	0.9	5.5	0.1	0.9
	24	15.8	75.5	14.7	66.4	0.3	2.9	0.7	5.3	0.1	0.9
	25	15.0	79.3	14.0	69.9	0.3	3.2	0.6	5.4	-	0.8
	26	14.6	81.3	13.7	72.0	0.3	3.0	0.6	5.5	-	0.8
	27	14.4	83.3	13.5	73.7	0.3	3.3	0.6	5.5	-	0.8
	28	13.9	86.2	13.1	76.4	0.3	3.3	0.5	5.8	-	0.8
	29	13.8	90.0	13.1	79.8	0.3	3.5	0.5	5.9	-	0.8
	30+	247.5	2,822.5	236.1	2,488.6	3.7	113.9	7.4	200.8	0.3	19.1
	Unknown	3.8	51.2	3.7	47.7	0.1	2.9	-	-	-	0.6
	All ages	1,011.3	4,118.9	918.8	3,570.3	32.9	167.2	44.0	338.7	15.5	42.7
Males											
Age[3]	<16	8.5	48.7	6.8	27.5	0.6	2.7	1.1	16.4	0.1	2.1
	16	134.4	46.6	117.9	35.7	6.7	1.7	5.5	7.1	4.4	2.0
	17	82.9	42.1	73.5	32.4	3.2	1.7	4.3	6.6	2.0	1.3
	18	46.0	45.5	40.2	37.8	1.6	1.9	2.9	4.8	1.2	1.0
	19	23.4	37.2	20.9	30.9	0.8	1.8	1.4	3.8	0.4	0.7
	20	15.3	33.7	13.7	28.4	0.5	1.5	0.9	3.3	0.1	0.5
	21	12.3	33.7	11.3	28.8	0.3	1.5	0.6	3.0	0.1	0.4
	22	10.2	32.3	9.5	27.8	0.2	1.4	0.5	2.8	-	0.3
	23	8.7	30.0	8.1	26.0	0.2	1.3	0.4	2.3	-	0.3
	24	7.9	29.6	7.4	26.0	0.1	1.2	0.3	2.1	-	0.3
	25	7.5	31.2	7.0	27.4	0.1	1.3	0.3	2.2	-	0.3
	26	7.4	32.1	7.0	28.4	0.1	1.2	0.2	2.3	-	0.3
	27	7.3	32.7	6.9	28.9	0.1	1.3	0.3	2.2	-	0.2
	28	7.0	33.5	6.7	29.6	0.1	1.3	0.2	2.4	-	0.3
	29	6.9	34.8	6.6	30.7	0.1	1.4	0.2	2.4	-	0.3
	30+	123.4	1,025.3	119.4	901.3	1.3	43.4	2.6	74.7	0.1	5.8
	Unknown	2.2	19.2	2.2	17.7	-	1.3	-	-	-	0.2
	All ages	511.3	1,588.2	465.1	1,365.6	16.0	67.9	21.7	138.5	8.4	16.2
Females											
Age[3]	<16	6.9	43.4	5.8	23.6	0.4	1.9	0.7	16.8	0.1	1.1
	16	136.7	44.1	122.5	30.7	6.6	1.9	4.2	9.0	3.3	2.5
	17	83.3	42.5	74.2	31.5	3.2	1.6	4.0	7.7	1.8	1.7
	18	42.4	44.9	37.1	38.3	1.5	1.6	2.9	4.0	1.0	1.0
	19	18.8	42.2	16.6	36.2	0.6	1.6	1.3	3.7	0.3	0.7
	20	12.7	42.1	11.4	36.6	0.4	1.6	0.8	3.2	0.1	0.7
	21	11.3	46.6	10.3	40.8	0.3	1.9	0.6	3.2	0.1	0.7
	22	9.9	47.7	9.1	41.8	0.2	1.9	0.5	3.4	0.1	0.6
	23	8.8	46.6	8.0	40.9	0.2	1.8	0.5	3.2	-	0.6
	24	7.8	45.8	7.3	40.3	0.2	1.7	0.4	3.2	-	0.6
	25	7.5	48.1	7.0	42.4	0.2	1.8	0.3	3.2	-	0.6
	26	7.2	49.2	6.7	43.6	0.2	1.9	0.3	3.2	-	0.5
	27	7.1	50.6	6.6	44.8	0.2	2.0	0.3	3.3	-	0.5
	28	7.0	52.8	6.5	46.8	0.2	2.0	0.3	3.5	-	0.5
	29	7.0	55.2	6.5	49.1	0.2	2.1	0.3	3.5	-	0.6
	30+	124.1	1,797.2	116.7	1,587.3	2.4	70.5	4.8	126.1	0.2	13.3
	Unknown	1.5	32.0	1.5	30.0	-	1.6	-	-	-	0.3
	All ages	500.0	2,530.7	453.7	2,204.7	16.9	99.4	22.3	200.2	7.1	26.4

Sources: Department for Education and Skills; National Assembly for Wales; Scottish Executive; Northern Ireland Department for Employment and Learning

1 Further education (FE) institution figures are whole year counts except for Northern Ireland, which are collected on a snapshot basis. Higher education (HE) institution figures are based on the HESA July 'standard registration' count and are not directly comparable with previous years.
2 Full-time includes sandwich. Part-time comprises both day and evening, including block release and open/distance learning.
3 Ages as at 31 August 2001 (1 July for Northern Ireland and 31 December for Scotland).
4 Further education institution figures for England include colleges and LSC funded external institutions, but exclude Specialist designated colleges. Figures for 2001/02 are not therefore directly comparable with those shown for 2000/01.
5 Figures for Scotland further education colleges are enrolments rather than headcounts.

3.12

New entrants to higher education[1] by level, mode of study[2], gender and age[3], 2001/02[4,5]

United Kingdom | Home and Overseas Students | Thousands

Age	Postgraduate level						First degree		Other Undergraduate		Total higher education students[6]	
	PhD & equivalent		Masters and Others		Total Postgraduate							
	Full-time	Part-time	Full-time	Part-time	Full-time	Part-time	Full-time	Part-time	Full-time	Part-time	Full-time[6]	Part-time[6]
All												
Age[3] <16	-	-	-	-	-	-	-	-	-	0.3	-	0.3
16	-	-	-	-	-	-	0.4	-	0.8	1.0	1.1	1.0
17	-	-	-	-	-	-	9.8	0.1	4.9	1.7	14.6	1.8
18	-	-	-	-	-	-	144.1	0.8	21.9	6.8	166.2	7.7
19	-	-	0.1	-	0.1	0.1	75.8	0.8	16.6	8.5	92.6	9.3
20	0.1	-	1.2	0.2	1.2	0.2	29.7	1.2	10.2	9.8	41.2	11.3
21	0.8	-	14.1	1.4	14.9	1.4	19.5	1.8	7.1	10.5	41.4	13.7
22	2.0	0.1	18.7	2.7	20.7	2.8	12.7	1.9	5.3	10.7	38.6	15.4
23	1.5	0.1	14.3	3.5	15.8	3.6	7.8	1.6	4.0	10.5	27.6	15.7
24	1.1	0.1	10.5	3.7	11.7	3.8	5.4	1.6	3.1	10.2	20.1	15.7
25	0.8	0.1	8.0	3.9	8.8	4.0	4.1	1.5	2.7	10.3	15.7	15.9
26	0.8	0.1	6.3	3.9	7.1	4.1	3.4	1.5	2.5	10.2	12.9	15.8
27	0.6	0.2	5.2	4.2	5.9	4.4	2.7	1.4	2.2	10.0	10.8	15.8
28	0.5	0.2	4.3	4.2	4.8	4.3	2.5	1.4	1.9	10.6	9.3	16.4
29	0.4	0.2	3.8	4.3	4.2	4.5	2.2	1.4	1.9	10.4	8.3	16.3
30+	3.1	3.6	26.2	70.3	29.3	73.9	23.4	24.5	22.4	222.9	75.1	321.6
Unknown	-	-	0.1	1.1	0.1	1.1	0.2	0.1	0.2	11.4	0.5	12.7
All ages	**11.7**	**4.8**	**112.9**	**103.4**	**124.6**	**108.2**	**343.6**	**41.7**	**107.6**	**355.9**	**576.1**	**506.3**
Males												
Age[3] <16	-	-	-	-	-	-	-	-	-	0.1	-	0.1
16	-	-	-	-	-	-	0.2	-	0.3	0.5	0.4	0.5
17	-	-	-	-	-	-	4.4	-	2.0	0.8	6.3	0.8
18	-	-	-	-	-	-	65.1	0.4	10.3	3.8	75.4	4.3
19	-	-	-	-	-	-	36.5	0.4	8.4	4.6	45.0	5.0
20	-	-	0.5	0.1	0.6	0.1	15.2	0.6	5.1	4.9	20.9	5.6
21	0.4	-	5.8	0.5	6.2	0.5	10.5	0.8	3.6	4.9	20.3	6.1
22	1.3	-	8.4	1.0	9.6	1.0	6.8	0.8	2.6	4.4	19.0	6.3
23	0.8	0.1	6.5	1.2	7.4	1.2	4.3	0.7	1.8	4.0	13.4	5.9
24	0.6	0.1	4.9	1.3	5.5	1.3	2.9	0.6	1.3	3.9	9.7	5.9
25	0.4	0.1	3.9	1.4	4.3	1.5	2.1	0.6	1.2	3.9	7.6	6.0
26	0.4	0.1	3.0	1.5	3.4	1.5	1.7	0.5	1.0	3.8	6.1	5.9
27	0.3	0.1	2.6	1.6	2.9	1.7	1.3	0.5	0.9	3.9	5.1	6.1
28	0.3	0.1	2.2	1.8	2.5	1.9	1.1	0.5	0.8	4.1	4.3	6.5
29	0.2	0.1	1.9	1.9	2.2	2.0	0.9	0.5	0.8	4.1	3.9	6.6
30+	1.9	2.0	13.5	29.8	15.4	31.8	8.1	7.6	7.0	78.3	30.5	117.7
Unknown	-	-	0.1	0.4	0.1	0.4	0.1	0.1	0.1	3.9	0.2	4.3
All ages	**6.7**	**2.6**	**53.3**	**42.3**	**60.0**	**44.9**	**161.0**	**14.6**	**47.0**	**133.8**	**268.2**	**193.6**
Females												
Age[3] <16	-	-	-	-	-	-	-	-	-	0.2	-	0.2
16	-	-	-	-	-	-	0.2	-	0.5	0.5	0.7	0.6
17	-	-	-	-	-	-	5.4	-	2.9	0.9	8.3	0.9
18	-	-	-	-	-	-	79.0	0.4	11.7	3.0	90.7	3.4
19	-	-	0.1	-	0.1	-	39.2	0.4	8.2	3.9	47.6	4.3
20	-	-	0.6	0.1	0.7	0.1	14.5	0.6	5.1	4.9	20.3	5.7
21	0.4	-	8.3	0.9	8.7	1.0	9.0	1.0	3.5	5.7	21.1	7.6
22	0.8	0.1	10.3	1.8	11.1	1.8	5.8	1.0	2.7	6.3	19.6	9.1
23	0.6	0.1	7.8	2.3	8.4	2.3	3.6	1.0	2.2	6.4	14.2	9.7
24	0.5	0.1	5.7	2.4	6.2	2.5	2.5	1.0	1.7	6.3	10.4	9.8
25	0.4	0.1	4.1	2.4	4.5	2.5	2.1	1.0	1.5	6.4	8.1	9.9
26	0.4	0.1	3.3	2.5	3.7	2.5	1.7	1.0	1.5	6.4	6.9	9.9
27	0.3	0.1	2.7	2.6	2.9	2.7	1.5	0.9	1.3	6.1	5.7	9.7
28	0.2	0.1	2.2	2.4	2.4	2.5	1.4	0.9	1.1	6.5	4.9	9.9
29	0.2	0.1	1.8	2.4	2.0	2.5	1.2	0.9	1.2	6.3	4.4	9.8
30+	1.2	1.6	12.7	40.5	13.9	42.2	15.3	16.9	15.4	144.6	44.7	203.8
Unknown	-	-	0.1	0.7	0.1	0.7	0.1	0.1	0.1	7.5	0.2	8.3
All ages	**4.9**	**2.3**	**59.6**	**61.0**	**64.6**	**63.3**	**182.6**	**27.1**	**60.7**	**222.0**	**307.9**	**312.7**

Sources: Department for Education and Skills; National Assembly for Wales; Scottish Executive; Northern Ireland Department for Employment and Learning

1 Figures reflect those on a first year of study, i.e. not necessarily brand new entrants to higher education. Higher Education Statistics Agency (HESA) institution figures include Open University students.
2 Full-time includes sandwich. Part-time comprises both day and evening, including block release and open/distance learning.
3 Ages as at 31 August 2001 (1 July for Northern Ireland and 31 December for Scotland).
4 Figures for higher education (HE) institutions are based on the HESA July 'standard registration' count and are not directly comparable with previous years. Figures for further education (FE) institutions (other than in Scotland FE colleges) are snapshots counted at a particular point in the year [November for FE institutions in England and Northern Ireland, and December for FE institutions in Wales]. Students starting courses after these dates will not therefore be counted. Figures for Scotland, however, are whole year (not snapshot) enrolments (rather than headcounts).
5 Revised to include HESA July 'standard registration' count data, and 2001/02 figures for HE students in FE institutions in Wales and Northern Ireland, and FE colleges in Scotland.
6 Includes data for HE students in FE institutions in Wales which cannot be split by level.

POST COMPULSORY EDUCATION AND TRAINING: STUDENTS AND STARTERS
Starts in Government-Supported Work-Based Learning[1] for Young People programmes by region - time series

England and Wales

Thousands

	1990-91	1995-96	2000-01[2]	2001-02[2,3,4]	2002-03[2]
Work-Based Learning for Young People[1,5,6]					
Government Office Region[7]					
England & Wales[8]	244.1	279.9	271.9	270.0	..
North East	23.9	20.5	20.3	19.1	..
North West	46.5	52.2	47.2	45.8	..
Yorkshire and the Humber	30.7	31.3	31.7	30.3	..
East Midlands[9]	30.9	25.2	21.8	22.3	..
West Midlands	33.9	28.0	29.2	32.3	..
Eastern[9]	..	23.3	21.7	21.5	..
London	13.6	23.9	26.1	20.3	..
South East	24.8	32.8	28.4	29.0	..
South West	21.5	22.7	21.2	23.1	..
England[8]	225.9	259.8	247.6	243.7	..
Wales	18.2	20.0	24.3	26.3	27.0
Advanced Modern Apprenticeships(AMA)[10]					
England & Wales[8]	.	28.4	89.5	66.1	..
North East	.	2.5	6.2	3.6	..
North West	.	6.8	16.0	11.0	..
Yorkshire and the Humber	.	4.3	9.4	6.0	..
East Midlands	.	2.7	7.3	5.3	..
West Midlands	.	2.4	10.3	9.2	..
Eastern	.	1.5	7.3	4.7	..
London	.	1.9	9.4	5.2	..
South East	.	1.9	10.6	7.9	..
South West	.	1.8	8.1	7.1	..
England[8]	.	25.8	84.6	60.0	..
Wales	.	2.6	4.9	6.1	6.4
Foundation Modern Apprenticeships(FMA)[11]					
England & Wales[8]	.	.	115.3	120.2	..
England	.	.	103.7	108.6	..
Wales	.	.	11.6	11.6	11.2
Other Training(OT)[12]					
England & Wales[8]	244.1	268.1	57.0	48.6	..
England	225.9	250.7	57.0	48.6	..
Wales	18.2	17.4	-	-	-
Life Skills/Skill Build					
England & Wales[8]	.	.	31.5	35.1	..
England	.	.	23.8	26.5	..
Wales	.	.	7.8	8.6	9.4

Sources: TEC Management Information; LSC Individualised Learner Record; National Council - ELWa

1 Work-Based Training for Young People in Wales. From 26 March 2001, responsibility for Work Based Learning for Adults (WBLA) in England transferred to the Employment Service (ES), which is now part of the Department for Work and Pensions (DWP). From April 2001, the National Council for Education and Training for Wales - ELWa, assumed responsibility for training programmes for Wales. WBLA figures are excluded from this table.
2 From 26 March 2001, the data source for England changed to the Learning and Skills Council's Individualised Learner Record, and there is a discontinuity in the time series. The number of young people in learning on this date from the new data source was 2,000 lower for AMA, 3,000 lower for FMA and 4,000 lower for OT.
3 Includes financial year data for Wales.
4 Includes revised data.
5 Includes Advanced Modern Apprenticeships, Foundation Modern Apprenticeships, Other Training, and, from October 1999, Life Skills (LS) and Skill Build.
6 From 1995-96, figures for Work-Based Learning do not equate the sum of the starts on Modern Apprenticeships, National Traineeships and Other Training because they exclude conversions between programmes whereas the figures for individual programmes include conversions from other programmes.
7 Government Office Regions in England plus country totals for England and for Wales.
8 Figures may not be the sum of the components shown due to rounding.
9 For 1991, Eastern figures were included with East Midlands.
10 Known as Modern Apprenticeships in Wales (and formerly in England).
11 Known as National Traineeships in Wales (and formerly in England).
12 Other Training includes Youth Credits & Youth Training.

3.14

POST COMPULSORY EDUCATION AND TRAINING: STUDENTS AND STARTERS
Work-Based Learning for Young People: characteristics of starts – time series[1]

England   Percentages

	1998/99	2000/01	2001/02	2002/03	Aug 02-Oct 02	Nov 02-Jan 03	Feb 03-Apr 03	May 03-Jul 03
ADVANCED MODERN APPRENTICESHIPS (AMA)[2]								
As a percentage of all starters								
gender								
Males	53	53	57	..	70	..	..	..
Females	47	47	43	..	30	..	..	..
ethnic origin								
White	95	95	96	..	89	..	..	..
Black/African/Caribbean	2	2	1	..	1	..	..	..
Asian	2	2	2	..	1	..	..	..
Other	1	1	1	..	9	..	..	..
special needs								
People with disabilities[3]	2	2	..	..	..	..	..	..
FOUNDATION MODERN APPRENTICESHIPS (FMA)[4]								
As a percentage of all starters								
gender								
Males	44	45	46	..	55	..	..	..
Females	56	55	54	..	45	..	..	..
ethnic origin								
White	94	94	95	..	92	..	..	..
Black/African/Caribbean	2	2	2	..	1	..	..	..
Asian	3	3	2	..	2	..	..	..
Other	1	1	1	..	4	..	..	..
special needs								
People with disabilities[3]	3	2	..	..	..	..	..	..
OTHER TRAINING (OT)[5]								
As a percentage of all starters								
gender								
Males	56	59	56	..	57	..	..	..
Females	44	41	44	..	43	..	..	..
ethnic origin								
White	91	97	97	..	80	..	..	..
Black/African/Caribbean	4	5	5	..	5	..	..	..
Asian	4	6	6	..	6	..	..	..
Other	1	2	2	..	10	..	..	..
special needs								
People with disabilities[3]	7	6	..	..	..	..	..	..
ALL WORK BASED LEARNING FOR YOUNG PEOPLE								
As a percentage of all starters								
gender								
Males	52	51	51	..	59	..	..	..
Females	48	49	49	..	41	..	..	..
ethnic origin								
White	93	93	94	..	88	..	..	..
Black/African/Caribbean	3	3	2	..	2	..	..	..
Asian	3	3	3	..	3	..	..	..
Other	1	1	1	..	7	..	..	..
special needs								
People with disabilities[3]	4	3	..	..	..	..	..	..

Sources: WBLYP trainee database; LSC Individualised Learner Record (ILR)

1 Data are collected on an academic year basis (1 August - 31 July).
2 Formerly known as Modern Apprenticeships.
3 Based on learner's self-assessment. For over half of those who started WBLYP in the last seven months of 2001/02, disability information was not recorded on the ILR. Data on people with disabilities has therefore been withdrawn after January 2002.
4 Formerly known as National Traineeships.
5 Other Training includes Youth Credits & Youth Training.

POST COMPULSORY EDUCATION AND TRAINING: STUDENTS AND STARTERS
Participants in Government-Supported Work-Based Learning[1] for Young People programmes by region - time series

England and Wales   Thousands

	March 91	March 96	March 01[2]	March 02[2,3]	March 03[2]
Work-Based Learning for Young People[1,4]					
Government Office Region[5]					
England & Wales[6]	209.5	252.0	280.8	299.0	..
North East	19.7	17.3	21.2	21.8	..
North West	30.6	46.4	49.3	50.9	..
Yorkshire and the Humber	28.8	26.3	33.3	32.5	..
East Midlands[7]	22.8	23.6	21.9	23.9	..
West Midlands	32.3	26.3	28.4	35.0	..
Eastern[7]	..	24.1	23.8	24.9	..
London	12.7	18.4	23.6	22.4	..
South East	25.8	31.8	32.1	34.2	..
South West	20.5	21.6	25.4	28.3	..
England[6]	193.2	235.8	259.1	273.9	..
Wales	16.4	16.2	21.7	25.1	27.0
Advanced Modern Apprenticeships(AMA)[8]					
England & Wales[6]	.	27.8	127.7	125.1	..
North East	.	2.4	9.2	8.7	..
North West	.	6.5	23.4	22.4	..
Yorkshire and the Humber	.	3.9	14.1	12.5	..
East Midlands	.	2.5	9.9	9.9	..
West Midlands	.	2.3	13.4	15.2	..
Eastern	.	1.6	10.4	8.9	..
London	.	2.0	10.1	9.7	..
South East	.	1.7	15.5	14.4	..
South West	.	1.9	12.7	13.3	..
England[6]	.	24.8	119.0	114.9	..
Wales	.	3.0	8.7	10.2	11.2
Foundation Modern Apprenticeships(FMA)[9]					
England & Wales	.	.	98.3	119.1	..
England	.	.	88.4	108.0	..
Wales	.	.	9.9	11.1	11.8
Other Training(OT)[10]					
England & Wales[6]	209.5	224.2	44.5	43.6	..
England	193.2	211.0	44.1	42.9	..
Wales	16.4	13.2	0.4	0.7	0.2
Life Skills/Skill Build					
England & Wales	.	.	10.5	11.2	..
England	.	.	7.7	8.1	..
Wales	.	.	2.8	3.1	3.7

Sources: TEC Management Information; LSC Individualised Learner Record; National Council - ELWa

1 Work-Based Training for Young People in Wales. From 26 March 2001, responsibility for Work Based Learning for Adults (WBLA) in England transferred to the Employment Service (ES), which is now part of the Department for Work and Pensions (DWP). From April 2001, the National Council for Education and Training for Wales - ELWa, assumed responsibility for training programmes for Wales. WBLA figures are excluded from this table.

2 From 26 March 2001, the data source for England changed to the Learning and Skills Council's Individualised Learner Record, and there is a discontinuity in the time series. The number of young people in learning on this date from the new data source was 2,000 lower for AMA, 3,000 lower for FMA and 4,000 lower for OT.

3 Includes revised figures.

4 Includes Advanced Modern Apprenticeships, Foundation Modern Apprenticeships, Other Training, and, from October 1999, Life Skills (LS) and Skill Build.

5 Government Office Regions in England plus country totals for England and for Wales.

6 Figures may not be the sum of the components shown due to rounding.

7 For 1991, Eastern figures were included with East Midlands.

8 Known as Modern Apprenticeships in Wales (and formerly in England).

9 Known as National Traineeships in Wales (and formerly in England).

10 Other Training includes Youth Credits & Youth Training.

THIS PAGE HAS BEEN LEFT BLANK

POST COMPULSORY EDUCATION AND TRAINING: JOB-RELATED TRAINING
Participation in job-related training[1] in the last four weeks by economic activity and region[2], 2003

United Kingdom: People of working age[3]

Thousands and percentages[4]

	Thousands			Percentages[4]		
	All	Males	Females	All	Males	Females
All people						
United Kingdom	5,141	2,445	2,696	13.8	12.5	15.3
North East	216	106	109	13.7	12.9	14.5
North West	587	277	310	13.9	12.4	15.5
Yorkshire and the Humber	466	219	246	14.9	13.3	16.8
East Midlands	345	149	197	13.2	10.8	15.8
West Midlands	435	198	237	13.4	11.5	15.4
Eastern	428	203	225	12.6	11.4	14.0
London	745	373	372	15.1	14.3	15.9
South East	690	330	359	13.6	12.5	14.9
South West	421	202	220	14.0	12.7	15.4
England	4,333	2,058	2,276	13.9	12.5	15.4
Wales	270	128	142	15.2	13.7	16.9
Scotland	418	205	213	13.2	12.5	13.9
Northern Ireland	120	54	66	11.5	10.1	13.1
Employees [5,6]						
United Kingdom	3,809	1,810	1,999	15.6	13.9	17.5
North East	157	77	80	16.0	14.8	17.3
North West	436	207	229	15.7	14.0	17.7
Yorkshire and the Humber	342	158	183	16.5	14.2	19.1
East Midlands	246	106	140	13.9	11.1	17.3
West Midlands	328	147	181	15.1	12.5	18.2
Eastern	342	162	180	14.7	13.1	16.5
London	478	248	230	16.3	15.4	17.4
South East	540	256	285	15.6	14.0	17.4
South West	328	156	172	16.1	14.5	17.8
England	3,197	1,516	1,681	15.6	13.8	17.6
Wales	205	93	112	18.3	16.0	20.7
Scotland	321	159	162	15.1	14.5	15.9
Northern Ireland	85	41	45	13.6	12.2	15.2
Self-employed [6,7]						
United Kingdom	244	143	101	7.6	6.0	12.2
North East	*	*	*	*	*	*
North West	22	14	*	6.9	5.9	*
Yorkshire and the Humber	19	12	*	8.4	7.1	*
East Midlands	16	10	*	7.8	6.4	*
West Midlands	17	11	*	7.7	6.2	*
Eastern	17	*	*	5.2	*	*
London	44	24	20	8.5	6.5	13.3
South East	43	24	19	8.2	6.4	12.8
South West	20	11	*	6.2	5.0	*
England	206	120	86	7.5	5.9	12.0
Wales	16	*	*	9.9	*	*
Scotland	18	11	*	8.3	6.5	*
Northern Ireland	*	*	*	*	*	*

Source: Labour Force Survey, Spring 2003 [10]

1 Job-related training includes both on and off-the-job training.
2 Government Office Regions in England and each UK country.
3 Working age is defined as males aged 16-64 and females aged 16-59.
4 Expressed as a percentage of the total number of people in each group.
5 Employees are those in employment excluding the self-employed, unpaid family workers and those on government employment and training programmes.
6 The split into employees and self-employed is based on respondents' own assessment of their employment status.
7 Self-employed are those in employment excluding employees, unpaid family workers and those on government employment and training programmes.
8 Unemployed according to the International Labour Organization (ILO) definition.
9 Economically inactive are those who are neither in employment nor ILO unemployed.
10 Users of these data should read the LFS entry in Annex A, as it contains important information about the LFS and the concepts and definitions used.

CONTINUED

POST COMPULSORY EDUCATION AND TRAINING: JOB-RELATED TRAINING

Participation in job-related training[1] in the last four weeks by economic activity and region[2], 2003

United Kingdom: People of working age[3]

Thousands and percentages[4]

	Thousands			Percentages[4]		
	All	Males	Females	All	Males	Females
ILO unemployed [8]						
United Kingdom	137	72	64	9.5	8.0	11.9
North East	*	*	*	*	*	*
North West	11	*	*	6.8	*	*
Yorkshire and the Humber	11	*	*	8.1	*	*
East Midlands	11	*	*	13.2	*	*
West Midlands	16	*	*	11.5	*	*
Eastern	12	*	*	11.1	*	*
London	32	18	14	12.6	11.8	13.8
South East	13	*	*	8.4	*	*
South West	13	*	*	14.2	*	*
England	124	66	58	10.3	8.7	12.9
Wales	*	*	*	*	*	*
Scotland	*	*	*	*	*	*
Northern Ireland	*	*	*	*	*	*
Economically inactive [9]						
United Kingdom	882	379	503	11.1	12.1	10.4
North East	43	20	23	10.1	11.5	9.1
North West	110	49	61	11.4	12.1	10.9
Yorkshire and the Humber	88	39	49	13.0	14.5	12.0
East Midlands	68	26	42	12.5	12.3	12.6
West Midlands	68	29	39	9.6	10.6	9.0
Eastern	53	22	31	8.7	9.8	8.1
London	185	80	105	15.2	17.4	13.9
South East	87	40	47	9.9	12.3	8.4
South West	57	24	33	10.1	10.6	9.8
England	759	329	430	11.5	12.8	10.7
Wales	38	19	20	9.1	9.8	8.4
Scotland	66	26	39	9.7	9.3	9.9
Northern Ireland	20	*	15	7.1	*	8.3

Source: Labour Force Survey, Spring 2003 [10]

See previous page for footnotes.

POST COMPULSORY EDUCATION AND TRAINING: JOB-RELATED TRAINING

3.17 Participation by employees[1] in job-related training[2] in the last four weeks by type of training and a range of personal characteristics, 2003

United Kingdom: Employees[1] of working age[3]

Thousands and percentages[4]

	Total number of employees (thousands)	of which: receiving off-the-job training only (%)	receiving on-the-job training only (%)	receiving both on and off-the-job training (%)	receiving any training (%)
All employees	24,413	7.5	4.9	3.1	15.6
By gender					
Males	13,010	6.6	4.6	2.7	13.9
Females	11,403	8.7	5.3	3.5	17.5
By age					
16-19	1,400	11.6	5.4	6.0	23.1
20-24	2,407	10.3	6.7	4.8	21.9
25-29	2,730	8.4	5.9	3.8	18.2
30-39	6,687	7.5	4.7	3.1	15.2
40-49	5,983	7.6	4.8	2.9	15.4
50-64	5,206	4.7	3.9	1.4	10.1
By ethnic origin					
White	22,858	7.4	4.9	3.1	15.5
Non-white	1,555	9.2	5.1	3.2	17.5
of which:					
Mixed	120	10.3	*	*	21.8
Asian or Asian British	747	6.6	4.5	3.1	14.1
Black or Black British	410	12.6	5.8	3.2	21.6
Chinese	96	12.6	*	*	18.0
Other ethnic group	172	9.7	6.7	*	19.2
By highest qualification held [5]					
Degree or equivalent	4,680	12.0	6.1	4.9	23.1
Higher Education qualification (below degree level)	2,441	10.7	6.9	4.4	22.1
GCE A level or equivalent	5,987	7.6	4.6	2.8	15.0
GCSE grades A* to C, or equivalent	5,525	6.6	4.8	3.0	14.5
Other	3,213	5.0	4.1	1.8	10.9
None	2,399	1.3	3.0	0.8	5.1
By region					
United Kingdom	24,413	7.5	4.9	3.1	15.6
North East	983	6.4	5.7	3.9	16.0
North West	2,773	7.3	5.2	3.3	15.7
Yorkshire and the Humber	2,073	7.5	5.8	3.1	16.5
East Midlands	1,766	6.1	4.8	3.0	13.9
West Midlands	2,170	7.0	5.1	3.0	15.1
Eastern	2,332	7.6	4.0	3.1	14.7
London	2,932	8.3	4.8	3.2	16.3
South East	3,472	8.1	4.6	2.8	15.6
South West	2,039	8.6	4.7	2.7	16.1
England	20,539	7.6	4.9	3.1	15.6
Wales	1,122	8.6	5.9	3.7	18.3
Scotland	2,124	6.9	4.8	3.5	15.1
Northern Ireland	628	6.9	4.8	1.9	13.6
Time series (Spring of each year) [6]					
1991	21,920	8.3	4.3	2.3	14.9
1996	22,092	8.5	3.9	2.4	14.8
2001	24,189	8.1	5.1	3.2	16.4
2002	24,319	8.1	5.2	3.3	16.6
2003	24,413	7.5	4.9	3.1	15.6

Source: Labour Force Survey, Spring 2003 [7]

1 Employees are those in employment excluding the self-employed, unpaid family workers and those on government employment and training programmes.

2 Job-related training includes both on and off-the-job training.

3 Working age is defined as males aged 16-64 and females aged 16-59.

4 Expressed as a percentage of the total number of people in each group.

5 Apart from rounding, figures may not sum to grand totals because of questions in the LFS which were unanswered or did not apply.

6 Data prior to Summer 1994 are not directly comparable with later years due to changes in the questionnaire.

7 Users of these data should read the LFS entry in Annex A, as it contains important information about the LFS and the concepts and definitions used.

POST COMPULSORY EDUCATION AND TRAINING: JOB-RELATED TRAINING

3.18

Participation by employees[1] in job-related training[2] in the last four weeks by a range of economic characteristics, 2003

United Kingdom: Employees[1] of working age[3]

Thousands and percentages[4]

	Thousands			Percentages[4]		
	All	Males	Females	All	Males	Females
All employees	3,809	1,810	1,999	15.6	13.9	17.5
By industry						
Agriculture, forestry & fishing	15	13	*	9.0	10.3	*
Energy and water supply	47	37	*	16.4	16.4	*
Manufacturing	378	294	84	9.5	9.8	8.8
Construction	159	145	14	11.7	12.2	8.6
Distribution, hotels & restaurants	579	269	309	11.7	11.6	11.9
Transport	191	135	56	11.0	10.4	12.9
Banking, finance & insurance	567	320	247	15.4	16.0	14.6
Public administration, education & health	1,685	511	1,174	24.0	23.1	24.4
Other services	188	85	103	14.8	13.8	15.8
By occupation						
Managers and senior officials	500	308	191	14.0	12.5	17.4
Professional occupations	724	368	356	24.9	21.6	29.6
Associate professional and technical	766	362	404	22.7	20.4	25.3
Administrative and secretarial	490	125	365	14.4	17.1	13.7
Skilled trades	259	242	17	11.5	11.7	8.9
Personal service occupations	408	66	341	22.2	20.6	22.6
Sales and customer service occupations	276	83	192	13.1	13.1	13.1
Process, plant and machine operatives	126	108	18	6.5	6.6	5.8
Elementary occupations	260	145	115	8.6	8.8	8.4
By full-time/part-time work [5]						
Full-time	2,899	1,612	1,287	15.7	13.6	19.5
Part-time	909	197	711	15.3	17.7	14.8
of which [6]:						
students	355	155	200	30.2	29.9	30.3
could not find full-time job	52	17	35	10.4	8.5	11.8
did not want full-time job	485	23	462	11.8	6.6	12.3
By employment status [6]						
Permanent job	3,522	1,693	1,829	15.4	13.8	17.2
Temporary job	271	108	163	19.7	16.9	22.2
of which:						
seasonal / casual work	54	26	28	17.8	17.4	18.1
contract for fixed term or task	161	57	105	23.9	19.2	27.6
agency temping	26	11	15	10.4	8.6	12.4
other	30	15	15	20.6	22.8	18.9

Source: Labour Force Survey, Spring 2003 [7]

1 Employees are those in employment excluding the self-employed, unpaid family workers and those on government employment and training programmes.

2 Job-related training includes both on and off-the-job training.

3 Working age is defined as males aged 16-64 and females aged 16-59.

4 Expressed as a percentage of the total number of people in each group.

5 The split between employees working full-time and part-time is based on respondents' own assessment.

6 Apart from rounding, figures may not sum to grand totals because of questions in the LFS which were unanswered or did not apply.

7 Users of these data should read the LFS entry in Annex A, as it contains important information about the LFS and the concepts and definitions used.

3.19 POST COMPULSORY EDUCATION AND TRAINING: JOB-RELATED TRAINING

Participation by employees[1] in job-related training[2] in the last four weeks by type of training and a range of economic characteristics, 2003

United Kingdom: Employees[1] of working age[3]

Thousands and percentages[4]

	Total number of employees (thousands)	of which: receiving off-the-job training only (%)	receiving on-the-job training only (%)	receiving both on and off-the-job training (%)	receiving any training (%)
All employees	24,413	7.5	4.9	3.1	15.6
By industry [5]					
Agriculture, forestry & fishing	161	*	*	*	9.0
Energy & water supply	286	7.9	5.0	*	16.4
Manufacturing	3,970	4.6	3.4	1.5	9.5
Construction	1,356	4.6	3.2	3.8	11.7
Distribution, hotels & restaurants	4,929	6.5	3.7	1.5	11.7
Transport	1,729	4.9	4.1	2.0	11.0
Banking, finance & insurance	3,691	7.4	4.8	3.2	15.4
Public administration, education & health	7,012	11.4	7.4	5.2	24.0
Other services	1,267	6.9	4.7	3.1	14.8
By occupation [5]					
Managers and senior officials	3,561	7.2	4.1	2.7	14.0
Professional occupations	2,912	12.7	6.8	5.3	24.9
Associate professional and technical	3,375	10.1	7.6	5.0	22.7
Administrative and secretarial	3,392	7.9	4.2	2.3	14.4
Skilled trades	2,260	4.3	3.7	3.4	11.5
Personal service occupations	1,832	8.6	8.0	5.7	22.2
Sales and customer service occupations	2,107	7.0	4.5	1.5	13.1
Process, plant and machine operatives	1,948	2.4	3.1	1.0	6.5
Elementary occupations	3,011	5.2	2.6	0.8	8.6
By full-time/part-time work [5,6]					
Full-time	18,482	7.0	5.3	3.4	15.7
Part-time	5,923	9.3	3.8	2.3	15.3
of which:					
students	1,178	24.4	2.7	2.8	30.2
could not find full-time job	499	4.5	4.3	1.7	10.4
did not want full-time job	4,110	5.5	4.0	2.2	11.8
By employment status [5]					
Permanent	22,864	7.3	5.0	3.1	15.4
Temporary	1,375	11.0	4.5	4.1	19.7
of which:					
seasonal / casual work	304	13.5	*	*	17.8
contract for fixed term or task	675	11.7	6.6	5.6	23.9
agency temping	252	6.4	*	*	10.4
other	144	10.6	*	*	20.6

Source: Labour Force Survey, Spring 2003 [7]

1 Employees are those in employment excluding the self-employed, unpaid family workers and those on government employment and training programmes.
2 Job-related training includes both on and off-the-job training.
3 Working age is defined as males aged 16-64 and females aged 16-59.
4 Expressed as a percentage of the total number of people in each group.
5 Apart from rounding, figures may not sum to grand totals because of questions in the LFS which were unanswered or did not apply.
6 The split between employees working full-time and part-time is based on respondents' own assessment.
7 Users of these data should read the LFS entry in Annex A, as it contains important information about the LFS and the concepts and definitions used.

THIS PAGE HAS BEEN LEFT BLANK

POST COMPULSORY EDUCATION AND TRAINING: JOB-RELATED TRAINING

3.20

Participation by employees[1] in job-related training[2] in the last four weeks by region[3] and a range of personal and economic characteristics, 2003

United Kingdom: Employees[1] of working age[4]

Thousands and percentages[5]

	United Kingdom	North East	North West	Yorkshire and the Humber	East Midlands	West Midlands	Eastern
All employees	3,809	157	436	342	246	328	342
By gender							
Males	1,810	77	207	158	106	147	162
Females	1,999	80	229	183	140	181	180
By age							
16-19	323	13	37	30	24	23	30
20-24	527	22	57	50	26	51	42
25-29	497	18	48	36	26	31	47
30-39	1,019	42	118	92	70	84	101
40-49	919	43	114	84	73	87	71
50-64	525	19	62	50	28	53	51
By highest qualification held [6]							
Degree or equivalent	1,080	35	109	91	64	79	98
Higher Education qualification (below degree level)	538	26	58	49	31	55	47
GCE A level or equivalent	901	38	112	80	55	77	76
GCSE grades A* to C, or equivalent	799	38	99	70	65	78	75
Other	349	13	37	37	24	24	33
None	122	*	19	14	*	13	11
By industry							
Agriculture & fishing	15	*	*	*	*	*	*
Energy & water	47	*	*	*	*	*	*
Manufacturing	378	20	43	34	30	43	32
Construction	159	*	22	16	12	13	15
Distribution, hotels & restaurants	579	20	73	51	38	43	55
Transport & communication	191	*	18	19	13	13	16
Banking, finance & insurance etc	567	15	55	48	21	37	56
Public admin, education & health	1,685	78	196	153	114	161	143
Other services	188	*	21	16	14	*	19
By occupation							
Managers and senior officials	500	16	54	39	34	38	57
Professional occupations	724	24	80	65	38	58	70
Associate professional and technical	766	31	82	63	51	63	70
Administrative and secretarial	490	25	60	45	32	44	40
Skilled trades	259	13	34	25	16	29	18
Personal service occupations	408	16	51	36	33	38	33
Sales and customer service occupations	276	13	33	31	17	22	22
Process, plant and machine operatives	126	*	14	17	*	15	12
Elementary occupations	260	*	28	21	16	22	19

Percentages [5]

	United Kingdom	North East	North West	Yorkshire and the Humber	East Midlands	West Midlands	Eastern
All employees	15.6	16.0	15.7	16.5	13.9	15.1	14.7
By gender							
Males	13.9	14.8	14.0	14.2	11.1	12.5	13.1
Females	17.5	17.3	17.7	19.1	17.3	18.2	16.5
By age							
16-19	23.1	26.0	24.6	22.1	20.8	18.5	20.9
20-24	21.9	22.4	19.9	24.3	16.9	24.5	20.0
25-29	18.2	17.9	16.6	17.4	14.4	15.4	18.6
30-39	15.2	16.2	15.4	16.6	14.7	14.2	15.6
40-49	15.4	16.0	16.6	16.0	16.4	15.8	13.0
50-64	10.1	9.1	10.4	11.1	7.0	10.6	9.6
By highest qualification held							
Degree or equivalent	23.1	24.7	24.7	27.8	23.3	23.6	22.7
Higher Education qualification (below degree level)	22.1	25.2	20.5	26.7	20.3	25.2	23.6
GCE A level or equivalent	15.0	13.8	15.7	14.7	12.4	14.8	14.4
GCSE grades A* to C, or equivalent	14.5	16.5	14.3	14.2	15.2	14.7	12.5
Other	10.9	11.6	12.2	12.6	9.9	8.0	10.5
None	5.1	*	6.0	6.1	*	5.1	4.6
By industry							
Agriculture & fishing	9.0	*	*	*	*	*	*
Energy & water	16.4	*	*	*	*	*	*
Manufacturing	9.5	10.9	8.9	9.0	7.5	8.4	8.9
Construction	11.7	*	14.0	12.2	11.3	11.6	12.3
Distribution, hotels & restaurants	11.7	10.4	13.1	11.7	10.5	10.3	11.4
Transport & communication	11.0	*	8.6	13.3	10.7	9.1	9.3
Banking, finance & insurance etc	15.4	14.5	15.3	18.6	11.2	14.3	13.5
Public admin, education & health	24.0	25.1	24.2	25.2	24.4	27.5	23.5
Other services	14.8	*	14.9	17.8	17.7	*	14.9
By occupation							
Managers and senior officials	14.0	15.3	15.4	16.0	13.8	12.5	14.5
Professional occupations	24.9	24.3	25.9	30.1	21.8	26.1	24.0
Associate professional and technical	22.7	25.6	23.6	24.6	23.8	24.5	22.4
Administrative and secretarial	14.4	19.5	14.6	16.8	14.0	15.3	11.6
Skilled trades	11.5	12.4	12.3	11.0	9.7	11.9	8.8
Personal service occupations	22.2	20.4	23.6	23.3	24.6	23.6	20.0
Sales and customer service occupations	13.1	13.6	13.2	15.0	11.4	12.2	10.9
Process, plant and machine operatives	6.5	*	5.6	7.6	*	6.0	7.5
Elementary occupations	8.6	*	7.7	7.4	6.5	8.2	7.3

Source: Labour Force Survey, Spring 2003 [7]

1 Employees are those in employment excluding the self-employed, unpaid family workers and those on government employment and training programmes.
2 Job-related training includes both on and off-the-job training.
3 Government Office Regions in England and each UK country.
4 Working age is defined as males aged 16-64 and females aged 16-59.
5 Expressed as a percentage of the total number of people in each group.
6 Apart from rounding, figures may not sum to grand totals because of questions in the LFS which were unanswered or did not apply.
7 Users of these data should read the LFS entry in Annex A, as it contains important information about the LFS and the concepts and definitions used.

POST COMPULSORY EDUCATION AND TRAINING: JOB-RELATED TRAINING

3.20

Participation by employees[1] in job-related training[2] in the last four weeks by region[3] and a range of personal and economic characteristics, 2003

United Kingdom: Employees[1] of working age[4]

Thousands and percentages[5]

	Region[3]						
	London	South East	South West	England	Wales	Scotland	Northern Ireland
All employees	478	540	328	3,197	205	321	85
By gender							
Males	248	256	156	1,516	93	159	41
Females	230	285	172	1,681	112	162	45
By age							
16-19	29	51	35	271	15	29	*
20-24	83	59	49	438	28	45	15
25-29	100	79	38	422	23	40	12
30-39	116	148	83	854	58	84	23
40-49	99	119	76	766	54	81	18
50-64	51	85	47	446	26	43	10
By highest qualification held [6]							
Degree or equivalent	191	153	84	903	61	94	22
Higher Education qualification (below degree level)	39	70	49	424	30	69	15
GCE A level or equivalent	88	130	84	740	49	84	27
GCSE grades A* to C, or equivalent	72	121	77	695	43	46	15
Other	77	49	24	317	12	18	*
None	10	15	*	101	*	*	*
By industry							
Agriculture & fishing	*	*	*	14	*	*	*
Energy & water	*	*	*	32	*	11	*
Manufacturing	25	50	37	315	22	33	*
Construction	15	19	10	132	11	12	*
Distribution, hotels & restaurants	68	90	55	494	27	44	14
Transport & communication	36	29	15	168	*	13	*
Banking, finance & insurance etc	110	104	49	495	20	45	*
Public admin, education & health	183	213	146	1,387	108	144	45
Other services	35	28	14	160	*	18	*
By occupation							
Managers and senior officials	64	88	43	432	19	42	*
Professional occupations	113	105	59	612	42	58	12
Associate professional and technical	94	110	70	635	44	68	20
Administrative and secretarial	63	62	43	414	24	38	14
Skilled trades	17	33	25	209	16	29	*
Personal service occupations	44	56	33	338	27	34	*
Sales and customer service occupations	35	41	22	235	*	23	*
Process, plant and machine operatives	10	11	*	103	*	11	*
Elementary occupations	39	35	26	217	14	20	*
Percentages [5]							
All employees	16.3	15.6	16.1	15.6	18.3	15.1	13.6
By gender							
Males	15.4	14.0	14.5	13.8	16.0	14.5	12.2
Females	17.4	17.4	17.8	17.6	20.7	15.9	15.2
By age							
16-19	27.1	23.1	26.0	23.0	21.8	23.7	*
20-24	26.7	18.5	24.7	22.1	23.1	20.4	19.6
25-29	20.8	20.6	17.7	18.3	21.1	17.4	13.8
30-39	13.4	15.4	15.5	15.1	19.5	14.8	13.5
40-49	14.8	14.5	15.4	15.3	19.5	14.5	12.0
50-64	10.3	11.1	10.2	10.1	10.7	9.9	8.7
By highest qualification held							
Degree or equivalent	21.5	19.9	23.0	22.7	29.4	23.9	19.8
Higher Education qualification (below degree level)	18.5	20.9	21.6	22.2	24.8	20.4	22.8
GCE A level or equivalent	16.5	15.6	16.5	15.1	18.5	13.2	15.5
GCSE grades A* to C, or equivalent	14.6	15.3	15.1	14.6	15.8	13.4	10.8
Other	13.6	10.6	8.7	11.1	9.5	9.5	*
None	4.2	5.8	*	5.1	*	*	*
By industry							
Agriculture & fishing	*	*	*	10.9	*	*	*
Energy & water	*	*	*	15.4	*	20.1	*
Manufacturing	10.1	10.1	11.7	9.3	10.8	11.6	*
Construction	13.6	11.3	9.5	12.1	16.4	8.8	*
Distribution, hotels & restaurants	11.9	12.5	12.8	11.8	12.0	10.6	12.0
Transport & communication	14.5	11.5	10.9	11.2	*	8.9	*
Banking, finance & insurance etc	15.1	15.8	17.7	15.2	18.8	15.5	*
Public admin, education & health	23.6	23.1	22.9	24.2	28.1	21.9	18.5
Other services	15.1	14.9	14.8	14.8	*	17.1	*
By occupation							
Managers and senior officials	12.0	13.3	15.2	13.9	15.4	16.3	*
Professional occupations	25.7	21.8	24.9	24.8	29.8	24.0	20.0
Associate professional and technical	19.0	20.9	23.1	22.4	28.3	22.5	24.2
Administrative and secretarial	13.6	13.1	16.0	14.4	17.1	13.5	14.6
Skilled trades	10.5	12.7	12.9	11.4	13.7	12.6	*
Personal service occupations	22.5	22.0	20.0	22.3	27.6	20.0	*
Sales and customer service occupations	16.9	14.4	12.0	13.4	*	11.2	*
Process, plant and machine operatives	8.1	6.3	*	6.4	*	6.4	*
Elementary occupations	12.5	9.8	10.1	8.6	10.0	7.3	*

Source: Labour Force Survey, Spring 2003 [7]

See previous page for footnotes.

POST COMPULSORY EDUCATION AND TRAINING: JOB-RELATED TRAINING

3.21

Length of job-related training[1], 2003

United Kingdom: People of working age[2]

Thousands and percentages[3]

	Total receiving training[6] (thousands)	Length of training[4,5]							
		Under 1 week	1 week < 1 month	1 month < 6 months	6 months < 1 year	1 year < 2 years	2 years < 3 years	3 years or more	Ongoing or no definite limit
All people	5,141	28.7	3.2	5.8	6.3	8.9	8.3	14.9	14.7
Economic activity									
Employees [7,8]	3,809	35.7	3.8	5.8	5.6	7.6	6.8	9.4	16.6
Self-employed [8,9]	244	39.1	*	6.8	7.7	6.2	4.8	5.4	20.2
ILO unemployed [10]	137	*	*	14.6	10.4	13.2	10.1	16.5	12.2
Economically inactive [11]	882	*	*	3.7	8.3	13.7	15.0	40.7	5.5
All employees	3,809	35.7	3.8	5.8	5.6	7.6	6.8	9.4	16.6
By gender									
Males	1,810	35.8	4.8	5.0	4.0	6.9	6.8	10.6	17.2
Females	1,999	35.6	2.8	6.6	7.0	8.3	6.8	8.2	16.0
By age									
16-19	323	5.8	*	*	5.4	15.3	22.7	24.6	11.1
20-24	527	16.5	3.0	4.4	5.7	9.7	9.1	21.6	15.6
25-29	497	31.1	4.4	6.3	5.2	8.2	5.7	10.9	16.6
30-39	1,019	39.2	4.6	6.3	5.9	6.8	5.8	6.4	16.8
40-49	919	46.1	3.5	6.6	5.6	6.4	4.6	3.6	17.0
50-64	525	52.9	3.9	6.8	5.2	4.1	*	2.0	19.7
By highest qualification held [5]									
Degree or equivalent	1,080	45.3	3.7	4.3	4.9	6.3	5.0	6.9	15.1
Higher Education qualification (below degree level)	538	41.6	3.1	7.3	5.5	7.2	5.7	6.9	15.1
GCE A level or equivalent	901	30.6	4.8	6.3	5.3	6.2	7.0	15.9	15.5
GCSE grades A* to C, or equivalent	799	28.2	3.4	6.1	7.5	10.9	10.8	8.3	16.7
Other qualification	349	30.1	*	5.7	5.1	8.3	5.6	7.9	22.6
No qualification	122	33.2	*	9.6	*	8.9	*	*	24.7
By industry									
Agriculture, forestry & fishing	15	*	*	*	*	*	*	*	*
Energy & water supply	47	38.3	*	*	*	*	*	*	*
Manufacturing	378	34.5	5.4	6.3	4.6	5.8	6.0	10.1	17.8
Construction	159	30.3	*	*	*	*	10.8	23.7	11.1
Distribution, hotels & restaurants	579	21.6	3.0	6.0	4.8	11.1	11.7	14.9	16.1
Transport	191	38.2	5.6	5.5	5.9	5.6	*	6.0	17.9
Banking, finance & insurance	567	36.8	4.5	4.9	5.3	5.3	5.0	9.2	19.0
Public administration, education & health	1,685	41.4	3.3	6.5	6.3	7.8	5.5	5.8	16.4
Other services	188	27.5	*	*	7.3	9.2	8.8	15.0	15.4
By occupation									
Managers and senior officials	500	46.8	4.7	5.0	4.8	6.1	3.5	4.3	16.7
Professional occupations	724	48.8	3.1	2.9	4.4	5.8	5.9	7.2	14.9
Associate professional and technical	766	37.2	5.1	7.2	5.3	7.1	4.8	6.9	17.5
Administrative and secretarial	490	34.1	3.0	7.1	7.2	6.1	5.4	8.5	19.1
Skilled trades	259	27.3	4.2	5.2	*	7.6	10.0	22.5	11.1
Personal service occupations	408	26.6	2.4	6.0	9.4	12.8	8.5	7.3	18.0
Sales and customer service occupations	276	15.0	*	6.9	5.0	10.0	13.1	18.2	17.4
Process, plant and machine operatives	126	32.7	*	10.5	*	*	*	*	20.2
Elementary occupations	260	22.6	*	6.3	4.7	10.7	12.0	17.2	13.5
By region [12]									
United Kingdom	3,809	35.7	3.8	5.8	5.6	7.6	6.8	9.4	16.6
North East	157	36.8	2.1	8.2	4.6	6.3	7.0	10.3	18.3
North West	436	32.7	3.6	6.0	5.8	8.2	7.8	8.0	19.0
Yorkshire and the Humber	342	34.3	3.0	5.0	6.0	9.3	5.9	9.1	18.6
East Midlands	246	34.1	3.2	5.7	6.5	8.7	6.9	7.6	15.2
West Midlands	328	33.0	4.5	7.2	6.0	8.0	7.3	7.4	17.9
Eastern	342	40.7	4.0	6.3	5.4	6.1	6.2	7.7	16.5
London	478	36.0	2.5	4.7	4.5	7.6	6.8	10.8	15.3
South East	540	37.4	4.1	5.3	4.1	7.1	7.2	10.0	15.0
South West	328	38.7	6.0	5.7	7.1	7.7	7.1	7.9	12.9
England	3,197	36.0	3.7	5.8	5.4	7.7	7.0	9.0	16.4
Wales	205	37.5	*	5.3	5.0	6.4	7.3	11.3	14.8
Scotland	321	35.6	4.3	6.9	7.0	7.9	5.2	10.4	15.5
Northern Ireland	85	22.0	*	*	*	*	*	*	31.0

Source: Labour Force Survey, Spring 2003 [13]

1 Job-related training includes both on and off-the-job training.
2 Working age is defined as males aged 16-64 and females aged 16-59. These figures include unpaid family workers, those on government employment and training programmes, or those who did not answer, who are excluded from the Economic activity analyses below.
3 Expressed as a percentage of those in the group who received training in the last four weeks.
4 The total length of the course was recorded not just the part completed. For people engaged on day or block release, the total length of training is given. For people who dropped out of a course the time spent on the course, not the total length is recorded.
5 Apart from rounding, figures may not sum to grand totals because of questions in the LFS which were unanswered or did not apply.
6 People of working age who received on or off-the-job training in the last four weeks.
7 Employees are those in employment excluding the self-employed, unpaid family workers and those on government employment job-training programmes.
8 The split into employees and self-employed is based on respondents' own assessment of their employment status.
9 Self-employed are those in employment excluding employees, unpaid family workers and those on government employment and training programmes.
10 Unemployed according to the International Labour Organization (ILO) definition.
11 Economically inactive are those who are neither in employment nor ILO unemployed.
12 Government Office Regions in England and each UK country.
13 Users of these data should read the LFS entry in Annex A, as it contains important information about the LFS and the concepts and definitions used.

POST COMPULSORY EDUCATION AND TRAINING: JOB-RELATED TRAINING

3.22

Location of off-the-job training[1], 2003

United Kingdom: People of working age[2]

Thousands and percentages[3]

	Total receiving training[1] (thousands)	Main place of training (percentages)[4]						
		Employer's premises	Another employer's premises	Private training centre	At home[5]	Further Education college or University	Other educational institution	Others
All people[2]	3,878	22.2	3.9	6.5	6.3	40.3	3.8	8.3
Economic activity								
Employees [6,7]	2,599	31.3	5.0	7.8	6.6	29.7	3.0	8.4
Self-employed [7,8]	203	7.1	6.7	14.0	13.0	28.5	7.4	18.0
ILO unemployed [9]	137	*	*	*	9.4	51.9	*	14.1
Economically inactive [10]	882	1.2	*	1.5	3.3	72.8	5.3	4.4
All employees	2,599	31.3	5.0	7.8	6.6	29.7	3.0	8.4
By gender								
Males	1,212	31.5	5.3	8.1	6.8	28.8	2.4	8.8
Females	1,387	31.2	4.7	7.6	6.5	30.4	3.5	8.1
By age								
16-19	246	14.8	*	*	*	64.3	4.7	*
20-24	364	22.4	*	5.2	4.6	47.6	2.7	3.6
25-29	335	28.7	4.4	8.9	10.9	27.5	*	6.1
30-39	705	34.1	5.0	10.3	7.1	23.8	2.8	9.3
40-49	628	37.5	7.0	7.7	7.7	19.7	2.9	10.4
50-64	322	38.9	6.8	9.5	4.9	17.4	*	15.6
By highest qualification held [4]								
Degree or equivalent	794	32.5	6.9	11.3	8.5	17.9	3.4	11.5
Higher Education qualification (below degree level)	368	33.4	5.6	7.7	6.0	28.7	2.9	8.0
GCE A level or equivalent	626	28.4	4.0	5.9	5.3	38.1	2.6	7.7
GCSE grades A* to C, or equivalent	532	31.9	3.6	6.3	5.9	36.8	3.0	5.7
Other qualification	217	29.2	*	6.0	6.9	33.2	*	6.5
No qualification	50	39.3	*	*	*	24.3	*	*
By industry [4]								
Agriculture, forestry & fishing	10	*	*	*	*	*	*	*
Energy & water supply	33	41.3	*	*	*	*	*	*
Manufacturing	245	30.8	*	12.7	6.2	28.9	*	7.5
Construction	115	24.5	*	8.9	*	42.6	*	*
Distribution, hotels & restaurants	397	20.7	2.5	3.7	4.3	51.1	3.6	3.8
Transport	119	33.3	*	8.7	8.6	19.9	*	9.1
Banking, finance & insurance	390	30.6	4.2	10.5	12.3	21.4	*	10.7
Public administration, education & health	1,164	36.5	6.4	7.2	6.0	23.6	3.5	9.9
Other services	126	23.5	*	*	*	42.3	*	*
By occupation								
Managers and senior officials	354	35.3	8.1	11.3	8.6	15.1	*	11.9
Professional occupations	526	33.3	6.7	10.9	7.3	18.3	4.2	12.0
Associate professional and technical	510	36.4	6.9	8.2	7.8	23.9	2.3	6.6
Administrative and secretarial	348	35.4	*	7.3	8.2	26.7	*	8.6
Skilled trades	174	27.1	*	6.9	*	45.6	*	*
Personal service occupations	261	29.3	*	4.3	6.4	35.3	*	9.4
Sales and customer service occupations	179	16.2	*	*	*	62.3	*	*
Process, plant and machine operatives	66	33.5	*	*	*	29.6	*	*
Elementary occupations	181	17.1	*	*	*	57.3	*	*
By region [11]								
United Kingdom	2,599	31.3	5.0	7.8	6.6	29.7	3.0	8.4
North East	101	30.4	*	*	*	31.0	*	*
North West	292	31.9	5.0	6.5	8.5	29.3	*	9.4
Yorkshire and the Humber	219	30.6	*	6.8	6.0	31.2	*	9.1
East Midlands	161	31.0	*	9.2	6.8	28.7	*	*
West Midlands	217	36.1	*	8.5	*	29.7	*	6.4
Eastern	249	32.8	7.5	9.9	8.7	23.9	*	8.9
London	336	28.3	5.7	8.6	4.1	31.1	4.3	7.4
South East	380	32.0	4.9	9.0	7.6	27.1	2.8	8.1
South West	231	29.6	*	6.5	6.9	32.7	*	10.3
England	2,186	31.4	5.0	8.2	6.6	29.2	3.1	8.3
Wales	138	32.3	*	*	*	31.0	*	8.9
Scotland	220	32.8	4.9	*	7.3	29.1	*	10.1
Northern Ireland	55	*	21.9	*	*	*	47.1	*

Source: Labour Force Survey, Spring 2003 [12]

1 Excludes those receiving on-the-job training only.
2 Working age is defined as males aged 16-64 and females aged 16-59. These figures include unpaid family workers, those on government employment and training programmes, or those who did not answer, who are excluded from the Economic activity analyses below.
3 Expressed as a percentage of those in the group who received training in the last four weeks.
4 Apart from rounding, figures may not sum to grand totals because of questions in the LFS which were unanswered or did not apply.
5 Includes open university, open tech, correspondence course and college.
6 Employees are those in employment excluding the self-employed, unpaid family workers and those on government employment and training programmes.
7 The split into employees and self-employed is based on respondents' own assessment of their employment status.
8 Self-employed are those in employment excluding employees, unpaid family workers and those on government employment and training programmes.
9 Unemployed according to the International Labour Organization (ILO) definition.
10 Economically inactive are those who are neither in employment nor ILO unemployed.
11 Government Office Regions in England and each UK country.
12 Users of these data should read the LFS entry in Annex A, as it contains important information about the LFS and the concepts and definitions used.

3.23 POST COMPULSORY EDUCATION AND TRAINING: JOB-RELATED TRAINING

Hours spent on job-related training[1] in the last week, 2003

United Kingdom: People of working age[2]

Thousands and percentages[3]

	Total receiving training[5] (thousands)	Hours spent on training[4]						
		Less than 7.5 hours	7.5 to <15 hours	15 to < 22.5 hours	22.5 to < 30 hours	30 to < 37.5 hours	37.5 hours or more	Average number of hours per week
All people[2]	2,641	36.6	21.2	10.4	11.0	6.3	14.4	18.4
Economic activity								
Employees [6,7]	1,782	45.1	24.4	9.1	7.5	5.1	8.9	14.5
Self-employed [7,8]	113	65.2	15.0	*	*	*	*	11.0
ILO unemployed [9]	85	21.0	28.4	18.6	11.5	*	14.2	21.9
Economically inactive [10]	611	10.5	11.6	13.8	21.8	10.5	31.7	30.3
All employees	1,782	45.1	24.4	9.1	7.5	5.1	8.9	14.5
By gender								
Males	842	39.4	25.5	10.5	8.0	5.6	10.9	16.2
Females	940	50.2	23.3	7.7	7.1	4.6	7.1	12.9
By age								
16-19	205	18.0	21.9	12.1	18.9	12.0	17.1	22.8
20-24	271	31.9	22.2	12.0	11.6	8.3	14.2	19.3
25-29	243	41.7	26.4	11.5	5.6	4.2	10.5	14.8
30-39	448	49.1	26.2	8.0	5.8	3.7	7.2	13.3
40-49	393	56.7	23.2	7.8	4.3	3.0	5.0	11.0
50-64	221	61.5	25.5	4.4	*	*	*	9.1
By highest qualification held [4]								
Degree or equivalent	457	49.6	25.9	7.9	4.9	3.9	7.7	13.1
Higher Education qualification (below degree level)	244	51.4	24.3	8.5	7.0	*	5.8	12.3
GCE A level or equivalent	450	37.3	24.7	11.4	9.5	6.3	10.7	16.6
GCSE grades A* to C, or equivalent	399	43.5	23.2	8.9	8.5	6.7	9.4	14.9
Other qualification	167	46.8	23.8	7.7	8.1	*	9.4	14.3
No qualification	59	49.8	19.1	*	*	*	*	14.8
By industry [4]								
Agriculture, forestry & fishing	*	*	*	*	*	*	*	*
Energy & water supply	20	*	*	*	*	*	*	18.0
Manufacturing	178	43.7	27.0	9.2	5.6	6.2	8.4	14.5
Construction	73	29.7	32.5	*	*	*	17.0	17.8
Distribution, hotels & restaurants	305	32.8	18.2	11.9	18.1	7.1	11.9	18.5
Transport	89	38.7	27.4	11.0	*	*	11.6	16.5
Banking, finance & insurance	252	49.7	22.7	8.9	6.6	6.0	6.1	13.3
Public administration, education & health	758	52.4	25.3	7.0	4.4	3.7	7.1	12.4
Other services	99	38.9	25.7	12.7	10.3	*	*	15.4
By occupation								
Managers and senior officials	215	51.2	25.2	10.5	5.0	*	5.6	12.3
Professional occupations	302	54.9	24.4	6.7	4.3	4.1	5.5	11.7
Associate professional and technical	349	42.7	27.5	9.9	4.7	4.7	10.5	15.1
Administrative and secretarial	231	54.6	26.3	4.7	4.6	4.4	5.4	11.5
Skilled trades	129	29.8	32.0	*	8.5	8.3	14.7	17.6
Personal service occupations	201	51.3	24.1	8.1	7.0	*	7.6	12.3
Sales and customer service occupations	150	29.6	15.7	12.9	20.8	9.0	12.0	19.8
Process, plant and machine operatives	56	42.4	23.9	*	*	*	*	16.1
Elementary occupations	149	29.0	15.5	15.5	17.3	9.2	13.5	20.5
By region [11]								
United Kingdom	1,782	45.1	24.4	9.1	7.5	5.1	8.9	14.5
North East	78	40.5	27.2	*	*	*	*	15.9
North West	216	49.4	23.4	8.1	7.8	*	7.2	13.2
Yorkshire and the Humber	152	52.3	22.4	8.3	*	*	*	12.2
East Midlands	111	50.3	21.3	*	*	*	*	14.1
West Midlands	160	48.4	28.7	8.9	*	*	6.8	12.0
Eastern	160	47.5	25.0	6.9	6.4	*	8.9	14.4
London	222	35.5	21.5	12.6	9.9	6.6	13.9	18.1
South East	243	43.0	25.9	9.2	7.8	5.3	8.7	14.3
South West	154	46.4	23.6	9.1	7.4	*	8.5	14.3
England	1,497	45.6	24.3	9.0	7.4	4.9	8.9	14.3
Wales	87	43.3	22.2	*	*	*	*	15.4
Scotland	154	43.1	25.4	10.9	6.9	*	7.8	14.4
Northern Ireland	44	40.1	28.9	*	*	*	*	17.3

Source: Labour Force Survey, Spring 2003 [12]

1 Job-related training includes both on and off-the-job training.
2 Working age is defined as males aged 16-64 and females aged 16-59. These figures include unpaid family workers, those on government employment and training programmes, or those who did not answer, who are excluded from the Economic activity analyses below.
3 Expressed as a percentage of those in the group who received training in the last week, who specified a valid length of training.
4 Apart from rounding, figures may not sum to grand totals because of questions in the LFS which were unanswered or did not apply.
5 Those who specified a valid length of training.
6 Employees are those in employment excluding the self-employed, unpaid family workers and those on government employment and training programmes.
7 The split into employees and self-employed is based on respondents' own assessment of their employment status.
8 Self-employed are those in employment excluding employees, unpaid family workers and those on government employment and training programmes.
9 Unemployed according to the International Labour Organization (ILO) definition.
10 Economically inactive are those who are neither in employment nor ILO unemployed.
11 Government Office Regions in England and each UK country.
12 Users of these data should read the LFS entry in Annex A, as it contains important information about the LFS and the concepts and definitions used.

THIS PAGE HAS BEEN LEFT BLANK

3.24 POST COMPULSORY EDUCATION AND TRAINING: JOB-RELATED TRAINING

Participation by employees[1] in job-related training[2] in the last thirteen weeks by a range of personal and economic characteristics - time series

United Kingdom: Employees[1] of working age[3]

Thousands

	1995			1999			2003		
	All	Males	Females	All	Males	Females	All	Males	Females
All employees [1]	5,559	2,856	2,703	6,740	3,415	3,325	7,360	3,623	3,737
By age									
16-19	288	151	137	472	248	225	448	225	224
20-24	694	348	346	799	410	388	855	426	428
25-29	925	492	433	1,008	526	482	934	482	452
30-39	1,619	861	759	1,957	1,038	919	2,092	1,076	1,016
40-49	1,382	663	719	1,551	717	834	1,836	850	986
50-64	651	342	309	953	476	477	1,194	563	632
By highest qualification held [4,5]									
Degree or equivalent	1,297	752	545	1,722	945	777	2,035	1,070	965
Higher Education qualification (below degree level)	900	378	523	1,004	401	603	1,052	402	650
GCE A level or equivalent	1,314	853	461	1,627	998	629	1,727	1,003	724
GCSE grades A* to C, or equivalent	1,162	471	691	1,474	636	838	1,520	636	884
Other	595	279	316	658	328	330	717	361	356
None	282	119	164	218	90	128	274	128	146
By industry [4]									
Agriculture, forestry & fishing	30	19	10	35	26	*	25	21	*
Energy & water supply	111	88	23	92	68	24	102	82	20
Manufacturing	839	636	204	964	729	235	783	613	170
Construction	193	164	29	260	230	30	331	303	28
Distribution, hotels & restaurants	784	376	408	992	492	500	1,053	512	541
Transport	313	221	92	366	251	115	416	298	118
Banking, finance & insurance	900	517	383	1,136	618	517	1,103	624	479
Public administration, education & health	2,145	719	1,426	2,601	869	1,732	3,199	1,005	2,194
Other services	236	111	125	290	129	160	346	162	184
By occupation [4]									
Managers and senior officials	978	624	354	1,097	688	409	1,056	681	376
Professional occupations	1,030	544	486	1,235	638	597	1,358	715	644
Associate professional and technical	832	363	469	1,012	422	591	1,473	715	758
Administrative and secretarial	884	242	642	1,055	296	760	937	228	709
Skilled trades	387	362	24	476	452	24	512	479	33
Personal service occupations	636	253	383	849	329	520	759	121	638
Sales and customer service occupations	366	149	217	475	191	284	494	154	339
Process, plant and machine operatives	258	221	37	324	274	50	292	260	32
Elementary occupations	178	92	85	217	126	90	476	268	208
By full-time/part-time work [6]									
Full-time	4,529	2,693	1,836	5,360	3,153	2,207	5,796	3,346	2,449
Part-time	1,030	163	867	1,380	262	1,118	1,563	275	1,287
of which:									
students	247	106	141	388	170	218	430	185	245
could not find full-time job	127	35	91	121	39	82	108	32	76
did not want full-time job	643	19	624	850	50	800	993	53	940
By employment status [4]									
Permanent	5,132	2,670	2,462	6,205	3,177	3,028	6,879	3,432	3,447
Temporary	401	172	230	509	223	286	456	176	280
of which:									
seasonal/casual work	60	27	33	91	35	58	75	34	41
contract for fixed term or task	275	117	157	316	142	174	280	98	182
agency temping	27	11	16	53	23	29	49	22	27
other	40	17	23	49	23	25	52	22	30

Source: Labour Force Survey, Spring 1995, 1999, 2003 [7]

1 Employees are those in employment excluding the self-employed, unpaid family workers and those on government employment and training programmes.
2 Job-related training includes both on and off-the-job training.
3 Working age is defined as males aged 16-64 and females aged 16-59.
4 Apart from rounding, figures may not sum to grand totals because of questions in the LFS which were unanswered or did not apply.
5 Highest qualifications held figures for 1995 are not directly comparable with later years due to changes in the level of detail collected for qualifications from the 1996 LFS onwards.
6 The split between employees working full-time and part-time is based on respondents' own assessment.
7 Users of these data should read the LFS entry in Annex A, as it contains important information about the LFS and the concepts and definitions used.
8 Expressed as a percentage of the total number of people in each group.

POST COMPULSORY EDUCATION AND TRAINING: JOB-RELATED TRAINING

3.24 Participation by employees[1] in job-related training[2] in the last thirteen weeks by a range of personal and economic characteristics
- time series

United Kingdom: Employees[1] of working age[3]

Percentages[8]

	1995			1999			2003		
	All	Males	Females	All	Males	Females	All	Males	Females
All employees[1]	25.6	24.9	26.5	28.8	27.3	30.4	30.1	27.8	32.8
By age									
16-19	25.6	27.5	23.8	33.9	35.4	32.4	32.0	32.2	31.9
20-24	28.8	27.8	29.9	35.6	34.7	36.7	35.5	33.5	37.8
25-29	29.7	29.6	29.8	32.4	31.2	34.0	34.2	32.7	36.1
30-39	27.6	27.1	28.2	29.6	29.1	30.2	31.3	29.7	33.1
40-49	26.2	24.9	27.4	28.4	26.0	30.9	30.7	27.8	33.7
50-64	16.8	15.7	18.1	20.6	18.3	23.6	22.9	19.5	27.1
By highest qualification held[5]									
Degree or equivalent	42.6	39.7	47.5	44.1	41.1	48.4	43.5	40.0	48.2
Higher Education qualification (below degree level)	42.7	38.5	46.5	43.1	37.3	48.0	43.1	36.0	49.1
GCE A level or equivalent	25.7	24.2	29.1	29.0	26.5	34.2	28.8	26.0	34.0
GCSE grades A* to C, or equivalent	24.8	25.0	24.7	27.1	27.7	26.6	27.5	27.2	27.8
Other	17.9	16.6	19.3	19.9	18.9	21.0	22.3	21.1	23.7
None	8.4	8.1	8.7	8.3	7.5	9.0	11.4	10.7	12.2
By industry									
Agriculture, forestry & fishing	14.0	12.6	17.5	18.0	17.6	*	15.3	16.9	*
Energy & water supply	33.8	33.4	35.7	32.5	31.3	36.9	35.5	35.8	34.4
Manufacturing	18.4	19.3	16.2	21.1	21.6	19.7	19.7	20.4	17.6
Construction	19.7	19.5	20.8	21.3	21.3	21.0	24.4	25.5	16.6
Distribution, hotels & restaurants	18.2	19.5	17.2	21.4	23.1	19.9	21.4	22.0	20.8
Transport	22.1	20.4	27.6	23.0	21.4	27.6	24.1	23.0	27.2
Banking, finance & insurance	30.3	34.0	26.4	32.5	33.7	31.2	29.9	31.2	28.4
Public administration, education & health	37.5	39.4	36.7	41.5	43.3	40.6	45.6	45.5	45.7
Other services	20.4	20.9	19.9	24.7	24.1	25.1	27.3	26.3	28.2
By occupation									
Managers and senior officials	30.1	28.6	33.2	31.0	29.0	35.1	29.7	27.7	34.1
Professional occupations	46.2	42.8	50.8	48.7	44.3	54.6	46.7	41.8	53.5
Associate professional and technical	41.4	36.7	46.0	43.5	37.7	48.9	43.6	40.2	47.5
Administrative and secretarial	24.6	26.4	24.0	27.3	29.2	26.6	27.6	31.0	26.7
Skilled trades	17.2	18.5	8.7	20.2	21.1	11.1	22.7	23.2	17.2
Personal service occupations	25.9	28.9	24.2	30.7	34.7	28.6	41.4	37.8	42.2
Sales and customer service occupations	20.2	24.1	18.2	23.5	27.2	21.5	23.4	24.3	23.1
Process, plant and machine operatives	11.7	12.7	8.2	14.5	15.2	11.8	15.0	15.8	10.5
Elementary occupations	9.6	10.4	8.9	12.1	13.2	10.9	15.8	16.2	15.3
By full-time/part-time work[6]									
Full-time	27.2	25.0	31.2	30.0	27.3	35.1	31.4	28.1	37.2
Part-time	20.5	23.2	20.0	24.6	27.5	24.1	26.4	24.7	26.8
of which:									
students	33.2	31.6	34.5	38.7	38.6	38.7	36.5	35.6	37.2
could not find full-time job	17.9	16.5	18.6	20.2	17.5	21.9	21.7	15.4	26.0
did not want full-time job	18.4	14.4	18.5	21.8	19.1	22.0	24.2	15.4	25.0
By employment status[4]									
Permanent	25.7	25.1	26.4	28.6	27.3	30.0	30.1	28.0	32.5
Temporary	26.8	24.6	28.8	32.5	29.5	35.2	33.2	27.5	38.1
of which:									
seasonal/casual work	16.9	17.3	16.5	23.7	21.1	26.6	24.7	23.1	26.3
contract for fixed term or task	33.6	30.1	36.8	39.5	35.8	43.0	41.4	33.2	47.9
agency temping	17.1	14.3	19.7	21.0	17.7	24.8	19.6	16.9	22.7
other	24.4	22.1	26.4	36.5	38.0	35.2	36.3	34.5	37.7

Source: Labour Force Survey, Spring 1995, 1999, 2003[7]

See previous page for footnotes.

3.25

POST COMPULSORY EDUCATION AND TRAINING: JOB-RELATED TRAINING
Employees[1] of working age[2] in the UK — summary of job-related training[3] received, 2003

United Kingdom: Employees[1] of working age[2]

Thousands and percentages

	Total number of employees (thousands)	Number who received training in the last			Never offered training by current employer (thousands)	Percentage who received training in the last			Never offered training by current employer (percentage)
		13 weeks	4 weeks	1 week		13 weeks	4 weeks	1 week	
All employees[1]	24,413	7,360	3,809	2,048	7,019	30.1	15.6	8.4	28.8
By gender									
Males	13,010	3,623	1,810	973	3,891	27.8	13.9	7.5	29.9
Females	11,403	3,737	1,999	1,075	3,128	32.8	17.5	9.4	27.4
By age									
16-19	1,400	448	323	245	434	32.0	23.1	17.5	31.0
20-24	2,407	855	527	341	756	35.5	21.9	14.2	31.4
25-29	2,730	934	497	286	727	34.2	18.2	10.5	26.6
30-39	6,687	2,092	1,019	505	1,763	31.3	15.2	7.6	26.4
40-49	5,983	1,836	919	436	1,604	30.7	15.4	7.3	26.8
50-64	5,206	1,194	525	235	1,735	22.9	10.1	4.5	33.3
By ethnic origin									
White	22,858	6,866	3,537	1,872	6,549	30.0	15.5	8.2	28.6
Non-white	1,555	493	272	176	469	31.7	17.5	11.3	30.3
Mixed	120	43	26	18	38	35.4	21.8	15.0	31.1
Asian or Asian British	747	201	105	66	242	26.9	14.1	8.9	32.4
Black or Black British	410	155	88	62	99	37.8	21.6	15.1	24.2
Chinese	96	29	17	13	38	29.6	18.0	13.1	39.9
Other Ethnic Group	172	63	33	16	52	36.3	19.2	9.3	30.2
By highest qualification held [4]									
Degree or equivalent	4,680	2,035	1,080	516	751	43.5	23.1	11.0	16.0
Higher Education qualification (below degree level)	2,441	1,052	538	276	406	43.1	22.1	11.3	16.6
GCE A level or equivalent	5,987	1,727	901	509	1,722	28.8	15.0	8.5	28.8
GCSE grades A* to C, or equivalent	5,525	1,520	799	465	1,697	27.5	14.5	8.4	30.7
Other qualification	3,213	717	349	200	1,121	22.3	10.9	6.2	34.9
No qualification	2,399	274	122	69	1,271	11.4	5.1	2.9	53.0
By industry [4]									
Agriculture, forestry & fishing	161	25	15	*	75	15.3	9.0	*	46.9
Energy & water supply	286	102	47	23	57	35.5	16.4	7.9	20.1
Manufacturing	3,970	783	378	202	1,436	19.7	9.5	5.1	36.2
Construction	1,356	331	159	88	495	24.4	11.7	6.5	36.5
Distribution, hotels & restaurants	4,929	1,053	579	360	1,985	21.4	11.7	7.3	40.3
Transport	1,729	416	191	101	572	24.1	11.0	5.8	33.1
Banking, finance & insurance	3,691	1,103	567	294	1,003	29.9	15.4	8.0	27.2
Public administration, education & health	7,012	3,199	1,685	856	970	45.6	24.0	12.2	13.8
Other services	1,267	346	188	115	423	27.3	14.8	9.1	33.4
By occupation [4]									
Managers and senior officials	3,561	1,056	500	237	820	29.7	14.0	6.6	23.0
Professional occupations	2,912	1,358	724	342	372	46.7	24.9	11.8	12.8
Associate professional and technical	3,375	1,473	766	397	514	43.6	22.7	11.8	15.2
Administrative and secretarial	3,392	937	490	266	958	27.6	14.4	7.8	28.2
Skilled trades	2,260	512	259	150	821	22.7	11.5	6.6	36.3
Personal service occupations	1,832	759	408	233	340	41.4	22.2	12.7	18.5
Sales and customer service occupations	2,107	494	276	181	821	23.4	13.1	8.6	39.0
Process, plant and machine operatives	1,948	292	126	65	902	15.0	6.5	3.3	46.3
Elementary occupations	3,011	476	260	176	1,465	15.8	8.6	5.9	48.7
By region [5]									
United Kingdom	24,413	7,360	3,809	2,048	7,019	30.1	15.6	8.4	28.8
North East	983	307	157	88	285	31.2	16.0	9.0	29.0
North West	2,773	843	436	246	759	30.4	15.7	8.9	27.4
Yorkshire and the Humber	2,073	636	342	175	616	30.7	16.5	8.4	29.7
East Midlands	1,766	499	246	132	551	28.2	13.9	7.5	31.2
West Midlands	2,170	627	328	183	669	28.9	15.1	8.4	30.9
Eastern	2,332	682	342	179	646	29.3	14.7	7.7	27.7
London	2,932	928	478	270	784	31.6	16.3	9.2	26.7
South East	3,472	1,045	540	280	954	30.1	15.6	8.1	27.5
South West	2,039	640	328	175	554	31.4	16.1	8.6	27.2
England	20,539	6,207	3,197	1,728	5,817	30.2	15.6	8.4	28.3
Wales	1,122	364	205	99	326	32.4	18.3	8.8	29.0
Scotland	2,124	618	321	171	671	29.1	15.1	8.0	31.6
Northern Ireland	628	171	85	51	206	27.2	13.6	8.1	32.8

Source: Labour Force Survey, Spring 2003 [6]

1 Employees are those in employment excluding the self-employed, unpaid family workers and those on government employment and training programmes.
2 Working age is defined as males aged 16-64 and females aged 16-59.
3 Job-related training includes both on and off-the-job training.
4 Apart from rounding, figures may not sum to grand totals because of questions in the LFS which were unanswered or did not apply.
5 Government Office Regions in England and each UK country.
6 Users of these data should read the LFS entry in Annex A, as it contains important information about the LFS and the concepts and definitions used.

POST COMPULSORY EDUCATION AND TRAINING: JOB-RELATED TRAINING

Participation by employees in job-related training[1] in the last thirteen weeks by disability status and a range of personal characteristics, 2003

United Kingdom: Employees[2] of working age[3]

Thousands and percentages[4]

	Total number of employees by disability status (thousands)					Percentage receiving job-related training in the last thirteen weeks				
	Total number of employees (thousands)	Both DDA disabled and work-limiting disabled	DDA disabled only	Work-limiting disabled only	Not disabled	All employees	Both DDA disabled and work-limiting disabled	DDA disabled only	Work-limiting disabled only	Not disabled
All employees	24,413	1,187	1,062	734	21,430	30.1	24.4	29.1	30.3	30.5
By gender										
Males	13,010	609	540	420	11,442	27.8	21.9	23.7	27.9	28.4
Females	11,403	578	522	314	9,988	32.8	27.1	34.8	33.6	33.0
By age										
16-19	1,400	31	29	32	1,309	32.0	29.0	36.4	34.8	31.9
20-24	2,407	63	56	56	2,232	35.5	33.1	37.5	32.8	35.6
25-29	2,730	79	71	62	2,518	34.2	32.6	38.2	34.2	34.2
30-39	6,687	265	221	195	6,005	31.3	25.4	32.7	35.2	31.4
40-49	5,983	329	254	185	5,214	30.7	27.4	35.3	29.5	30.7
50-64	5,206	420	430	204	4,153	22.9	18.2	20.5	23.8	23.6
By highest qualification held[5]										
Degree or equivalent	4,680	135	171	118	4,256	43.5	38.8	51.1	49.0	43.2
Higher Education qualification (below degree level)	2,441	120	120	68	2,133	43.1	38.5	44.3	43.9	43.2
GCE A level or equivalent	5,987	295	265	178	5,248	28.8	26.4	26.6	27.2	29.1
GCSE grades A* to C, or equivalent	5,525	259	223	164	4,878	27.5	23.6	29.0	32.2	27.5
Other qualification	3,213	188	153	116	2,757	22.3	17.2	15.8	19.7	23.1
No qualification	2,399	185	127	86	2,001	11.4	10.6	7.5	15.4	11.7
By industry[5]										
Agriculture, forestry & fishing	161	11	*	*	140	15.3	*	*	*	15.6
Energy & water supply	286	11	15	*	251	35.5	*	*	*	36.1
Manufacturing	3,970	187	184	119	3,480	19.7	15.1	15.3	18.1	20.3
Construction	1,356	61	53	37	1,205	24.4	18.5	22.8	*	24.8
Distribution, hotels & restaurants	4,929	238	196	152	4,343	21.4	14.6	21.3	23.7	21.7
Transport	1,729	91	70	55	1,513	24.1	16.8	21.6	25.2	24.6
Banking, finance & insurance	3,691	143	146	95	3,307	29.9	23.4	26.7	30.3	30.3
Public administration, education & health	7,012	373	342	218	6,078	45.6	39.1	45.6	45.7	46.0
Other services	1,267	70	50	45	1,102	27.3	20.4	23.0	28.0	27.9
By occupation[5]										
Managers and senior officials	3,561	123	163	77	3,199	29.7	29.3	30.5	28.8	29.7
Professional occupations	2,912	98	123	79	2,613	46.7	41.6	51.9	47.1	46.6
Associate professional and technical	3,375	142	143	99	2,991	43.6	42.5	41.0	46.7	43.7
Administrative and secretarial	3,392	172	146	97	2,977	27.6	22.0	27.6	29.7	27.9
Skilled trades	2,260	119	97	75	1,969	22.7	16.5	14.5	18.8	23.6
Personal service occupations	1,832	107	87	61	1,577	41.4	37.4	35.2	41.2	42.0
Sales and customer service occupations	2,107	100	90	60	1,857	23.4	20.3	28.8	31.0	23.1
Process, plant and machine operatives	1,948	122	94	71	1,662	15.0	9.1	10.3	19.4	15.5
Elementary occupations	3,011	204	121	115	2,571	15.8	11.7	14.1	14.6	16.3
By full-time/part-time work[5]										
Full-time	18,432	798	824	540	16,320	31.4	26.5	30.1	32.0	31.6
Part-time	5,923	388	238	194	5,104	26.4	19.9	25.8	25.7	26.9
of which:										
Males										
Full-time	11,891	512	506	379	10,495	28.1	22.5	23.5	29.3	28.6
Part-time	1,116	96	34	41	944	24.7	18.4	25.4	14.7	25.7
Females										
Full-time	6,591	287	318	162	5,825	37.2	33.7	40.4	38.3	37.1
Part-time	4,807	291	204	152	4,159	26.8	20.4	25.9	28.7	27.2

Source: Labour Force Survey, Spring 2003[6]

1 Job-related training includes both on and off-the-job training.
2 Employees are those in employment excluding the self-employed, unpaid family workers and those on government employment and training programmes.
3 Working age is defined as males aged 16-64 and females aged 16-59.
4 Expressed as a percentage of those in the group who received training in the last thirteen weeks.
5 Apart from rounding, figures may not sum to grand totals because of questions in the LFS which were unanswered or did not apply.
6 Users of these data should read the LFS entry in Annex A, as it contains important information about the LFS and the concepts and definitions used.

Chapter 4
Qualifications

CHAPTER 4: QUALIFICATIONS

Key Facts

GCE, GCSE, SCE and Vocational qualifications

- In 2001/02, 38.5 per cent of young people in the United Kingdom achieved 2 or more GCE A level passes or equivalent in schools and FE colleges. At GCSE/Standard Grade level, of pupils in their last year of compulsory schooling:

    - 52.5 per cent gained 5 or more passes at grades A*–C/1–3

    - 23.7 per cent gained 1–4 passes at grades A*–C/1–3

    - 18.4 per cent gained no passes at grades A*–C/1–3 but gained at least one grade D–G

    - 5.4 per cent had no graded results. **(Table 4.1)**

- Over 5.9 million entries were made for GCSE/Standard Grade examinations by pupils in their last year of compulsory education in schools in the United Kingdom in 2001/02. 59% of all entries achieved passes at grade A*–C. **(Table 4.2)**

- A total of 871,700 entries were made by young people for GCE A level/Higher Grade examinations in the United Kingdom in 2001/02. 67% of all entries achieved grades A–C. **(Table 4.3)**

- Of the 72,500 Intermediate and Foundation GNVQ entries in England, Wales and Northern Ireland in 2001/02, 48% achieved GNVQ Part One, and 24% achieved a Full GNVQ. Of the VCE A/AS and Double Award passes in 2001/02, 33,900 were Double Awards, 25,800 were A level and 10,600 were AS passes. **(Table 4.4)**

Subject Choice

- Most frequently studied subjects at GCE A level/Higher Grade were English (English 42,400, English Literature 64,300), Mathematics (73,400), Social Studies (72,900), Biological Sciences (60,600) and General Studies (59,000). **(Table 4.3)**

- Of the 70,300 VCE A/AS and Double Award qualifications obtained in England, Wales and Northern Ireland in 2001/02, the largest subject areas were Business and Information Technology with 19,100 and 18,700 qualifications obtained respectively. **(Table 4.4)**

Full Vocational Awards

- There were 408,000 NVQs awarded in the United Kingdom in 2001/02. Almost three-fifths (57%) were awarded at level 2. Almost 0.5 million

"Other" vocational qualifications were awarded in 2001/02, and around half of these (49%) were awarded at level 1. **(Table 4.5)**

National Learning Targets

- In Spring/Summer 2003, progress towards selected targets in England was:

    - 75% of 11-year-olds achieving level 4 or above in *English* (target 85%)

    - 73% of 11-year-olds achieving level 4 or above in *mathematics* (target 85%)

    - 68% of 14-year-olds achieving level 5 or above in *English*, 70% in *mathematics*, and 67% in ICT (target 75%)

    - 68% of 14-year-olds achieving level 5 or above in *science* (target 70%)

    - 53% of 16-year-olds gaining at least five GCSEs at grades A*–C (target: on average, a 2 percentage point increase each year between 2002 and 2006)

    - 86% of 16-year-olds gaining at least five GCSEs at grades A*–G (target 92%)

    - 76% of 19-year-olds with a "level 2" qualification (target 85%)

    - 52% of 19-year-olds with a "level 3" qualification (target 55%)

    - 49% of adults with a "level 3" qualification (target 52%). **(Table 4.7)**

- In Summer 2003, progress towards selected targets in Wales was:

    - 79% of 11-year-olds achieving level 4 or above in *English*, 78% in *Welsh (first language)*, 75% in *mathematics*, and 88% in *science* (target 80–85%)

    - 63% of 14-year-olds achieving level 5 or above in *English*, 74% in *Welsh (first language)*, 68% in *mathematics*, and 69% in *science* (target 80–85%)

    - 51% of 15-year-olds gaining at least five GCSEs at grades A*–C (target 58%)

    - 85% of 15-year-olds gaining at least five GCSEs at grades A*–G (target 95%). **(Table 4.7)**

Higher Education Qualifications

- A total of 486,400 higher education qualifications were awarded in higher education institutions in the United Kingdom in 2001/02. Of these, 83,100 were sub-degree qualifications, 267,100 were first degrees, 11,400 were PhD or equivalents and 124,800 were at Masters / other postgraduate level. 57% of these qualifications were awarded to women. **(Table 4.8)**

Highest Qualification Held

- 44% of people of working age were qualified to NVQ level 3 equivalent or above in Spring 2003, with 25% of people of working age qualified to NVQ level 4 equivalent or above, and 15% having no qualification. **(Table 4.9)**

- Attainment levels vary by Government Office region, with London having a higher proportion of highly qualified people (i.e. qualified to NVQ level 4 and 5 or equivalent) than any other UK region in Spring 2003. **(Table 4.9)**

- Attainment levels varied greatly by economic activity with 31% of the economically inactive and 21% of the unemployed having no qualifications, compared to 10% of employees and 12% of the self-employed. **(Table 4.9)**

- 90% of employees in professional occupations held two or more A levels, or a higher level qualification, compared with 62% of managers and senior officials, 22% of process, plant and machine operatives and 20% of those in elementary occupations. **(Table 4.9)**

People Working Towards a Qualification

- In 2001/02, of the 206,700 LSC Work-based learning provision programme leavers in England, 36% met the requirements of their Modern Apprenticeship Framework or NVQ. The proportion for those aged 16–18 meeting these was 37%, and for those aged 19 and over, 33%. **(Table 4.6)**

- 18% of all people of working age were studying towards a qualification in Spring 2003. Young people aged 16–24 were far more likely to be working towards a qualification than people in any other age group. **(Table 4.10)**

- People of non-white ethnic origin were far more likely to be studying towards a qualification than people of white ethnic origin; 27% compared to 17%. **(Table 4.10)**

CHAPTER 4: QUALIFICATIONS – LIST OF TABLES

4.1 GCE, GCSE, SCE and vocational qualifications obtained by pupils and students at a typical age, and students of any age – time series

4.2 GCSE and SCE Standard Grade entries and achievements for pupils in their last year of compulsory education in all schools by subject and gender by the end of 2001/02

4.3 GCE A level/SCE Higher Grade entries and achievements for young people in all Schools and Further Education Sector Colleges by subject and gender, 2001/02

4.4 GNVQ entries and results, and VCE A/AS and Double Awards qualifications obtained, by subject and gender, 2001/02

4.5 Full vocational awards by type of qualification, equivalent level and gender – time series

4.6 Success rates in Learning and Skills Council funded Work-Based Learning provision: by programme type and age group, 2001/02

4.7 Progress towards selected National Targets – time series

4.8 Students obtaining higher education qualifications by level, gender and subject group, 2001/02

4.9 Highest qualification held by people of working age, by gender, age, region and economic activity and, for employees of working age, by occupation, 2003

4.10 People currently working towards a qualification, 2003

4.1 QUALIFICATIONS

GCE, GCSE, SCE[1] and vocational qualifications obtained by pupils and students at a typical age[2,3], and students of any age – time series

United Kingdom   (i) Students at a typical age   Percentages and thousands

| | Pupils in their last year of compulsory education[2] | | | | | Pupils/students in education[3] | | | |
| | | | | | | % Achieving GCE A Levels and equivalent | | | |
	5 or more grades A*-C[4] (%)	1-4 grades A*-C[4] (%)	Grades D-G[5] only (%)	No graded results (%)	Total (=100%) (thousands)	2 or more passes[6,7]	1 pass[8]	1 or more passes	population aged 17 (thousands)
1995/96									
All	45.5	25.9	21.2	7.4	722.8	29.6	7.8	37.4	672.1
Males	40.6	25.5	25.3	8.6	369.0	26.7	7.1	33.8	345.8
Females	50.5	26.4	16.9	6.2	353.7	32.7	8.6	41.2	326.3
1999/00[1]									
All	50.4	24.5	19.7	5.5	703.7	34.5	6.5	41.0	732.2
Males	45.0	25.0	23.6	6.4	357.7	30.5	6.0	36.6	376.0
Females	55.9	23.9	15.7	4.5	346.0	38.6	7.1	45.6	356.3
2000/01[1]									
All	51.0	24.1	19.4	5.5	729.7	37.2	4.7	41.9	735.4
Males	45.7	24.6	23.1	6.5	372.1	32.9	4.5	37.4	378.5
Females	56.5	23.6	15.5	4.4	357.6	41.7	4.9	46.6	356.9
2001/02[1]									
All	52.5	23.7	18.4	5.4	732.5	38.5	4.6	43.1	735.2
Males	47.2	24.4	22.0	6.4	374.0	34.1	4.4	38.5	377.0
Females	58.0	23.1	14.6	4.3	358.5	43.2	4.8	48.0	358.2

United Kingdom   (ii) Students of any age achieving   Thousands

| | GCSE and SCE S Grade/Standard Grade (SG) | | | | GCE A Level and SCE/NQ Higher Grade | | |
	5 or more grades A*-C[4,9]	1-4 grades A*-C[4,9]	Grades D-G[5,10] only	No graded results[11]	2 or more passes[6,7]	1 pass[8]	Total 1 or more passes
1995/96							
All	331.4	371.7	236.5	40.0	204.5	78.2	282.6
Males	151.3	175.3	130.9	20.0	95.2	33.8	129.0
Females	180.1	196.4	105.6	20.0	109.3	44.3	153.6
1999/00[1]							
All	357.7	311.6	224.4	30.3	258.8	65.6	324.4
Males	162.8	150.9	125.3	15.2	118.0	28.7	146.6
Females	194.9	160.7	99.1	15.1	140.9	36.9	177.7
2000/01[1]							
All	375.1	335.0	227.3	31.8	280.8	64.2	345.1
Males	171.8	164.1	127.3	16.0	128.4	29.1	157.5
Females	203.3	170.9	100.1	15.8	152.4	35.2	187.6
2001/02[1]							
All	394.9	381.1	234.2	50.6	286.7	67.8	354.5
Males	182.4	188.7	131.1	27.9	130.0	31.6	161.6
Females	212.4	192.3	103.1	22.7	156.7	36.2	192.9

Source: Department for Education and Skills; National Assembly for Wales; Scottish Executive; Northern Ireland Department of Education

1 From 1999/00 National Qualifications (NQ) were introduced in Scotland but are not all shown until 2000/01. NQs include Standard Grades, Intermediate 1 & 2 and Higher Grades. The figures for Higher Grades combine the new NQ Higher and the old SCE Higher and include Advanced Highers.

2 Pupils aged 15 at the start of the academic year, pupils in Year S4 in Scotland.

3 Up to 1999/00, pupils in schools and students in further education institutions aged 16-18 at the start of the academic year in England, Wales and Northern Ireland as a percentage of the 17 year old population. From 2000/01, pupils in schools and students in further education institutions aged 17-18 at the start of the academic year in England, aged 17 in Wales, and aged 16-18 in Northern Ireland, as a percentage of the 17 year old population. Pupils in Scotland generally sit Highers one year earlier and the figures relate to the results of pupils in Year S5/S6.

4 Standard Grades 1-3/Intermediate 2 A-C/Intermediate 1 A-B in Scotland.

5 Grades D-G at GCSE and Scottish Standard Grades 4-6/Intermediate 1(C)/Access 3 (pass).

6 3 or more SCE/NQ Higher Grades/2 or more Advanced Highers/1 Advanced Higher with more than 2 Higher Passes in Scotland.

7 Includes Vocational Certificates of Education (VCE) and, previously, Advanced level GNVQ/GSVQ, which is equivalent to 2 GCE A levels or AS equivalents/3 SCE/NQ Higher grades.

8 2 AS levels or 2 Highers/1 Advanced Higher or 1 each in Scotland, count as 1 A level pass. Includes those with 1.5 A level passes.

9 Includes GNVQ/GSVQ Intermediate Part 1, Full and Language unit which are equivalent to 2, 4 and 0.5 GCSE grades A*-C/SCE Standard grades 1-3 respectively. Figures include those with 4.5 GCSEs.

10 Includes GNVQ/GSVQ Foundation Part 1, Full and Language unit which are equivalent to 2, 4 and 0.5 GCSE grades D-G/SCE Standard grades 4-7 respectively.

11 Figures for Scotland include students in Year S4 only.

4.2 QUALIFICATIONS

GCSE and SCE Standard grade[1] entries and achievements[2] for pupils in their last year of compulsory education[3], in all schools by subject and gender* by the end of 2001/02

United Kingdom

Thousands and percentages

Subject group	Number of entries (000s)			Percentage achieving grade A*–C			Percentage achieving grade D–G		
	All	Males	Females	All	Males	Females	All	Males	Females
Biological Science	68.5	32.9	35.7	86	87	85	13	12	14
Chemistry	66.9	37.1	29.8	88	87	88	12	12	11
Physics	63.4	40.0	23.4	88	87	89	11	12	10
Science Single Award[4]	78.8	40.2	38.5	21	19	23	71	72	70
Science Double Award	518.2	257.6	260.6	54	52	55	45	46	43
Other Science[5]	5.4	3.6	1.8	49	47	51	47	47	45
Mathematics[6]	709.0	359.1	349.9	53	53	54	44	44	43
Computer Studies[7]	139.8	83.7	56.1	60	57	64	36	38	32
Design and Technology[8]	462.6	249.6	213.0	53	47	61	43	49	36
Business Studies	127.4	66.2	61.3	57	54	61	38	41	36
Home Economics	49.1	4.2	44.9	51	34	52	44	57	43
Art and Design	221.7	94.8	126.9	69	57	77	29	40	21
Geography	253.6	142.4	111.2	61	58	64	37	39	33
History	236.9	118.5	118.3	63	60	66	34	37	31
Economics	5.7	4.1	1.6	70	70	71	26	27	25
Humanities[5]	20.9	10.3	10.7	44	38	51	52	57	46
Religious Studies	123.4	51.6	71.9	61	53	67	34	41	30
Social Studies	16.1	4.5	11.5	54	42	58	41	50	37
English	676.8	339.2	337.6	61	54	69	37	44	30
Welsh[9]	4.5	2.2	2.3	75	67	83	25	32	17
English Literature[5]	539.0	261.0	278.0	65	58	72	33	40	26
Drama	104.5	37.8	66.8	71	63	76	27	36	22
Communication Studies[5]	40.0	17.5	22.5	57	49	63	40	47	34
Modern Languages									
French	374.1	177.7	196.5	54	46	61	44	52	38
German	142.9	68.3	74.6	59	51	65	40	47	34
Spanish	54.9	23.2	31.7	58	50	65	40	48	34
Other languages[10]	36.6	16.4	20.3	71	63	77	27	34	22
Classical Studies	15.9	8.3	7.7	88	86	89	11	12	9
Physical Education	140.2	90.5	49.7	58	58	59	40	41	39
Vocational Studies	21.9	9.7	12.2	48	43	52	45	48	42
Modern Studies[11]	13.9	5.8	8.2	66	61	69	33	38	30
Music	57.9	24.5	33.4	73	68	76	24	27	21
Other subjects[12]	6.9	3.4	3.5	63	57	69	34	40	29
All entries[13]	5,908.9	2,939.9	2,968.9	59	54	63	39	43	35
English and Mathematics[14,15,16]	667.9	334.7	333.2	48	45	51	49	51	46
English, Maths and a Science[14,15,16]	654.5	327.7	326.9	44	41	47	52	54	50
English, Maths, Science and Modern Languages[16,17]	521.5	250.1	271.4	42	37	46	54	58	51
Mathematics and Science[16,17]	633.1	318.9	314.2	47	46	48	50	50	49
Any Subject	701.4	355.0	346.4	77	73	81	23	27	19

Source: Department for Education and Skills; National Assembly for Wales; Scottish Executive; Northern Ireland Department of Education

1 Or equivalent.
2 Where a candidate attempted an examination in the same subject more than once, only the highest value pass has been counted. However, some double counting may occur if a student enters for more than one subject within a subject category.
3 Those in all schools who were 15 at the start of the academic year, i.e. 31 August 2001. Pupils in Year S4 in Scotland.
4 Standard Grade in General Science in Scotland.
5 England and Wales only.
6 Includes related subjects such as Statistics.
7 Includes Information Systems in England and Wales.
8 Craft and Design, Graphic Communications and Technological Studies in Scotland.
9 Welsh as a first language.
10 Includes Welsh as a second language.
11 Scotland only.
12 Includes combined syllabuses, Area studies, Gaelic, Welsh literature, Creative Arts and General Studies.
13 Science Double Award are counted twice in this row.
14 English or Welsh as a first language in Wales.
15 Only includes successful entries (grade A*–G) in Wales so the number of entries is an underestimate.
16 Percentages are those achieving grades A*–C or D–G respectively in all these subjects.
17 England and Scotland only.

4.3 QUALIFICATIONS

GCE A level[1]/SCE Higher grade[2] entries and achievements for young people[3] in all Schools and Further Education Sector Colleges by subject and gender, 2001/02

United Kingdom

Thousands and percentages

Subject group	Number of entries(000s)			Percentage achieved grades A–C			Percentage achieved grades D–E[4]			Percentage with no graded results		
	All	Males	Females	All	Males	Females	All	Males	Females	All	Males	Females
Biological Sciences	60.6	22.4	38.1	62	59	64	28	30	27	10	10	9
Chemistry	45.7	22.4	23.3	71	69	73	22	23	20	7	8	6
Physics	40.4	30.6	9.8	68	65	75	24	25	19	9	10	6
Other Science	11.1	4.8	6.4	61	58	64	28	32	26	10	10	11
Mathematics	73.4	44.3	29.1	72	70	75	17	19	15	11	11	10
Computer Studies[5]	32.6	24.0	8.6	49	48	51	39	39	39	12	13	10
Design and Technology[6]	22.6	15.2	7.4	63	60	70	28	29	24	9	11	5
Business Studies[7]	51.0	26.7	24.3	64	61	68	27	31	23	9	8	9
Home Economics	2.2	0.1	2.0	67	58	68	22	24	22	11	18	10
Art and Design	41.6	13.0	28.6	74	66	77	21	27	19	5	7	4
Geography	43.1	23.4	19.7	72	67	77	23	27	19	5	6	4
History	47.9	22.6	25.4	73	72	75	23	24	22	4	4	4
Economics	15.8	10.9	5.0	74	73	76	22	23	20	4	4	4
Religious Studies	12.5	3.3	9.2	74	72	75	21	22	20	5	6	5
Social Studies[8]	72.9	21.3	51.5	62	57	64	32	35	31	6	8	6
English	42.4	16.3	26.1	67	65	69	21	21	21	12	14	11
Welsh Second Language[9]	0.6	0.1	0.5	69	70	69	29	29	29	2	1	2
Gaelic	0.2	-	0.1	98	98	98	1	2	-	1	-	2
English Literature[8]	64.3	19.5	44.8	72	70	72	27	28	26	2	2	1
Welsh[9]	0.4	0.1	0.3	85	83	86	14	16	14	-	1	-
Drama	15.3	4.2	11.2	74	67	76	23	28	21	3	5	2
Communication studies[8]	25.1	9.8	15.2	69	64	72	29	33	26	2	3	2
Modern Languages	39.9	12.3	27.5	79	79	79	17	17	17	4	4	4
of which												
French	20.4	5.9	14.5	78	78	78	18	18	18	4	4	4
German	9.2	2.9	6.3	75	75	75	20	19	20	5	5	5
Spanish	5.9	1.7	4.2	80	79	80	17	17	17	3	3	3
Other Languages	4.5	1.9	2.6	87	86	89	9	11	7	4	4	4
Classical Studies[10]	6.1	2.6	3.5	81	78	84	16	19	14	3	4	3
Creative Arts[11]	10.7	4.6	6.0	78	74	81	19	22	17	3	4	2
Physical Education	22.3	13.9	8.4	59	55	66	34	38	29	6	7	5
Vocational Studies[8]	2.7	1.6	1.2	43	43	43	40	40	41	17	17	16
General Studies[8]	59.0	28.2	30.8	49	47	51	39	40	39	12	13	10
Modern Studies[12]	7.5	2.9	4.6	79	76	81	9	10	9	12	14	11
Other subjects	1.7	0.6	1.1	66	58	69	9	10	8	26	32	23
All entries	**871.7**	**401.8**	**469.9**	**67**	**64**	**70**	**26**	**28**	**24**	**7**	**9**	**6**

Sources: Department for Education and Skills; National Assembly for Wales; Scottish Executive; Northern Ireland Department of Education

1 Figures for Wales include Advanced Supplementary (AS), Advanced Vocational Certificates of Education (AVCEs) and Advanced Subsidiary Vocational Certificates of Education (ASVCEs). Each AVCE double award is counted as two entries, however a double award is allocated two grades which may not be the same.

2 Includes the new Scottish qualification framework from 1999/00 which contains different subject categories to those previously used. The new Intermediate 1 and 2 qualifications (which overlap with Standard Grades and Highers) are not included in the table.

3 Pupils in schools and students in further education institutions aged 16–18 at the start of the academic year in England and in Northern Ireland, and aged 17 in Wales. Pupils in Scotland generally sit Highers one year earlier and the figures relate to the result of pupils in Year S5/S6.

4 Compensatory Award in Scotland.

5 Includes Information Systems.

6 Craft and Design, Graphic Communication and Technological Studies in Scotland and Northern Ireland.

7 Includes Accounting, Management and Information Studies and Secretarial Studies in Scotland. Includes Business Studies and Accounting in Northern Ireland.

8 England and Wales only.

9 Wales only.

10 Includes Classical Greek and Latin.

11 Includes music.

12 Scotland only.

4.4 QUALIFICATIONS

GNVQ entries and results, and VCE A/AS and Double Awards qualifications obtained, by subject and gender, 2001/02[1]

England, Wales and Northern Ireland

Thousands

	Intermediate and Foundation GNVQ Pupils aged 15 in all schools[2]								VCE A/AS and Double Award passes for young people[3] in schools and colleges[4]		
			Qualifications obtained								
	Total Entries		GNVQ Part One		Full GNVQ[5]		GNVQ Language Unit[6]		Qualification obtained		
	Interm-ediate	Found-ation	Interm-ediate	Found-ation	Interm-ediate	Found-ation	Interm-ediate	Found-ation	Double Award	A Level	AS
All											
Art & Design	2.1	0.5	1.0	0.2	0.6	0.1	-	-	3.3	1.2	-
Business	9.4	2.8	6.2	1.3	1.2	0.2	-	-	9.5	6.5	3.1
Health & Social Care	6.5	3.7	4.3	2.0	0.7	0.4	-	-	5.0	3.7	1.7
Leisure and Recreation	5.5	3.3	3.5	1.8	0.8	0.3	-	-	2.2	1.6	-
Manufacturing	1.8	0.9	1.1	0.5	0.2	-	-	-	-	-	-
Construction	0.1	0.2	-	-	-	0.1	-	-	0.3	0.1	-
Hospitality and Catering	0.1	0.2	-	-	0.1	0.1	-	-	0.5	0.2	-
Science	0.8	0.1	-	-	0.6	0.1	-	-	0.9	0.5	-
Engineering	1.3	0.6	0.8	0.3	0.2	-	-	-	0.6	0.3	0.1
Information Technology	29.2	2.7	10.8	0.9	8.4	0.1	-	-	5.3	7.6	5.8
Media: Communication and Production	0.1	-	-	-	0.1	-	-	-	1.1	0.5	-
Retail and Distribution	-	-	-	-	-	-	-	-	-	0.2	-
Performing Arts	0.3	-	-	-	0.3	-	-	-	0.5	0.5	-
Other subjects[7]	0.1	0.3	-	-	-	-	-	0.2	4.1	2.9	-
Total	**57.3**	**15.2**	**27.9**	**7.0**	**13.1**	**1.5**	**-**	**0.2**	**33.9**	**25.8**	**10.6**
Males											
Art & Design	0.9	0.3	0.4	0.1	0.2	-	-	-	1.2	0.4	-
Business	5.1	1.7	3.3	0.8	0.6	0.1	-	-	4.8	3.2	1.4
Health & Social Care	0.5	0.5	0.2	0.2	-	-	-	-	0.2	0.1	0.1
Leisure and Recreation	2.2	1.8	1.3	0.9	0.3	0.1	-	-	1.4	1.0	-
Manufacturing	1.4	0.7	0.8	0.4	0.1	-	-	-	-	-	-
Construction	0.1	0.2	-	-	-	0.1	-	-	0.3	0.1	-
Hospitality and Catering	0.1	0.1	-	-	-	-	-	-	0.2	0.1	-
Science	0.4	0.1	-	-	0.3	0.1	-	-	0.5	0.2	-
Engineering	1.2	0.6	0.8	0.3	0.1	-	-	-	0.6	0.3	0.1
Information Technology	17.3	1.7	6.3	0.6	4.9	0.1	-	-	4.3	4.9	3.0
Media: Communication and Production	0.1	-	-	-	-	-	-	-	0.5	0.2	-
Retail and Distribution	-	-	-	-	-	-	-	-	-	0.1	-
Performing Arts	0.1	-	-	-	0.1	-	-	-	0.1	0.1	-
Other subjects[7]	-	0.2	-	-	-	-	-	0.1	0.6	0.6	-
Total	**29.3**	**7.7**	**13.1**	**3.2**	**6.8**	**0.7**	**-**	**0.1**	**14.8**	**11.4**	**4.6**
Females											
Art & Design	1.2	0.2	0.6	0.1	0.4	-	-	-	2.1	0.7	-
Business	4.4	1.1	2.9	0.6	0.7	0.1	-	-	4.4	3.0	1.4
Health & Social Care	6.1	3.3	4.1	1.8	0.7	0.3	-	-	4.8	3.2	1.4
Leisure and Recreation	3.2	1.4	2.2	0.8	0.5	0.2	-	-	0.7	0.5	-
Manufacturing	0.4	0.1	0.3	0.1	0.1	-	-	-	-	-	-
Construction	-	-	-	-	-	-	-	-	-	-	-
Hospitality and Catering	0.1	0.1	-	-	0.1	0.1	-	-	0.3	0.2	-
Science	0.4	0.1	-	-	0.3	-	-	-	0.4	0.2	-
Engineering	0.1	-	-	-	-	-	-	-	-	-	-
Information Technology	11.9	1.0	4.5	0.4	3.5	-	-	-	0.8	2.5	2.7
Media: Communication and Production	-	-	-	-	-	-	-	-	0.6	0.3	-
Retail and Distribution	-	-	-	-	-	-	-	-	-	0.1	-
Performing Arts	0.2	-	-	-	0.2	-	-	-	0.4	0.3	-
Other subjects[7]	-	0.1	-	-	-	-	-	0.1	3.4	2.3	-
Total	**28.1**	**7.5**	**14.7**	**3.8**	**6.4**	**0.8**	**-**	**0.1**	**18.0**	**13.4**	**5.5**

Source: Department for Education and Skills; National Assembly for Wales; Northern Ireland Department of Education

1 Including attempts and achievements by these students in previous years.
2 Those in all schools who were 15 at the start of the academic year, i.e. 31 August 2001.
3 Pupils in schools and students in further education institutions aged 16-18 at the start of the academic year (i.e. 31 August 2001) in England and in Northern Ireland, and aged 17 in Wales.
4 Data for Wales are not included by gender.
5 In Northern Ireland, Full Intermediate and Foundation GNVQ figures relate to pupils aged 16 and 17 in schools and FE colleges at the start of the academic year.
6 England and Wales only. In England, GNVQ Language Units include French, German and Spanish, but the composition is not known for Wales.
7 Includes subjects in England which are not specified in the table (e.g. Travel & Tourism), and Language Units in Wales.

QUALIFICATIONS

4.5

Full vocational awards by type of qualification, equivalent level and gender[1] - time series

United Kingdom

Thousands and percentages

	Year[2]			
	1995/96	1999/00	2000/01[3]	2001/02
All (thousands)[4]				
Full vocational awards:				
By qualification & level				
NVQs/SVQs				
Level 1	62	65	50	47
Level 2	218	262	231	231
Level 3	65	113	103	114
Level 4 and 5	9	15	15	17
Total[5,6]	**354**	**454**	**428**	**408**
GNVQs/GSVQs				
Level 1/Foundation	6	13	..	..
Level 2/Intermediate	44	55	..	..
Level 3/Advanced	34	49	..	..
Total[5]	**84**	**117**	**..**	**..**
Other Vocational Qualifications[7,8]				
Level 1	188	266	299	244
Level 2	89	114	134	119
Level 3	94	83	82	87
Level 4 and 5	53	39	37	49
Total[5]	**423**	**502**	**553**	**499**
Of which:				
Vocationally Related Qualifications (VRQs)[9]				
Level 1	.	.	.	3
Level 2	.	.	.	6
Level 3	.	.	.	14
Level 4 and 5	.	.	.	2
Total[5]	**.**	**.**	**.**	**25**
Males (percentages)[4]				
Full vocational awards:				
By qualification				
NVQs/SVQs[10,11]	41	48	47	45
GNVQs/GSVQs	47	50	..	..
Other vocational qualifications[8,12]	57	46	45	45
VRQs[12]	.	.	.	69
Females (percentages)[4]				
Full vocational awards:				
By qualification				
NVQs/SVQs[10,11]	59	52	53	55
GNVQs/GSVQs	53	50	..	..
Other vocational qualifications[8,12]	43	54	55	55
VRQs[12]	.	.	.	31

Source: National Information System for Vocational Qualifications/Qualifications & Curriculum Authority (QCA)

1 Based on all awards where the gender of the candidate is identified.
2 Academic years from October to September.
3 Includes revised data.
4 Awards are excluded if the centre or qualification was not identified.
5 Numbers may not add to column totals due to rounding.
6 For 2000/01, numbers do not add to column totals because SVQ data are excluded from the respective individual levels.
7 Numbers of Other VQ awards in 2001/02 include VRQs for comparability with previous years.
8 For Other Vocational Qualifications, notional NVQ levels are allocated by QCA for analytical purposes as part of the NISVQ project. Up to 1997/98, includes Other Vocational Qualifications made by City & Guilds, Edexcel, OCR and Scottish Qualifications Agency (SQA) only, not UK estimates. From 1998/99 - 2000/01, numbers of awards are for City & Guilds, Edexcel and OCR only. For 2001/02 numbers of awards are for 7 awarding bodies (see technical notes, paragraph 7 of the Statistical Bulletin 'Vocational Qualifications in the UK: 2001/02' available through the DfES Research and Statistics Gateway 'http://www.dfes.gov.uk/rsgateway').
9 Number of awards are for ASDAN, OCR and City & Guilds Only and are not full UK estimates.
10 Prior to 1997/98 data available on gender for NVQs/SVQs was limited therefore this table may not be representative of the gender split for all NVQs/SVQs awarded nationally for these years.
11 Percentage figures for 2000/01 are calculated excluding SVQ data.
12 Due to limited data available, awards for VRQs and other non regulated vocational qualifications in this table may not be representative of the gender split for all other vocational qualifications awarded nationally.

4.6 QUALIFICATIONS

Success rates[1] in Learning and Skills Council funded Work-Based Learning provision: by programme type and age group, 2001/02[2]

England   Percentages and thousands

| Age at start of learning | Work-Based Learning Provision | | | Total Leavers[4] (000s) |
	Framework[3] (x%)	NVQ Only (y%)	Framework or NVQ (x% + y%)	
Programme Type				
Advanced Modern Apprenticeships (AMA)				
16 - 18	31	10	41	33.5
19+	21	10	31	31.8
All	26	10	36	65.4
Foundation Modern Apprenticeships (FMA)				
16 - 18	24	11	35	60.3
19+	19	12	31	31.4
All	22	11	34	91.8
All Modern Apprenticeships				
16 - 18	27	11	37	93.9
19+	20	11	31	63.3
All	24	11	35	157.1
NVQ Training – level 1				
16 - 18	-	31	31	14.5
19+	-	35	35	0.7
All	-	31	31	15.1
NVQ Training – level 2				
16 - 18	-	41	41	19.6
19+	-	48	48	8.1
All	-	43	43	27.7
NVQ Training – level 3				
16 - 18	-	52	52	3.0
19+	-	36	36	2.7
All	-	45	45	5.7
NVQ Training – level 4				
16 - 18	-	63	63	0.2
19+	-	48	48	0.8
All	-	51	51	1.0
All Frameworks or NVQs				
16 - 18	-	-	37	131.1
19+	-	-	33	75.6
All	-	-	36	206.7

Source: Learning and Skills Council (LSC)

1 For Modern Apprenticeships: the proportion who either meet all the requirements of their apprenticeship framework, or achieve an NVQ required by the framework. For NVQ learning: the proportion of learners who achieved the NVQ.
2 1st August 2001 to 31st July 2002.
3 A set of requirements drawn up by a National Training Organisation (NTO) which need to be fulfilled for the recognition of training as a modern apprenticeship in the sector concerned.
4 Total leavers have been rounded to the nearest 100.

THIS PAGE HAS BEEN LEFT BLANK

4.7

QUALIFICATIONS
Progress towards selected National Targets[1] — time series

<table>
<tr><td rowspan="3"></td><td colspan="9" align="center">(i) England</td><td align="right">Percentages</td></tr>
<tr><td colspan="3" align="center">2001</td><td colspan="3" align="center">2002</td><td colspan="3" align="center">2003[2]</td></tr>
<tr><td>All</td><td>Males</td><td>Females</td><td>All</td><td>Males</td><td>Females</td><td>All</td><td>Males</td><td>Females</td></tr>
<tr><td colspan="10">Targets for 11-year-olds [Key Stage 2 tests]</td></tr>
<tr><td colspan="10">By 2006</td></tr>
<tr><td>85% of 11-year-olds to achieve level 4 or above in
English</td><td>75</td><td>70</td><td>80</td><td>75</td><td>70</td><td>79</td><td>75</td><td>70</td><td>80</td></tr>
<tr><td>35% of 11-year-olds to achieve level 5 or above in
English</td><td>29</td><td>22</td><td>35</td><td>29</td><td>24</td><td>34</td><td>27</td><td>21</td><td>33</td></tr>
<tr><td>85% of 11-year-olds to achieve level 4 or above in
mathematics</td><td>71</td><td>71</td><td>70</td><td>73</td><td>73</td><td>73</td><td>73</td><td>73</td><td>72</td></tr>
<tr><td>35% of 11-year-olds to achieve level 5 or above in
mathematics</td><td>25</td><td>27</td><td>23</td><td>28</td><td>30</td><td>25</td><td>29</td><td>32</td><td>26</td></tr>
<tr><td colspan="10">Targets for 14-year-olds [Key Stage 3 tests]</td></tr>
<tr><td colspan="10">By 2004</td></tr>
<tr><td colspan="10">75% of 14-year olds to achieve level 5 or above in:</td></tr>
<tr><td>English</td><td>65</td><td>57</td><td>73</td><td>67</td><td>59</td><td>76</td><td>68</td><td>61</td><td>75</td></tr>
<tr><td>mathematics</td><td>66</td><td>65</td><td>67</td><td>67</td><td>67</td><td>68</td><td>70</td><td>69</td><td>72</td></tr>
<tr><td>ICT (teacher assessment)</td><td>65</td><td>61</td><td>69</td><td>66</td><td>62</td><td>70</td><td>67</td><td>63</td><td>71</td></tr>
<tr><td>70% of 14-year-olds to achieve level 5 or above in
science</td><td>66</td><td>66</td><td>66</td><td>67</td><td>67</td><td>67</td><td>68</td><td>68</td><td>68</td></tr>
<tr><td colspan="10">Targets for 16-year-olds [Key Stage 4]</td></tr>
<tr><td>Between 2002 and 2006, the proportion of those aged 16
who get qualifications equivalent to 5 GCSEs at Grades
A*-C to rise by 2 percentage points each year on average</td><td>50</td><td>45</td><td>55</td><td>52</td><td>46</td><td>57</td><td>53</td><td>48</td><td>58</td></tr>
<tr><td colspan="10">By 2004</td></tr>
<tr><td>92% of 16-year-olds to achieve 5+ GCSE/GNVQ Grades A*-G
(including English and Mathematics)</td><td>87</td><td>85</td><td>89</td><td>87</td><td>85</td><td>89</td><td>86</td><td>84</td><td>89</td></tr>
<tr><td colspan="10">Targets for Young people</td></tr>
<tr><td colspan="10">By 2004</td></tr>
<tr><td>85% of 19-year-olds[3] to attain a NVQ "level 2"
or equivalent qualification[4,5]</td><td>76</td><td>74</td><td>78</td><td>75</td><td>72</td><td>77</td><td>76</td><td>73</td><td>78</td></tr>
<tr><td>55% of 19-year-olds[3] to attain a NVQ "level 3"
or equivalent qualification[6]</td><td>53</td><td>52</td><td>53</td><td>50</td><td>48</td><td>53</td><td>52</td><td>50</td><td>53</td></tr>
<tr><td colspan="10">Targets for Adults[7]</td></tr>
<tr><td>Reduce by at least 40% the number of adults who lack "level 2"
by 2010, working towards this, 1 million adults already
in the workforce to achieve "level 2" between 2003 and 2006[4,8]</td><td>69</td><td>72</td><td>65</td><td>70</td><td>72</td><td>67</td><td>70</td><td>72</td><td>68</td></tr>
<tr><td colspan="10">By 2004</td></tr>
<tr><td>52% of adults to attain a NVQ "level 3"
or equivalent qualification[6]</td><td>47</td><td>51</td><td>43</td><td>48</td><td>51</td><td>44</td><td>49</td><td>52</td><td>45</td></tr>
</table>

Source: Department for Education and Skills; Labour Force Survey, Spring Quarter of each year; National Assembly for Wales [9]

1 There are further Spending Review 2002 targets in England, and BEST/ETAP targets in Wales which are not included in this table.
2 2003 figures against the targets for 11-year-olds to 16-year-olds are provisional and subject to change.
3 The attainment of those aged 19-21 is used as a proxy for achievement at age 19.
4 "level 2" is defined here as 5 GCSEs at grades A*-C, an NVQ level 2, an Intermediate GNVQ or equivalent.
5 Between 2002 and 2004 the proportion of 19-year-olds who get qualifications equivalent to 5 GCSEs at Grades A*-C to rise by 3 percentage points.
6 "level 3" is 2 A levels, an NVQ level 3, an Advanced GNVQ or equivalent.
7 Adults consist of males aged 18-64 and females aged 18-59, who are in employment or actively seeking employment.
8 The percentage figures are those who have achieved "level 2".
9 More up-to-date information may be available through the DfES Research and Statistics Gateway 'www.dfes.gov.uk/rsgateway', or the National Assembly for Wales 'www.wales.gov.uk'.
10 Age at the start of the academic year.
11 The corresponding figure for 1999 was 1,322 pupils and the target for 2004 is to reduce to 992 pupils.

4.7
QUALIFICATIONS
Progress towards selected National Targets[1] — time series

	(ii) Wales								Percentages
	2001			**2002**			**2003**[2]		
	All	Males	Females	All	Males	Females	All	Males	Females
Targets for 11-year-olds [Key Stage 2 task/test]									
By 2004									
80-85% of 11-year-olds to achieve **level 4 or above** in									
English	77	72	82	79	75	84	79	74	84
Welsh (first language)	71	65	78	75	68	82	78	72	83
mathematics	74	73	76	73	72	74	75	74	76
science	82	81	83	86	85	87	88	87	88
Targets for 14-year-olds [Key Stage 3 task/test]									
By 2004									
80–85% of 14-year-olds to achieve **level 5 or above** in									
English	62	53	71	61	53	70	63	55	72
Welsh (first language)	71	63	79	71	63	79	74	66	81
mathematics	62	60	63	62	62	62	68	67	69
science	63	63	64	67	67	67	69	70	69
Targets for 15-year-olds[10] **[Key Stage 4]**									
By 2004									
58% of 15-year-olds to achieve at least **5 GCSEs at Grades A*–C** or vocational equivalent	50	45	55	50	45	56	51	45	57
95% of 15-year-olds to achieve at least **5 GCSEs at Grades A*–G** or vocational equivalent	85	82	87	85	82	88	85	82	88
									Numbers
the number of pupils leaving full-time education without a recognised qualification to be 25% lower than in 1999[11]	1,122	625	497	1,113	613	500	..	..	..

Source: Department for Education and Skills; Labour Force Survey, Spring Quarter of each year; National Assembly for Wales [9]

See previous page for footnotes.

QUALIFICATIONS

Students[1] obtaining higher education qualifications[2,3] by level, gender and subject group, 2001/02

United Kingdom

Thousands

	Sub-degree[4]	First Degree	Postgraduate			Total Higher Education
			PhD & equivalent	Masters and Others	Total	
All						
Medicine & Dentistry	0.1	6.1	1.0	2.4	3.5	9.6
Subjects Allied to Medicine	25.1	20.9	0.7	5.5	6.2	52.2
Biological Sciences	1.1	18.2	1.8	3.1	4.9	24.2
Vet. Science, Agriculture & related	1.3	2.9	0.3	0.9	1.2	5.4
Physical Sciences	0.8	12.2	1.6	2.4	4.0	17.0
Mathematical and Computer Sciences	6.2	17.9	0.6	7.1	7.8	31.9
Engineering & Technology	4.8	19.8	1.5	6.3	7.9	32.4
Architecture, Building & Planning	1.8	6.2	0.1	3.3	3.4	11.4
Social Sciences[5]	5.8	31.6	1.1	19.0	20.1	57.5
Business & Administrative Studies	9.5	32.6	0.4	24.5	24.9	67.0
Librarianship & Info Science	0.6	5.2	0.1	2.9	2.9	8.8
Languages	1.9	15.5	0.6	3.1	3.7	21.1
Humanities	1.0	9.8	0.7	2.8	3.5	14.3
Creative Arts & Design	3.4	23.0	0.2	4.6	4.8	31.2
Education[6]	6.0	12.5	0.5	30.5	31.0	49.5
Combined, general	13.8	32.6	0.2	6.4	6.6	52.9
All subjects	**83.1**	**267.1**	**11.4**	**124.8**	**136.2**	**486.4**
Males						
Medicine & Dentistry	-	2.8	0.5	1.0	1.5	4.3
Subjects Allied to Medicine	3.0	4.1	0.3	1.4	1.7	8.8
Biological Sciences	0.6	6.6	0.8	1.0	1.8	8.9
Vet. Science, Agriculture & related	0.6	1.1	0.2	0.4	0.6	2.3
Physical Sciences	0.6	7.3	1.1	1.3	2.4	10.3
Mathematical and Computer Sciences	4.4	13.3	0.5	4.8	5.3	23.0
Engineering & Technology	4.3	16.8	1.3	5.1	6.4	27.4
Architecture, Building & Planning	1.3	4.5	0.1	2.0	2.1	7.8
Social Sciences[5]	1.7	12.2	0.6	8.0	8.6	22.5
Business & Administrative Studies	4.0	14.6	0.3	12.8	13.1	31.8
Librarianship & Info Science	0.3	2.0	-	1.0	1.0	3.3
Languages	0.7	4.0	0.3	0.9	1.2	5.9
Humanities	0.4	4.4	0.4	1.3	1.7	6.5
Creative Arts & Design	1.5	8.9	0.1	1.8	1.9	12.4
Education[6]	1.8	2.9	0.2	8.4	8.7	13.4
Combined, general	5.0	13.4	0.1	3.7	3.8	22.2
All subjects	**30.2**	**118.8**	**6.7**	**55.1**	**61.8**	**210.8**
Females						
Medicine & Dentistry	0.1	3.3	0.5	1.4	1.9	5.3
Subjects Allied to Medicine	22.1	16.8	0.4	4.1	4.5	43.4
Biological Sciences	0.5	11.6	1.0	2.1	3.1	15.3
Vet. Science, Agriculture & related	0.7	1.8	0.1	0.5	0.6	3.1
Physical Sciences	0.3	4.9	0.5	1.1	1.6	6.8
Mathematical and Computer Sciences	1.8	4.7	0.1	2.3	2.4	8.9
Engineering & Technology	0.5	3.0	0.3	1.2	1.5	5.0
Architecture, Building & Planning	0.6	1.7	-	1.3	1.4	3.6
Social Sciences[5]	4.1	19.4	0.5	11.0	11.5	35.0
Business & Administrative Studies	5.4	18.0	0.1	11.6	11.8	35.2
Librarianship & Info Science	0.3	3.3	-	1.9	1.9	5.5
Languages	1.2	11.5	0.4	2.1	2.5	15.1
Humanities	0.6	5.4	0.3	1.5	1.8	7.8
Creative Arts & Design	1.9	14.1	0.1	2.8	2.8	18.8
Education[6]	4.2	9.6	0.3	22.1	22.4	36.1
Combined, general	8.8	19.2	0.1	2.7	2.8	30.7
All subjects	**53.0**	**148.2**	**4.7**	**69.7**	**74.4**	**275.6**

Sources: Department for Education and Skills; Higher Education Statistics Agency (HESA)

1 Includes students on Open University courses.
2 Excludes qualifications from the private sector.
3 Includes higher education in higher education institutions in the United Kingdom only. Higher education qualifications in further education institutions (approximately 6% of the total number of students) are excluded.
4 Excludes students who successfully completed courses for which formal qualifications are not awarded.
5 Including Law.
6 Including ITT and INSET.

4.9 QUALIFICATIONS

Highest qualification held by people of working age[1], by gender, age, region and economic activity and, for employees of working age[1], by occupation, 2003

United Kingdom

Thousands and percentages

	All people of working age[1] (000s)	Percentage of people of working age					
		NVQ level 5[2]	NVQ level 4[3]	NVQ level 3[4]	NVQ level 2[5]	Below NVQ level 2[6]	No qualifications
Personal and economic characteristics							
By gender							
Males	19,528	5	20	23	21	17	14
Females	17,671	4	20	15	22	22	17
By age							
16-19	3,006	*	1	21	37	21	21
20-24	3,712	2	18	35	22	16	7
25-29	3,693	7	30	19	20	16	8
30-39	9,397	6	23	16	21	23	10
40-49	8,414	6	22	18	20	19	15
50-64	8,976	5	18	17	19	16	24
By ethnic origin[7]							
White	34,057	5	20	20	22	19	15
Non-white	3,127	6	19	15	20	21	19
of which:							
Mixed	223	5	21	17	21	20	17
inc Asian or British Asian	1,567	5	18	15	19	21	22
Black or Black British	734	5	21	17	22	23	13
Chinese	184	10	24	17	18	20	12
Other Ethnic Group	420	8	18	12	20	22	20
By Government Office region[8]							
United Kingdom	37,199	5	20	19	22	19	15
North East	1,577	3	17	20	21	19	19
North West	4,228	4	18	20	22	18	18
Yorkshire & the Humber	3,120	4	17	21	22	20	16
East Midlands	2,621	4	17	21	22	19	17
West Midlands	3,258	3	18	19	22	20	18
Eastern	3,393	5	19	18	23	20	14
London	4,943	8	23	16	20	19	13
South East	5,055	6	23	20	21	20	11
South West	3,013	5	22	20	22	21	11
England	31,207	5	20	19	22	20	15
Wales	1,777	5	19	19	23	17	17
Scotland	3,172	4	24	22	20	15	15
Northern Ireland	1,042	4	16	19	24	12	24
By economic activity							
Employees[7,9,10]	24,413	6	24	20	22	19	10
of which:							
Managers and senior officials	3,561	8	33	21	19	14	6
Professional occupations	2,912	27	55	8	6	4	-
Associate professional and technical	3,375	6	45	19	17	11	2
Administrative and secretarial	3,392	2	17	20	30	26	6
Skilled trades	2,260	1	7	38	27	16	12
Personal service occupations	1,832	1	15	22	28	24	11
Sales and customer service occupations	2,107	1	9	22	29	25	14
Process, plant and machine operatives	1,948	*	4	18	25	32	20
Elementary occupations	3,011	*	5	15	25	29	27
Self-employed[8,11]	3,215	5	23	24	20	16	12
ILO unemployed[12]	1,444	3	12	16	23	25	21
Inactive[13]	7,966	2	10	17	20	19	31
Time series							
2001	36,759	4	19	19	22	20	16
2002	36,997	5	20	19	22	19	16
2003	37,199	5	20	19	22	19	15

Labour Force Survey, Spring Quarters[14,15]

1 Working age is defined as males aged 16-64 and females 16-59. These figures include unpaid family workers, those on government employment and training programmes, or those who did not answer, who are excluded from the economic activity analyses below.
2 Includes Higher degrees and other qualifications at Level 5.
3 Includes First degree, Other degree and sub-degree higher education qualifications such as teaching and nursing certificates, HNC/HNDs, other HE diplomas and other qualifications at Level 4.
4 Vocational qualifications include those with RSA Advanced Diploma, BTEC Nationals, ONC/ONDs, City and Guilds Advanced Craft or trade apprenticeships and other professional or vocational qualifications at Level 3. Academic qualifications include those with more than one GCE A level or SCE Highers/Scottish Certificates of Sixth Year Studies (CSYS) at Level 3.
5 Vocational qualifications include those with RSA Diplomas, City and Guilds Craft, BTEC Firsts or trade apprenticeships and other professional or vocational qualifications at Level 2. Academic qualifications include those with one GCE A level, five or more GCSE grades A*-C or equivalent or AS examinations/SCE Highers/CSYS at Level 2.
6 Vocational qualifications include those with BTEC general certificates, YT certificates, other RSA qualifications, other City and Guilds or other professional or vocational qualifications at Level 1. Academic qualifications include those with one or more GCSE grade G or equivalent (but less than five at grades A*-C) or AS examinations at Level 1.
7 Apart from rounding, figures may not sum to grand totals because of questions in the LFS which were unanswered or did not apply.
8 Usual region of residence - Government Office Regions in England and each UK country.
9 Employees are those in employment excluding the self-employed, unpaid family workers and those on government employment and training programmes.
10 The split into employees and self-employed is based on respondents' own assessment of their employment status.
11 Self-employed are those in employment excluding employees, unpaid family workers and those on government employment and training programmes.
12 Unemployed according to the International Labour Organization (ILO) definition.
13 People who are neither in employment nor ILO unemployed.
14 Users of these data should read the LFS entry Annex A, as it contains important information about the LFS and the concepts and definitions used.
15 More up-to-date information may be available through the DfES Research and Statistics Gateway 'www.dfes.gov.uk/rsgateway'.

QUALIFICATIONS
People[1] currently working towards a qualification[2], 2003

United Kingdom   Thousands and percentages

	Total working towards a qualification		Of which, percentage working towards[3,4]				
	Number (thousands)	Percentage (%)[5]	Degree or equivalent	Higher Education qualification (below degree level)	GCE A level or equivalent	GCSE grades A* to C or equivalent	Other qualification
All people[1]	6,543	17.6	28.5	8.1	21.6	12.9	27.9
Economic activity							
Employees[6,7]	3,888	15.9	24.4	9.8	21.9	9.4	33.8
Self-employed[7,8]	206	6.4	19.1	9.2	9.3	7.0	54.0
ILO unemployed[9]	251	17.4	22.6	4.5	19.0	19.7	32.2
Economically inactive[10]	2,118	26.6	38.6	5.5	21.7	19.0	14.0
All aged							
All	6,543	17.6	28.5	8.1	21.6	12.9	27.9
16-19	2,112	70.2	12.9	3.5	47.5	26.1	8.9
20-24	1,320	35.6	58.5	9.1	10.3	4.5	16.7
25-29	670	18.2	37.3	11.0	6.8	5.0	38.8
30-39	1,180	12.6	27.0	10.6	9.2	9.2	42.9
40-49	851	10.1	21.6	12.4	9.9	6.5	48.7
50-64	410	4.0	16.6	7.7	8.1	8.1	58.2
Males aged							
All	3,076	15.6	30.4	6.2	22.3	12.1	27.7
16-19	1,040	67.6	11.8	3.1	50.3	25.2	8.2
20-24	669	35.4	61.0	8.3	10.8	3.4	15.2
25-29	340	18.1	39.6	8.5	5.6	5.0	40.3
30-39	531	11.0	29.9	7.2	6.2	7.8	47.4
40-49	328	7.7	23.6	8.6	7.2	5.1	54.2
50-64	168	3.3	19.7	*	8.9	6.9	58.9
Females aged							
All	3,467	19.6	26.8	9.8	20.9	13.6	28.1
16-19	1,072	73.0	13.9	3.9	44.9	27.0	9.5
20-24	651	35.8	56.0	9.9	9.7	5.6	18.3
25-29	330	18.3	34.9	13.5	8.1	5.0	37.3
30-39	649	14.1	24.7	13.3	11.5	10.4	39.2
40-49	523	12.5	20.4	14.8	11.6	7.3	45.3
50-59	242	6.3	14.4	9.8	7.6	8.8	57.7
By highest qualification held[4]							
Degree or equivalent	1,029	16.7	46.3	9.9	3.8	2.3	37.5
Higher Education qualification (below degree level)	565	17.9	38.5	19.2	4.9	2.1	34.3
GCE A level or equivalent	2,055	22.9	46.6	8.4	20.2	3.9	20.1
GCSE grades A* to C, or equivalent	1,673	20.7	5.0	5.9	48.9	13.2	26.0
Other qualification	618	12.1	19.6	6.6	11.8	15.1	45.1
No qualification	575	10.3	*	*	6.0	71.5	19.2
By ethnic origin							
White	5,694	16.7	27.2	8.0	22.1	13.1	28.7
Non-white	849	27.3	37.3	8.9	18.2	11.4	23.0
Mixed	69	32.1	23.1	*	30.6	*	27.3
Asian or British Asian	348	22.3	35.7	6.4	20.5	13.2	23.2
Black or Black British	242	32.5	31.9	14.2	15.0	12.9	24.5
Chinese	75	41.0	67.2	*	14.7	*	*
Other ethnic group	113	28.8	42.8	9.3	12.8	9.8	23.9
Employees							
Full-time & part-time							
All	3,888	15.9	24.4	9.8	21.9	9.4	33.8
Males	1,786	13.7	25.6	7.9	22.3	7.9	35.3
Females	2,102	18.4	23.3	11.3	21.6	10.6	32.6
Full-time							
All	2,310	12.5	21.9	10.4	15.2	7.6	44.1
Males	1,261	10.6	22.4	8.4	15.6	6.6	45.7
Females	1,049	15.9	21.2	12.8	14.7	8.6	42.0
Part-time							
All	1,577	26.6	28.0	8.8	31.8	12.0	18.8
Males	524	46.7	33.4	6.6	38.4	10.9	10.1
Females	1,053	21.9	25.4	9.9	28.5	12.6	23.2

Source: Labour Force Survey, Spring 2003[11]

1 Only those of working age; males aged 16-64 and females aged 16-59. These figures include unpaid family workers, those on government employment and training programmes, or those who did not answer, who are excluded from the Economic activity analyses below.
2 For those who are working towards more than one qualification the highest is recorded.
3 Expressed as a percentage of those in the group working towards a qualification.
4 Apart from rounding, figures may not sum to grand totals because of questions in the LFS which were unanswered or did not apply.
5 Expressed as a percentage of the total number of people in the group.
6 Employees are those in employment excluding the self-employed, unpaid family workers and those on government employment and training programmes.
7 The split into employee and self-employed is based on respondents' own assessment of their employment status.
8 Self-employed are those in employment excluding employees, unpaid family workers and those on government employment and training programmes.
9 Unemployed according to the International Labour Organization (ILO) definition.
10 People who are neither in employment nor ILO unemployed.
11 Users of these data should read the LFS entry in Annex A, as it contains important information about the LFS and the concepts and definitions used.

Chapter 5
Destinations

CHAPTER 5: DESTINATIONS

Key Facts

- The number of school leavers in the United Kingdom increased by 8,700 between 2001 and 2002, to 711,500. The proportion of pupils at the end of compulsory education continuing their education in England remained at 72% – 11 percentage points higher than in 1991. In Northern Ireland, the proportion increased to 68% in 2002 – 10 percentage points higher than in 1991. In Scotland the percentage of all school leavers continuing their education remained at 52% in 2002, some 20 percentage points higher than in 1991. The percentage of school leavers continuing their education in Wales in 2002 fell to 73% – still 11 percentage points higher than in 1991 **(Table 5.1)**

- By 25th March 2001, 76% of leavers from *Work-Based Learning for Young People* in England were in a job 6 months after leaving the programme, compared to 70% in 1999/00. The proportion who were unemployed 6 months after leaving was 9% – a reduction of 2 percentage points from 1999/00. **(Table 5.2)**

- 120,300 first-degree graduates from the academic year 2001/02 were known to go into employment, 12,400 graduates were believed to be unemployed and 36,400 graduates continued their education/training. **(Table 5.3)**

- Of those with a known destination, 65.8% were in employment, 19.9% continued their education/training and 6.8% were believed unemployed. **(Table 5.3)**

CHAPTER 5: DESTINATIONS – LIST OF TABLES

5.1 Destination of school leavers by country – time series

5.2 Work-based Learning for Young People: destinations of leavers – time series

5.3 Destinations of full-time first-degree home and EU graduates by gender and subject group, 2001/02

DESTINATIONS
5.1
Destinations of school leavers by country – time series

United Kingdom

Thousands and percentages[1]

	1991	1996	2000	2001	2002
United Kingdom					
Number of school leavers	638.3	683.3	686.8	702.8	711.5
Destination at end of compulsory schooling					
England					
Number of school leavers	522.8	562.1	570.3	582.8	592.3
of which(%):					
Education	61	68	71	72	72
Government supported training[2]	15	10	8	7	7
Employment	10	8	9	12	11
Unemployed or not available for work	9	7	6	7	8
Unknown or left area	6	8	5	5	5
Wales[3]					
Number of school leavers	34.9	36.9	35.4	36.9	36.4
of which(%):					
Education	62	70	75	74	73
Government supported training[2]	16	8	8	8	9
Employment	8	9	7	7	6
Unemployed or not available for work	8	7	6	6	7
Unknown or left area	6	6	6	6	5
Northern Ireland					
Number of school leavers	25.4	26.9	25.6	26.1	26.3
of which(%):					
Education	58	67	67	67	68
Training	27	22	21	21	19
Employment	5	5	6	6	6
Unemployed or not available for work	4	4	3	3	3
Unknown or left area	6	3	3	3	4
Destination of all school leavers					
Scotland[4]					
Number of school leavers	55.2	57.4	55.5	57.0	56.4
of which(%):					
Education	32	45	50	52	52
Training	25	14	7	6	6
Employment	24	23	26	24	23
Unemployed[5]	9	..	..	..	..
Miscellaneous/other known destinations	11	14	13	14	16
Destinations not known	..	4	3	4	3

Sources: School Leavers Destinations Surveys; Careers Service Activity Survey (England); Careers Wales Association Ltd; Scottish Executive; Northern Ireland Department of Employment and Learning

1 Figures may not sum to 100% due to rounding.
2 Including those who have employed status under Work-based training/learning for young people schemes.
3 Figures recorded in the table for Wales, after 1996, are not classified as 'National Statistics'.
4 These figures cannot be directly compared with those for England, Wales and Northern Ireland as they cover the destinations of pupils from classes S4, S5 and S6 who left Education Authority schools during or at the end of the years academic session. England and Wales figures relate to destinations of year 11 pupils leaving secondary school, while figures for Northern Ireland relate to year 12 pupils.
5 Other than for 1991, figures for 'unemployed' cannot be identified separately and are included within the 'other known destinations' category.

Period of leaving[2,6]	Advanced Modern Apprenticeships (AMA)[3] survey respondents who were:			Foundation Modern Apprenticeships (FMA)[4] survey respondents who were:		
	In a job	In a positive outcome[5]	Unemployed	In a job	In a positive outcome[5]	Unemployed
1990/91	.	.	.	.	.	.
1991/92	.	.	.	.	.	.
1992/93	.	.	.	.	.	.
1993/94	.	.	.	.	.	.
1994/95	..	..	..	.	.	.
1995/96	69	88	11	.	.	.
1996/97	76	89	9	.	.	.
1997/98	81	91	7	..	..	..
1998/99	82	92	6	..	..	..
1999/00	85	93	5	67	88	10
Aug 2000 to Oct 2000	85	93	4	62	87	11
Nov 2000 to Jan 2001	88	95	4	72	89	11
Feb 2001 to 25 Mar 2001	88	94	4	74	91	8

Period of leaving[2,6]	Other Training (OT)[7] survey respondents who were:			Work-Based Learning for Young People survey respondents who were:		
	In a job	In a positive outcome[5]	Unemployed	In a job	In a positive outcome[5]	Unemployed
1990/91	52	67	25	52	67	25
1991/92	50	66	27	50	66	27
1992/93	50	67	27	50	67	27
1993/94	56	71	23	56	71	23
1994/95	59	73	21	59	73	21
1995/96	64	77	17	64	78	17
1996/97	66	79	15	67	81	14
1997/98	65	79	14	68	81	12
1998/99	63	77	15	69	82	12
1999/00	61	75	17	70	84	11
Aug 2000 to Oct 2000	57	73	17	69	85	10
Nov 2000 to Jun 2001	63	74	17	75	87	10
Feb 2001 to 25 Mar 2001	62	74	18	76	88	9

Sources: WBLYP trainee database

1 There was a discontinuity in the survey from which outcomes are derived after March 2001, due to changes in response patterns and better identification of leavers.

2 Data are now collected on an academic year basis (1 August–31 July) rather than financial years (1 April–31March), as in previous editions.

3 Formerly known as Modern Apprenticeships. AMA was launched as an initiative in September 1994 and was fully operational from September 1995.

4 Formerly known as National Traineeships; introduced nationally in September 1997. FMA follow up survey results are for leavers from November 1999 onwards.

5 In a positive outcome = in a job, full-time education or other Government Supported Training.

6 Leavers to September 1990 surveyed three months after leaving. Leavers in October and November 1990 surveyed in June 1991. Leavers from December 1990 surveyed six months after leaving.

7 From April 1995 the definition of Other Training leavers changed, no longer counting those making planned transfers from one training provider to another as leavers. Many of these transferring trainees will not have gained a job or qualification or completed their training. Therefore the change in definition will increase slightly the proportions with jobs and qualifications and those completing their training. The way that data on qualifications gained are collected was changed from August 1991 on. The effect appears to have been to decrease the proportion recorded as gaining full qualifications, but to increase by a similar amount the proportion gaining part qualifications. Data for 1990/91 are therefore not strictly comparable with those for later years.

THIS PAGE HAS BEEN LEFT BLANK

5.3 DESTINATIONS

Destinations of full-time first degree home and EU graduates[1] by gender and subject group, 2001/02[2]

United Kingdom   (i) Numbers of first degree graduates – by destination   Thousands

| | UK Employment | | Overseas | Total | Continuing education/ | Believed | Other known | Unknown | All First Degree |
	Permanent[3]	Temporary	employment[4]	Employment	training[5]	unemployed	destinations[6]	destinations[7]	Graduates[8]
All									
Medicine & Dentistry	1.1	3.4	-	4.4	0.4	-	-	0.4	5.2
Subjects Allied to Medicine	7.2	2.9	0.2	10.3	1.5	0.3	0.5	2.2	14.8
Biological Sciences	5.2	2.6	0.3	8.2	3.9	0.9	1.2	2.8	16.9
Vet. Science, Agriculture & related	1.1	0.4	0.1	1.6	0.3	0.1	0.2	0.5	2.7
Physical Sciences	3.3	1.5	0.2	5.0	3.1	0.7	0.8	1.9	11.5
Mathematical Sciences	5.5	2.0	0.2	7.7	2.1	1.6	0.9	3.1	15.5
Engineering & Technology	5.6	1.5	0.3	7.4	2.2	1.1	0.9	3.4	15.0
Architecture, Building & Planning	1.7	0.7	0.1	2.6	0.6	0.2	0.2	0.8	4.4
Social Sciences	8.3	3.7	0.5	12.5	7.0	1.3	1.9	5.1	27.8
Business & Financial Studies	11.5	3.7	0.6	15.9	2.2	1.4	1.8	5.5	26.7
Librarianship & Info Science	1.9	0.8	0.1	2.8	0.4	0.4	0.3	1.0	4.9
Languages	3.8	2.2	0.8	6.8	3.2	0.8	1.0	2.8	14.6
Humanities	2.4	1.5	0.2	4.0	2.3	0.6	0.7	1.6	9.2
Creative Arts & Design	7.6	3.3	0.4	11.3	2.6	1.6	1.6	4.5	21.4
Education	5.1	3.5	0.1	8.7	0.6	0.2	0.3	1.3	11.1
Combined, general	7.2	3.3	0.7	11.1	4.0	1.3	1.5	4.3	22.1
All subjects	**78.5**	**36.9**	**4.9**	**120.3**	**36.4**	**12.4**	**13.6**	**41.1**	**223.9**
Males									
Medicine & Dentistry	0.5	1.5	-	2.0	0.2	-	-	0.2	2.4
Subjects Allied to Medicine	1.1	0.8	-	1.9	0.5	0.1	0.1	0.5	3.2
Biological Sciences	1.9	0.9	0.1	2.9	1.3	0.4	0.4	1.1	6.1
Vet. Science, Agriculture & related	0.4	0.1	-	0.6	0.1	0.1	0.1	0.2	1.0
Physical Sciences	1.9	0.9	0.1	2.9	1.8	0.5	0.5	1.2	6.9
Mathematical Sciences	4.1	1.4	0.2	5.7	1.5	1.3	0.6	2.4	11.5
Engineering & Technology	4.7	1.3	0.3	6.2	1.8	1.0	0.7	2.9	12.6
Architecture, Building & Planning	1.3	0.5	0.1	1.9	0.4	0.1	0.1	0.6	3.1
Social Sciences	2.9	1.4	0.2	4.5	2.6	0.6	0.8	2.1	10.7
Business & Financial Studies	5.0	1.5	0.3	6.8	1.0	0.8	0.8	2.7	12.1
Librarianship & Info Science	0.7	0.3	-	1.0	0.2	0.2	0.1	0.4	1.8
Languages	0.9	0.5	0.2	1.7	0.8	0.3	0.3	0.8	3.8
Humanities	1.1	0.6	0.1	1.7	1.0	0.3	0.3	0.8	4.1
Creative Arts & Design	2.9	1.2	0.1	4.3	0.9	0.8	0.6	1.9	8.4
Education	1.2	0.6	-	1.8	0.1	0.1	0.1	0.4	2.5
Combined, general	2.8	1.3	0.3	4.4	1.5	0.7	0.6	1.9	9.1
All subjects	**33.3**	**14.8**	**2.2**	**50.3**	**15.7**	**7.1**	**6.3**	**20.1**	**99.4**
Females									
Medicine & Dentistry	0.6	1.9	-	2.5	0.2	-	-	0.2	2.9
Subjects Allied to Medicine	6.1	2.1	0.1	8.4	1.0	0.2	0.4	1.7	11.6
Biological Sciences	3.4	1.8	0.2	5.3	2.6	0.5	0.7	1.8	10.8
Vet. Science, Agriculture & related	0.7	0.3	0.1	1.0	0.2	0.1	0.1	0.3	1.7
Physical Sciences	1.3	0.7	0.1	2.1	1.3	0.2	0.3	0.7	4.6
Mathematical Sciences	1.4	0.6	0.1	2.0	0.6	0.3	0.3	0.7	3.9
Engineering & Technology	0.9	0.2	0.1	1.2	0.4	0.1	0.1	0.5	2.4
Architecture, Building & Planning	0.4	0.2	-	0.7	0.2	-	0.1	0.2	1.3
Social Sciences	5.4	2.3	0.3	8.0	4.3	0.7	1.1	3.0	17.1
Business & Financial Studies	6.5	2.2	0.4	9.1	1.2	0.6	1.0	2.8	14.7
Librarianship & Info Science	1.2	0.5	-	1.8	0.3	0.2	0.2	0.6	3.0
Languages	2.9	1.6	0.6	5.1	2.4	0.5	0.7	2.0	10.8
Humanities	1.4	0.8	0.1	2.3	1.3	0.3	0.4	0.8	5.1
Creative Arts & Design	4.6	2.1	0.2	7.0	1.7	0.8	1.0	2.6	13.0
Education	3.9	2.9	0.1	6.9	0.5	0.2	0.2	0.9	8.6
Combined, general	4.3	2.0	0.4	6.7	2.5	0.6	0.9	2.4	13.1
All subjects	**45.2**	**22.2**	**2.8**	**70.1**	**20.7**	**5.3**	**7.3**	**21.0**	**124.4**

Source: Department for Education and Skills; Higher Education Statistics Agency (HESA)

1 Home and EU students graduating from higher education institutions in 2002. As from 1999/00 the target population excludes non-EU overseas domiciled students, consequently direct comparisons with earlier years cannot be made.
2 Destinations from the academic year 2001/02.
3 Includes the self-employed.
4 Home and overseas students.
5 Continuing education/training in the United Kingdom or overseas.
6 Including students not available for employment.
7 Includes those overseas graduates reported as returning overseas (no other information available).
8 Includes known and unknown destinations.
9 As a percentage of known destinations.

CONTINUED
DESTINATIONS
Destinations of full-time first degree home and EU graduates[1] by gender and subject group, 2001/02[2]

United Kingdom   (ii) Percentage of known destinations   Percentages[9] and thousands

	UK Employment		Overseas	Total	Continuing education/	Believed	Other known	Total of known	All First Degree
	Permanent[3]	Temporary	employment[4]	Employment	training[5]	unemployed	destinations[6]	destinations (000s) (=100%)	Graduates[8] (000s)
All									
Medicine & Dentistry	22.1	69.2	0.3	91.5	7.8	0.1	0.5	4.9	5.2
Subjects Allied to Medicine	57.4	23.1	1.4	81.9	12.0	2.3	3.8	12.6	14.8
Biological Sciences	37.0	18.7	2.2	57.9	27.7	6.1	8.3	14.1	16.9
Vet. Science, Agriculture & related	50.7	17.8	4.4	73.0	13.6	6.1	7.4	2.2	2.7
Physical Sciences	33.7	15.9	2.4	52.0	32.5	7.4	8.1	9.7	11.5
Mathematical Sciences	44.9	16.2	1.6	62.7	17.1	12.9	7.3	12.3	15.5
Engineering & Technology	48.3	13.0	2.9	64.2	18.8	9.6	7.5	11.6	15.0
Architecture, Building & Planning	48.9	19.5	3.7	72.0	18.0	4.3	5.6	3.6	4.4
Social Sciences	36.4	16.1	2.4	54.9	30.7	5.9	8.5	22.7	27.8
Business & Financial Studies	54.2	17.6	3.0	74.9	10.2	6.5	8.4	21.3	26.7
Librarianship & Info Science	49.7	20.4	1.8	71.9	11.0	9.2	7.9	3.8	4.9
Languages	32.2	18.5	6.9	57.6	27.2	6.7	8.5	11.8	14.6
Humanities	31.8	19.2	2.5	53.5	30.2	7.6	8.8	7.6	9.2
Creative Arts & Design	44.8	19.6	2.1	66.5	15.1	9.2	9.2	16.9	21.4
Education	51.4	35.2	1.5	88.1	6.4	2.5	3.0	9.8	11.1
Combined, general	40.3	18.2	3.7	62.2	22.2	7.4	8.2	17.9	22.1
All subjects	**43.0**	**20.2**	**2.7**	**65.8**	**19.9**	**6.8**	**7.4**	**182.8**	**223.9**
Males									
Medicine & Dentistry	22.0	68.8	0.4	91.2	8.3	0.1	0.3	2.2	2.4
Subjects Allied to Medicine	42.7	28.7	1.4	72.8	18.9	3.5	4.8	2.7	3.2
Biological Sciences	36.8	17.5	2.4	56.7	26.5	8.0	8.8	5.0	6.1
Vet. Science, Agriculture & related	49.9	15.8	5.9	71.7	12.1	7.4	8.8	0.8	1.0
Physical Sciences	33.3	15.3	2.4	51.0	31.4	9.0	8.6	5.7	6.9
Mathematical Sciences	45.1	15.8	1.7	62.6	16.3	14.1	7.0	9.1	11.5
Engineering & Technology	48.0	13.1	3.0	64.1	18.4	10.2	7.4	9.7	12.6
Architecture, Building & Planning	51.1	18.4	3.6	73.0	16.6	4.7	5.6	2.5	3.1
Social Sciences	33.8	16.0	2.8	52.7	30.6	7.2	9.6	8.6	10.7
Business & Financial Studies	52.9	16.4	3.0	72.4	10.7	8.1	8.8	9.4	12.1
Librarianship & Info Science	47.4	18.3	2.4	68.1	11.9	11.6	8.4	1.4	1.8
Languages	30.5	18.0	7.2	55.8	26.1	8.3	9.8	3.0	3.8
Humanities	31.7	18.4	2.3	52.4	29.5	9.4	8.7	3.3	4.1
Creative Arts & Design	45.0	18.7	2.0	65.8	13.3	11.8	9.1	6.5	8.4
Education	54.6	27.9	2.1	84.6	6.4	4.1	4.9	2.1	2.5
Combined, general	39.8	17.9	3.6	61.2	20.7	9.4	8.7	7.2	9.1
All subjects	**42.0**	**18.6**	**2.7**	**63.3**	**19.7**	**9.0**	**8.0**	**79.3**	**99.4**
Females									
Medicine & Dentistry	22.1	69.6	0.2	91.8	7.4	0.1	0.6	2.7	2.9
Subjects Allied to Medicine	61.3	21.6	1.4	84.4	10.1	2.0	3.6	9.9	11.6
Biological Sciences	37.1	19.4	2.1	58.5	28.5	5.1	7.9	9.1	10.8
Vet. Science, Agriculture & related	51.2	19.0	3.5	73.7	14.4	5.3	6.5	1.4	1.7
Physical Sciences	34.2	16.8	2.4	53.4	34.1	5.0	7.5	3.9	4.6
Mathematical Sciences	44.3	17.2	1.6	63.1	19.5	9.4	8.0	3.2	3.9
Engineering & Technology	49.7	12.3	2.7	64.7	20.8	6.7	7.8	1.9	2.4
Architecture, Building & Planning	43.4	22.3	3.9	69.6	21.4	3.4	5.6	1.0	1.3
Social Sciences	38.0	16.2	2.2	56.3	30.7	5.1	7.8	14.1	17.1
Business & Financial Studies	55.2	18.6	3.0	76.8	9.7	5.3	8.2	11.8	14.7
Librarianship & Info Science	51.1	21.6	1.5	74.2	10.4	7.7	7.7	2.4	3.0
Languages	32.8	18.6	6.8	58.2	27.6	6.1	8.1	8.8	10.8
Humanities	31.9	19.8	2.6	54.4	30.8	6.1	8.8	4.2	5.1
Creative Arts & Design	44.6	20.2	2.2	66.9	16.3	7.6	9.2	10.4	13.0
Education	50.5	37.3	1.3	89.0	6.4	2.1	2.5	7.7	8.6
Combined, general	40.6	18.4	3.7	62.8	23.2	6.1	8.0	10.7	13.1
All subjects	**43.7**	**21.4**	**2.7**	**67.8**	**20.0**	**5.1**	**7.0**	**103.4**	**124.4**

Source: Department for Education and Skills; Higher Education Statistics Agency (HESA)

See previous page for footnotes

Chapter 6
Population

CHAPTER 6: POPULATION

Key Facts

- UK population aged 2 and over at January 2003 was 57.9 million (28.2 million males and 29.7 million females). **(Table 6.1)**

- UK working age population at Spring 2003 was 37.2 million, of which 24.4 million were Employees, 3.2 million were Self employed, 1.4 million were ILO unemployed and 8.0 million were Economically inactive. **(Table 6.1)**

- UK population aged 2 and over increased by 3.8 per cent between 1991 (55.7 million) and 2003 (57.9 million). Over the same period the working age population increased by 6.0 per cent, from 35.1 million to 37.2 million. **(Table 6.2)**

- Of people of working age, between 1991 and 2003, Employees increased by 11.4 per cent (21.9 million to 24.4 million), Self employed decreased by 1.1 per cent (3.3 million to 3.2 million), Economically inactive increased by 14.1 per cent (7.0 million to 8.0 million), and ILO unemployed decreased by over 40 per cent from 2.5 million to 1.4 million. **(Table 6.2)**

CHAPTER 6: POPULATION - LIST OF TABLES

6.1

POPULATION

Population[1] at 1 January by age[2] and gender at the beginning of the academic year[2], 2003

United Kingdom

Thousands

| | 2003[2] | | | | | | | | | | | | | | |
| | All[3] | | | | | Males | | | | | Females | | | | |
	UK	England	Wales	Scotland	NI	UK	England	Wales	Scotland	NI	UK	England	Wales	Scotland	NI
Ages															
Under 5	2,078	1,745	100	164	69	1,065	893	51	84	36	1,013	851	49	80	33
5-10	4,451	3,720	222	363	147	2,280	1,905	113	186	76	2,172	1,815	108	177	72
11-15	3,902	3,249	197	324	133	2,000	1,665	102	166	68	1,902	1,584	96	157	65
16-19	2,999	2,484	153	257	104	1,534	1,273	77	131	53	1,464	1,211	75	127	51
20-24	3,636	3,030	174	320	111	1,809	1,506	86	161	56	1,827	1,523	88	160	55
25-29	3,714	3,149	157	297	111	1,837	1,561	76	145	55	1,877	1,588	81	152	56
30-39	9,131	7,697	407	770	257	4,504	3,810	197	371	126	4,627	3,886	210	399	131
40-49	8,107	6,759	388	733	227	4,020	3,359	190	359	112	4,088	3,401	198	374	115
50-59	7,506	6,275	392	649	191	3,714	3,107	194	320	94	3,792	3,168	198	329	97
60-64	2,896	2,402	157	262	76	1,417	1,178	77	125	37	1,480	1,224	80	137	39
65+	9,433	7,883	509	813	228	3,982	3,342	215	331	94	5,450	4,541	294	482	134
Total aged 2 +	**57,853**	**48,392**	**2,856**	**4,951**	**1,653**	**28,162**	**23,599**	**1,378**	**2,378**	**806**	**29,691**	**24,793**	**1,477**	**2,573**	**847**
of which working age [4]	37,199	31,207	1,777	3,172	1,042	19,529	16,414	935	1,642	538	17,671	14,793	843	1,530	504
of which															
Employees [5,6]	24,413	20,539	1,122	2,124	628	13,010	10,991	583	1,103	334	11,403	9,548	539	1,021	294
Self employed [6,7]	3,215	2,753	158	221	84	2,389	2,040	112	168	70	826	714	46	53	14
ILO unemployed [8]	1,444	1,205	62	137	41	905	753	44	82	25	540	452	17	55	16
Economically inactive [9]	7,966	6,587	425	678	277	3,146	2,573	191	281	101	4,820	4,014	234	397	176

Sources: Department for Education and Skills; Labour Force Survey [10]; Office for National Statistics; Government Actuary's Department

1 Estimated and projected numbers based on demographic data provided by the Office for National Statistics (ONS) and the Government Actuary's Department (GAD). Population estimates incorporate post-2001 Census revisions.

2 Age at 31 August 2002. For the Labour Force Survey economic data only, age is based on the age of respondents at the time of the survey.

3 Males and Females may not sum to All totals due to rounding.

4 Working age is defined as males aged 16-64 and females aged 16-59. These figures include unpaid family workers, those on government employment and training programmes, or those who did not answer, who are excluded from the separate analyses below.

5 Employees are those in employment excluding the self-employed, unpaid family workers and those on government employment and training programmes.

6 The split into employees and self-employed is based on respondents' own assessment of their employment status.

7 Self-employed are those in employment excluding employees, unpaid family workers and those on government employment and training programmes.

8 Unemployed according to the International Labour Organization (ILO) definition.

9 Economically inactive are those who are neither in employment nor ILO unemployed.

10 Users of these data should read the LFS entry in Annex A, as it contains important information about the LFS and the concepts and definitions used.

POPULATION

6.2

Population[1] at 1 January by age[2] at the beginning of the academic year - time series

United Kingdom   Thousands

Ages	1991[3]	1996[3]	2001[3]	2002[3]	2003
Under 5	2,289	2,319	2,161	2,130	2,078
5-10	4,379	4,598	4,569	4,508	4,451
11-15	3,391	3,614	3,834	3,860	3,902
16-19	3,180	2,686	2,880	2,936	2,999
20-24	4,502	3,872	3,506	3,580	3,636
25-29	4,668	4,486	4,022	3,904	3,714
30-39	7,870	8,722	9,157	9,215	9,131
40-49	7,522	7,835	7,816	7,957	8,107
50-59	6,027	6,364	7,288	7,417	7,506
60-64	2,904	2,790	2,894	2,882	2,896
65+	9,013	9,193	9,306	9,370	9,433
Total aged 2 +	**55,744**	**56,478**	**57,433**	**57,759**	**57,853**
of which working age [4]	35,103	35,663	36,759	36,997	37,199
of which					
Employees [5,6]	21,920	22,092	24,189	24,319	24,413
Self employed [6,7]	3,250	3,109	2,986	3,026	3,215
ILO unemployed [8]	2,501	2,321	1,398	1,498	1,444
Economically inactive [9]	6,980	7,790	7,950	7,968	7,966

Sources: Department for Education and Skills; Labour Force Survey[10]; Office for National Statistics; Government Actuary's Department

1 Estimated and projected numbers based on demographic data provided by the Office for National Statistics (ONS) and the Government Actuary's Department (GAD). Population estimates incorporate post-2001 Census revisions.

2 Age at 31 August of the previous year. For the Labour Force Survey economic data only, age is based on the age of respondents at the time of the survey.

3 Includes revised data.

4 Working age is defined as males aged 16-64 and females aged 16-59. These figures include unpaid family workers, those on government employment and training programmes, or those who did not answer, who are excluded from the separate analyses below.

5 Employees are those in employment excluding the self-employed, unpaid family workers and those on government employment and training programmes.

6 The split into employees and self-employed is based on respondents' own assessment of their employment status.

7 Self-employed are those in employment excluding employees, unpaid family workers and those on government employment and training programmes.

8 Unemployed according to the International Labour Organization (ILO) definition.

9 Economically inactive are those who are neither in employment nor ILO unemployed.

10 Users of these data should read the LFS entry in Annex A, as it contains important information about the LFS and the concepts and definitions used.

Chapter 7
International Comparisons

CHAPTER 7: INTERNATIONAL COMPARISONS

Introduction

International comparisons of the functioning of education and training systems can help countries to identify their strengths and weaknesses and evaluate their performance against their main competitors. Governments are increasingly looking towards these comparisons as they develop and monitor education and training policies.

The United Kingdom participates in the continuing development of international comparisons of education and training. With help from the National Assembly for Wales, Scottish Executive, the Northern Ireland Department of Education and the Northern Ireland Department for Employment and Learning, DfES supply detailed statistics on education and training in the UK, drawn from this volume and other sources, to the Organisation for Economic Co-operation and Development (OECD), the Statistical Office of the European Union (EUROSTAT) and the United Nations Educational, Scientific and Cultural Organisation (UNESCO).

Based on information supplied by various countries to the international bodies, and the results of international studies, a range of 'indicators' is now available, seeking to compare different aspects of countries' education and training systems and their respective performance.

The comparative tables shown here draw from OECD's "Education at a Glance" (2003 Edition), which includes trends in international comparisons.

It is important to note, however, that international comparisons of education and training are very difficult and should therefore be treated with caution. In addition, some knowledge of the underlying systems in different countries is extremely useful in interpreting the data.

To ensure comparability, most educational activity in different countries has been assigned to 6 internationally-agreed "ISCED" (International Standard Classification of Education) levels of education. The best comparisons are based on such internationally agreed definitions and procedures, backed up by controls to ensure that each country meets these. Despite these efforts, there may still be comparability problems that persist - some of the more important ones are noted below:

Notes:

Classifying education
- Coverage of what is considered to be "education" may vary, especially at the pre-compulsory and post-compulsory level e.g. early childhood provision, apprenticeships, adult learning etc.

Expenditure on education
- Where institutions cover more than one of the education levels (e.g. "lower" (age 11-13) and "upper" (age 14+) secondary school education in the UK), estimates are often required to assign expenditure figures between levels.

- The range of public and private provision varies considerably between countries. In Japan and Australia, private expenditure on educational institutions is almost one-third of that from public sources, and in the United States it is just under half. This figure for the UK is nearer one-fifth.

- Public expenditure on education, as a percentage of GDP, is influenced by a number of factors. An obvious one is the proportion of the population of school age, which can vary widely between different countries.

- Expenditure coverage, especially at the HE level, differs according to the extent to which countries include elements such as student support and research and development.

Participation in education
- Many of the measures shown are on the basis of headcounts, no distinction being possible between full-time and part-time study. Some countries do not even recognise the concept of part-time study, although many of their students would be classified as "part-time" in the UK.

- When comparing expected years of schooling in different countries, the length of the school year and the quality of education offered is not necessarily the same.

- The reasons why adults in some countries are so much less likely than others to participate in university-level education are varied. One important factor may be the extensive provision of vocational education and apprenticeships in continental Europe, likely to have reduced the perceived need to enrol in formal university-level studies as preparation for work.

Teachers

- A clear definition of a "teacher", especially in higher education, has not been well established in international data collections. Some countries include professional staff such as guidance counsellors and school psychologists in their "teacher" counts.

CHAPTER 7: INTERNATIONAL COMPARISONS

Explanatory Note

In the following 'Key Facts' section the UK position is sometimes compared to the 'OECD average'. This 'average' is calculated as the *unweighted* mean of the data values of all countries for which data are available or can be estimated.

Key Facts

- Public expenditure on all levels of education in the UK represented 4.8% of Gross Domestic Product in 2000, slightly below the OECD average of 5.2%. This was higher than Japan (3.6%) and Germany (4.5%), but lower than the US (5.0%), Australia (5.1%), France (5.8%), New Zealand (7.0%) and all of the Scandinavian countries. **(Table 7.1)**

- In 2000, average expenditure per student per year at the pre-primary level (US$6,677) was significantly above the OECD average (US$4,137). The average expenditure per secondary level student (US$5,991) was close to the OECD average (US$5,957). Spending per student at primary level (US$3,877) was below the OECD average (US$4,381). **(Table 7.2)**

- Average expenditure per higher education student in the UK in 2000 (US$9,657) was slightly above the OECD average (US$9,571) - however, the US spent over twice the amount per higher education student as the UK. **(Table 7.2)**

- The age range at which over 90% of the population are enrolled in education in the UK each year is 4 -15. In almost all other OECD countries, compulsory education does not start until age 6 or 7, compared with age 5 in the UK. **(Table 7.3)**

- In 2001, given current conditions, a UK 5 year old could expect to enrol in 18.9 years of full-time and part-time education during their lifetime, compared with the OECD average of 16.9 years. Expected years in education in the UK increased by 10% between 1995 and 2001. They are currently highest in Australia, where a 5 year old can expect to enrol in 20.6 years of full-time and part-time education. **(Table 7.3)**

- The ratio of students to teaching staff in the UK was above the OECD average at all levels of education in 2001. **(Table 7.4)**

- In 2000, 15 year olds in the UK were above the OECD average in reading, mathematical and scientific literacy. **(Table 7.5)**

- In 2001, the UK graduation rate for all first degrees (37.4%) was above the OECD average (30.3%). The UK had the highest rate for medium term first degree programmes (3-5 years duration) and the 5th highest for advanced research programmes. **(Table 7.6)**

- In 2001, the proportion of primary and secondary teachers in the United Kingdom aged less than 30 was well above the OECD average. **(Table 7.7)**

CHAPTER 7: INTERNATIONAL COMPARISONS – LIST OF TABLES

INTERNATIONAL COMPARISONS
Expenditure on education as a percentage of GDP, 1995 and 2000

| | Public expenditure on education[1] as a percentage of GDP | | | |
| | 2000 | | | 1995 |
	Primary and Secondary Education	Higher Education	All levels[2]	All levels[2]
Australia	3.9	1.2	5.1	5.2
Austria	3.8	1.4	5.8	6.2
Belgium	3.4	1.3	5.2	..
Canada[3]	3.3	2.0	5.5	6.5
Czech Republic	3.0	0.8	4.4	4.9
Denmark[4]	4.8	2.5	8.4	7.4
Finland	3.6	2.0	6.0	7.0
France	4.1	1.0	5.8	6.0
Germany	3.0	1.1	4.5	4.6
Greece	2.7	0.9	3.8	2.9
Hungary	3.1	1.0	4.9	5.4
Iceland	4.7	1.1	6.0	4.9
Ireland	3.0	1.3	4.4	5.1
Italy	3.2	0.8	4.6	4.9
Japan[4]	2.7	0.5	3.6	3.6
Korea	3.3	0.7	4.3	..
Luxembourg	..	..	..	..
Mexico	3.4	0.9	4.9	4.6
Netherlands	3.2	1.3	4.8	5.0
New Zealand	4.9	1.7	7.0	5.7
Norway	3.9	1.7	6.7	9.0
Poland	3.8	0.8	5.2	5.5
Portugal	4.2	1.0	5.7	5.4
Slovak Republic	2.7	0.7	4.1	4.7
Spain	3.1	1.0	4.4	4.7
Sweden	4.9	2.0	7.4	7.2
Switzerland	3.9	1.2	5.4	5.5
Turkey	2.4	1.1	3.5	2.4
United Kingdom	**3.4**	**1.0**	**4.8**	**5.1**
United States[3]	3.5	1.1	5.0	..
Country mean	**3.5**	**1.2**	**5.2**	**5.4**

Source: OECD, Education at a Glance, 2003

1 Direct expenditure for institutions and public subsidies to households e.g. for tuition fees and living costs. The definition of "education expenditure" used by OECD is different from the definition used in Chapter 1 of this Volume.
2 Includes expenditure for early childhood education and other miscellaneous expenditure.
3 Post-secondary non-tertiary is included in 'higher' education and is excluded from 'primary and secondary' education.
4 Post-secondary non-tertiary is included in both 'primary and secondary' and 'higher' education.

	Expenditure per full-time equivalent student per year[1]				Cumulative expenditure per student over the average duration of higher education studies[2]
	(US$ converted using purchasing power parities)				
	Early childhood education	Primary education	Secondary education	Higher Education	
Australia	..	4,967	6,894	12,854	32,521
Austria	5,471	6,560	8,578	10,851	66,948
Belgium	3,282	4,310	6,889	10,771	..
Canada	6,120	[3]	5,947	14,983	..
Czech Republic	2,435	1,827	3,239	5,431	..
Denmark[4]	4,255	7,074	7,726	11,981	50,199
Finland	3,944	4,317	6,094	8,244	50,469
France[4]	4,119	4,486	7,636	8,373	39,200
Germany	5,138	4,198	6,826	10,898	52,962
Greece[5]	[6]	3,318	3,859	3,402	17,723
Hungary[5]	2,511	2,245	2,446	7,024	28,448
Iceland[5]	..	5,854	6,518	7,994	21,424
Ireland	2,863	3,385	4,638	11,083	35,909
Italy[5]	5,771	5,973	7,218	8,065	44,278
Japan	3,376	5,507	6,266	10,914	..
Korea[4]	1,949	3,155	4,069	6,118	20,985
Luxembourg	..	..	..	..	..
Mexico[4]	1,385	1,291	1,615	4,688	16,044
Netherlands[4]	3,920	4,325	5,912	11,934	46,543
New Zealand	..	..	..	..	..
Norway[5]	13,170	6,550	8,476	13,353	..
Poland[5]	2,278	2,105	..	3,222	..
Portugal	2,237	3,672	5,349	4,766	..
Slovak Republic	1,644	1,308	1,927	4,949	..
Spain[4]	3,370	3,941	5,185	6,666	30,330
Sweden	3,343	6,336	6,339	15,097	69,561
Switzerland[4,5]	3,114	6,631	9,780	18,450	66,867
Turkey[5]	..	..	..	4,121	..
United Kingdom[7]	**6,677**	**3,877**	**5,991**	**9,657**	**34,202**
United States[8]	7,980	6,995	8,855	20,358	..
Country mean	**4,137**	**4,381**	**5,957**	**9,571**	**40,371**

Source: OECD, Education at a Glance, 2003

1 Calendar year 2000. Where the financial year and/or school year do not match the calendar year, corresponding weightings are made.
2 Calculated by multiplying the expenditure per full-time equivalent student per year by the average number of years of duration of higher education studies. Includes students who do not complete their course.
3 Included in secondary education figure.
4 The duration of higher education studies is obtained by a special survey conducted in 1997 for the academic year 1995.
5 Public institutions only.
6 Included in primary education figure.
7 Public and Government-dependent private institutions only.
8 Public and independent private institutions only.

	Context			Expected years of education[1]	
	Compulsory school starting age[2]	Ending age of compulsory schooling[3]	Age range at which over 90% of the population are enrolled	Expected years of full-time and part time education from age 5	Index of change between 1995 and 2001 (1995 = 100)
Australia	6	15	5-16	20.6	107
Austria	6	15	5-16	16.3	104
Belgium	6	18	3-17	19.2	107
Canada	6	16	6-17	16.6	98
Czech Republic	6	15	5-17	16.0	112
Denmark	7	16	4-15	18.0	106
Finland	7	16	6-17	19.2	112
France	6	16	3-17	16.6	101
Germany	6	18	6-17	17.3	106
Greece	6	15	6-16	16.1	116
Hungary	6	16	5-16	16.4	115
Iceland	6	16	4-16	18.0	108
Ireland	6	15	5-16	16.3	106
Italy	6	15	3-15	16.1	..
Japan	6	15	4-17	..	..
Korea	6	14	6-17	16.1	112
Luxembourg	6	15	4-15	..	..
Mexico	6	15	6-12	12.8	105
Netherlands	5	18	4-16	17.3	..
New Zealand	6	16	4-15	17.8	..
Norway	7	16	6-17	17.8	102
Poland	7	15	6-17	16.7	116
Portugal	6	14	5-15	17.1	104
Slovak Republic	6	16	6-16	14.9	..
Spain	6	16	4-16	17.3	102
Sweden	7	16	6-18	20.0	..
Switzerland	6	15	6-16	16.5	..
Turkey	6	14	7-12	11.5	121
United Kingdom[4]	**5**	**16**	**4-15**	**18.9**	**110**
United States	6	17	5-15	17.1	..
Country mean	**6**	**16**	**.**	**16.9**	**108**

Sources: OECD, Education at a Glance, 2003; UNESCO Statistical Yearbook, 1999

1 Calculated as the sum of the net enrolment rates in education for each single year of age from age 5 onwards, divided by 100.
2 Age at start of academic year.
3 Age at end of academic year.
4 Coverage of enrolments in further education has been expanded from a "snapshot" to a "whole year" count. This has had an effect on "school expectancy" figures which are not directly comparable with figures from before 1999.

INTERNATIONAL COMPARISONS
Ratio of students to teaching staff[1] by level of education (based on full-time equivalents), 2001

| | Level of education (full-time equivalents) | | | |
	Early childhood education	Primary education	Secondary education	Higher education
Australia[2]	..	17.0	..	..
Austria	18.1	14.3	9.8	15.8
Belgium	16.7	13.4	9.8	18.1
Canada	11.5	18.3	17.8	16.2
Czech Republic	12.7	19.4	13.8	14.9
Denmark	6.9	10.0	12.4	..
Finland	13.0	16.1	14.0	16.8
France	19.2	19.5	12.3	18.1
Germany	24.6	19.4	15.2	12.3
Greece	14.5	12.7	9.7	25.2
Hungary	11.4	11.3	11.8	13.3
Iceland	5.2	12.6	..	8.0
Ireland	14.5	20.3	15.2	16.0
Italy	12.8	10.8	10.2	22.4
Japan	18.5	20.6	15.1	11.3
Korea	22.2	32.1	20.1	53.9
Luxembourg[3]	17.4	11.0	9.1	..
Mexico	21.9	27.0	27.3	15.2
Netherlands	[4]	17.2	17.1	12.6
New Zealand	7.6	19.6	15.7	15.0
Norway	..	11.6	9.3	11.5
Poland	12.8	12.5	15.4	16.2
Portugal	16.9	11.6	8.9	..
Slovak Republic	10.0	20.7	13.8	10.8
Spain	16.0	14.7	11.0	13.4
Sweden	10.3	12.4	14.6	9.3
Switzerland[3]	..	..	..	..
Turkey	15.6	29.8	17.2	16.1
United Kingdom[2]	**22.1**	**20.5**	**14.5**	**17.6**
United States	14.9	16.3	15.9	13.7
Country mean	**14.9**	**17.0**	**13.9**	**16.5**

Source: OECD, Education at a Glance, 2003

1   Includes head teachers and administrative personnel involved in teaching, pro-rata.
2   Includes only general secondary education programmes.
3   Public institutions only.
4   Included in primary education figures.

	Area of literacy					
	Reading Literacy[1]		Mathematical Literacy[2]		Scientific Literacy[3]	
	Mean score[4]	Compared to OECD average[5]	Mean score[4]	Compared to OECD average[5]	Mean score[4]	Compared to OECD average[5]
Australia	528	+	533	+	528	+
Austria	507	+	515	+	519	+
Belgium	507	+	520	+	496	
Canada	534	+	533	+	529	+
Czech Republic	492	−	498		511	+
Denmark	497		514	+	481	−
Finland	546	+	536	+	538	+
France	505		517	+	500	
Germany	484	−	490	−	487	−
Greece	474	−	447	−	461	−
Hungary	480	−	488	−	496	
Iceland	507	+	514	+	496	
Ireland	527	+	503		513	+
Italy	487	−	457	−	478	−
Japan	522	+	557	+	550	+
Korea	525	+	547	+	552	+
Luxembourg	441	−	446	−	443	−
Mexico	422	−	387	−	422	−
New Zealand	529	+	537	+	528	+
Norway	505		499		500	
Poland	479	−	470	−	483	−
Portugal	470	−	454	−	459	−
Spain	493	−	476	−	491	−
Sweden	516	+	510	+	512	+
Switzerland	494		529	+	496	
United Kingdom	**523**	**+**	**529**	**+**	**532**	**+**
England	523	+	529	+	533	+
United States	504		493		499	
Country mean	**500**		**500**		**500**	

Source: OECD, PISA 2000

1 The ability to understand, use and reflect on written texts in order to achieve one's goals, to develop one's own knowledge and potential, and to participate effectively in society.

2 Concerns student's ability to recognise and interpret mathematical problems encountered in their world, to translate these problems into a mathematical context, to use mathematical knowledge and procedures to solve the problems within their mathematical context, to interpret the results in terms of the original problem, to reflect upon the methods applied, and to formulate and communicate the outcomes.

3 Reflects students' ability to use scientific knowledge, to recognise scientific questions and to identify what is involved in scientific investigations, to relate scientific data to claims and conclusions, and to communicate these aspects of science.

4 The OECD average score is set to 500.

5 '+' indicates a mean score significantly above the OECD average, '−' indicates a mean score significantly below the OECD average.

7.6

Higher education: participation and graduation, 2001

	Participation	Graduation rates[1]				
			University level[2]			
			First Degree			Postgraduate[3]
	Expected years of Higher Education for all 17 year-olds	Non-university level[2]	All First Degrees	Medium[4]	Long[5]	Doctorate
Australia	3.1	..	42.0	33.3	8.7	1.3
Austria	2.4	..	16.6	2.1	14.5	1.5
Belgium	2.8	..	..	..	..	1.0
Canada	2.8	..	..	..	..	..
Czech Republic	1.6	5.0	14.1	3.6	10.5	0.7
Denmark	2.6	8.0	38.8	33.5	4.5	1.0
Finland	4.2	7.3	40.7	22.4	17.7	1.8
France	2.6	17.9	25.0	10.2	14.0	1.4
Germany	2.1	10.7	19.0	6.4	12.7	2.0
Greece	3.1	..	..	..	..	0.4
Hungary	2.2	..	..	..	..	0.6
Iceland	2.4	7.6	39.5	33.9	5.6	0.1
Ireland	2.6	19.0	29.3	15.3	14.0	0.9
Italy	2.4	0.3	20.0	2.1	17.8	0.5
Japan	..	27.4	32.8	28.8	4.0	0.7
Korea	3.9	..	..	..	..	0.8
Luxembourg	..	..	..	..	..	..
Mexico	1.1	..	..	..	..	0.1
Netherlands	2.5	..	..	..	..	1.3
New Zealand	3.2	17.6	40.2	..	..	0.9
Norway	3.1	..	..	..	..	1.1
Poland	2.9	..	38.6	..	..	0.9
Portugal	2.5	..	..	..	..	..
Slovak Republic	1.6	2.3	..	..	..	0.7
Spain	3.0	10.9	32.1	..	..	0.9
Sweden	3.2	4.0	29.6	28.5	1.2	2.7
Switzerland	1.8	16.1	18.7	7.4	10.1	2.5
Turkey	1.3	..	..	..	..	0.2
United Kingdom	**2.6**	**11.5**	**37.4**	**34.8**	**2.5**	**1.6**
United States	3.5	..	..	..	..	1.3
Country mean	**2.6**	**11.0**	**30.3**	**18.7**	**9.8**	**1.1**

Source: OECD, Education at a Glance, 2003

1 Calculated as the ratio of graduates to the population at the typical age of graduation, multiplied by 100, except for Postgraduate.

2 "University-level" higher education refers to "largely theoretically based" courses with a minimum of 3 years full-time-equivalent duration. In the UK, this comprises first and higher degrees. "Non university-level higher education" courses are "more practically-oriented and occupationally specific". In the UK, this level comprises "sub-degree" higher education courses, such as HNCs, HNDs, Dip HEs.

3 Calculated by summing the graduation rates by single year of age, except for France, Italy, Japan, Korea, Mexico, the Netherlands and the United States.

4 Three to less than 5 years duration.

5 Five or more years duration.

INTERNATIONAL COMPARISONS
Age distribution of teachers in primary and secondary education, 2001

7.7

Percentages

	Primary education					Secondary education				
	Age range					Age range				
	< 30	30 - 39	40 - 49	50 - 59	>= 60	< 30	30 - 39	40 - 49	50 - 59	>= 60
Australia	..	..	..	..	..	..	..	..	..	..
Austria	..	..	..	..	..	..	..	..	..	..
Belgium	21.5	29.5	27.7	20.7	0.7	12.7	21.8	35.6	27.7	2.2
Canada	11.8	24.4	38.7	24.0	1.1	11.8	24.4	38.7	24.0	1.1
Czech Republic	..	..	..	..	..	..	..	..	..	..
Denmark	..	..	..	..	..	..	..	..	..	..
Finland	13.2	32.9	29.3	24.0	0.6	7.5	25.4	31.1	32.8	3.2
France	13.5	28.1	34.7	23.3	0.3	17.1	24.6	27.1	30.0	1.1
Germany	6.1	15.3	33.7	39.3	5.6	4.0	14.0	35.4	40.5	6.2
Greece	..	..	..	..	..	..	..	..	..	..
Hungary	..	..	..	..	..	..	..	..	..	..
Iceland[1]	15.4	29.2	30.2	19.0	6.2	7.7	21.9	32.8	26.0	11.5
Ireland	18.1	25.9	34.1	17.5	4.4	10.5	31.3	29.2	24.0	4.9
Italy	2.8	24.3	38.7	29.8	4.3	0.1	8.7	42.5	44.5	4.2
Japan	8.8	30.1	43.9	17.0	0.2	10.9	32.2	36.4	18.8	1.7
Korea	27.2	31.6	26.1	14.5	0.6	15.0	41.7	33.0	9.9	0.5
Luxembourg[2]	26.0	22.5	27.0	23.7	0.8	13.1	26.8	29.5	29.1	1.6
Mexico	..	..	..	..	..	..	..	..	..	..
Netherlands	18.4	21.1	37.4	21.7	1.5	8.3	17.2	37.5	34.5	2.6
New Zealand	16.0	20.1	32.0	26.0	5.9	13.8	19.4	31.9	28.2	6.7
Norway	[3]	[3]	[3]	[3]	[3]	12.9	22.1	28.7	29.7	6.6
Poland	15.5	41.3	28.6	13.4	1.2	19.0	29.7	30.1	17.8	3.3
Portugal	13.8	25.8	41.2	16.5	2.7	23.8	38.8	25.3	9.9	2.2
Slovak Republic	22.1	24.9	24.8	22.6	5.7	18.7	24.2	28.8	22.5	5.7
Spain	..	..	..	..	..	..	..	..	..	..
Sweden	12.7	17.3	28.2	35.5	6.2	11.7	19.1	24.6	36.4	8.3
Switzerland[2]	..	..	..	..	..	..	..	..	..	..
Turkey	..	..	..	..	..	..	..	..	..	..
United Kingdom	**21.9**	**21.3**	**30.8**	**25.3**	**0.7**	**17.8**	**22.8**	**33.4**	**25.1**	**0.9**
United States	..	..	..	..	..	..	..	..	..	..
Country mean	**16.2**	**26.0**	**32.4**	**22.8**	**2.6**	**12.6**	**24.5**	**32.4**	**26.8**	**3.8**

Source: OECD, Education at a Glance, 2003

1   Excluding lower secondary education.
2   Public institutions only.
3   Included in secondary education figures.

Annex A

SOURCES OF EDUCATION AND TRAINING STATISTICS

This section gives details of the current major sources of education and training statistics used in this publication. Previous editions of "Education and Training Statistics for the United Kingdom" and its predecessors, and "Training Statistics", give earlier sources used.

List of Sources

1   Education Expenditure

2   Further Education Statistics

3   Higher Education Statistics Agency (HESA)

4   Labour Force Survey (LFS)

5   Population

6   Public Examinations: GCSE/GNVQ, GCE, SCE Standard Grade and National Qualifications (NQ)

7   School Leaver Destinations

8   Schools Statistics

9   Government Supported Work-Based Learning for Young People (WBLYP)

10 Vocational Qualifications

11 International Comparisons

1 EDUCATION EXPENDITURE

HM Treasury provided education expenditure figures in Tables 1.1 and 1.2 from their Public Expenditure Statistical Analysis (PESA). Expenditure on services is a definition of aggregate public spending consistent with Total Managed Expenditure (TME), where TME is a measure of public sector expenditure drawn from components in national accounts produced by the Office for National Statistics (ONS). It is the consolidated sum of current and capital expenditure of central and local government, and public corporations, but excludes net public service pension payments in Annually Managed Expenditure (AME), debt interest payments and other accounting adjustments. Gross Domestic Product (GDP) figures and deflators are based on the September 2003 National Accounts release. Table 1.3 reports identifiable expenditure on education services by country, and is also derived from PESA.

2 FURTHER EDUCATION STATISTICS

In April 2001 the publication of data on further education in England became the responsibility of the Learning and Skills Council (LSC), which took over responsibility for funding the further education sector in England from the Further Education Funding Council (FEFC). The source used for the FE data for England is the Individualised Student Record (ISR). At the same time the National Council for Education and Training for Wales (ELWa) became responsible for collection of information in Wales - statistics are provided by the National Assembly for Wales (NAfW). Statistical information on further education students in Scotland are provided by the Scottish Executive, from the Scottish Further Education Funding Council (SFEFC), and institutes of further education provide data for Northern Ireland to the Department for Employment and Learning (DELNI). The Higher Education Statistics Agency (HESA) provides data on FE students in higher education institutions in the UK.

3 HIGHER EDUCATION STATISTICS AGENCY (HESA)

From the academic year 1994/95 onwards, the Higher Education Statistics Agency (HESA) has collected information for HE students within UK HE institutions. The data collected include enrolment numbers, qualifiers and first destinations (home and EU students only from 1999/00) of qualifiers. The 2001/02 HESA student figures in this volume are taken from the July 'standard registration' count and are not directly comparable with those previously recorded from the December 'snapshot' count.

4 LABOUR FORCE SURVEY (LFS)

Please note that in the LFS tables some separate analyses will not sum to base figures shown

because of unpaid family workers, those on government-supported training and employment programmes, or those who did not answer, who are excluded from the separate analyses (see below for details).

The Labour Force Survey (LFS) was first carried out in the United Kingdom in 1973, as part of the UK's obligations as members of the European Economic Community, and was repeated every two years until 1983. Between 1984 and 1991, the survey was carried out annually, with results published relating to the March to May quarter.

From spring (March to May) 1992 the survey was carried out in Great Britain on a quarterly basis. In Northern Ireland the LFS was conducted in spring 1992 and spring 1993, and was then carried out quarterly from winter (December to February) 1994-95. For about the last nine years, there has been a quarterly survey covering the whole of the UK. The International Labour Organization (ILO) - an agency of the United Nations - agrees the concepts and definitions used in the LFS.

The survey is based on a random sample throughout the whole of the United Kingdom. Every three months almost 65 thousand households are contacted and information is collected about the personal and work circumstances of everyone living in these households. As well as these private households, the survey covers two groups of people living in a type of accommodation called *communal establishments*. These two groups are students in halls of residence (whose parents usually answer the survey questions on the students' behalf) and people living in NHS accommodation (which used to be called nurses' homes). The survey does not sample people living in other forms of accommodation - for example, army camps, local authority homes, or hospitals.

The results of each survey are processed and 'grossed', to provide estimates that cover the whole population. This allows us to say that there are about 28 million people in employment, even though the sample itself has only identified about 60 thousand employed people.

In April 2002 ONS issued re-grossed figures revising LFS estimates back to the summer quarter 1998. This is reflected in time series data used in the 2002 and 2003 editions of *Education and Training Statistics for the United Kingdom*.

LFS data presented here have not been reweighted to post-2001 Census revised population estimates.

CONCEPTS AND DEFINITIONS

All People
This group includes everyone of working age (Males aged 16-64 and Females aged 16-59) and comprises; employees, the self-employed, those on government

supported programmes, unpaid family workers, the ILO unemployed and the economically inactive.

Economically active – people aged 16 and over who are either in employment (did some paid work in the reference week) or ILO unemployed.

Employees / Self-employed – the division between employees and self-employed is based on survey respondents' own assessment of their employment status.

Full-time / part-time – the classification of full-time and part-time is on the basis of self-assessment. People on Government-supported training and employment programmes who are at college in the survey reference week are classified, by convention, as part-time.

Temporary employees – in the LFS these are defined as those employees who say that their main job is non-permanent in one of the following ways: fixed period contract; agency temping; casual work; seasonal work; other temporary work.

Government-supported training and employment programmes – This group comprises all people aged 15 and over participating in one of the Government's employment and training programmes administered by the Learning and Skills Councils in England, the National Council for Education and Training (ELWa) in Wales, local enterprise companies in Scotland, or the Training and Employment Agency in Northern Ireland. This group of people has been excluded from the separate economic analyses in the tables as the LFS generally undercounts the numbers involved. Administrative sources provide much more reliable information about this group (see separate source number 9).

Unpaid Family Workers – This group comprises persons doing unpaid work for a business they own or for a business that a relative owns. This group of people has been excluded from the separate economic analyses as it is relatively small (around 100,000) and when disaggregated many of the estimates fall below the publication threshold of 10,000.

ILO unemployment – the International Labour Organization (ILO) measure of unemployment refers to people without a job who were available to start work in the two weeks following their LFS interview and who had either looked for work in the four weeks prior to interview or were waiting to start a job they had already obtained.

Economically inactive – people who are neither in employment nor unemployed on the ILO measure. This group includes, for example, all those who were looking after a home or retired (as well as those aged under 16).

Industry – the classification of respondents' industry of employment is based on the Standard Industrial Classification 1992, SIC (92).

Occupation – the classification of respondents' occupations are based on the Standard Occupational Classification (SOC2000), introduced in spring 2001.

5   POPULATION

The population figures in Chapter 6 are estimated and projected numbers based on demographic data provided by the Office for National Statistics and the Government Actuary's Department, which incorporate post-2001 Census revisions. Data for the 'working age' category and sub-analyses, however, are taken from the Labour Force Survey (see source No 4 for further information), which do not incorporate post-2001 Census revisions.

6   PUBLIC EXAMINATIONS: GCSE/GNVQ, GCE, SCE STANDARD GRADE AND NATIONAL QUALIFICATIONS (NQ)

Data for England and Wales are produced from data provided by the GCSE and GCE examining boards and groups. GCSE and GCE data for Northern Ireland are derived from the Summary of Annual Examination Results and Further Education examination results. In Scotland pupils study for the SCE Standard grade (a two-year course leading to examinations at the end of the fourth year of secondary schooling) and Higher grade, which requires at least a further year of secondary schooling. The data source is the Scottish Qualifications Authority (formerly Scottish Examination Board). From 1999/00 additional new National Qualifications (NQ) were introduced in Scotland to allow greater flexibility and choice in the Scottish examination system. NQ include Intermediate 1 & 2 designed primarily for candidates in the fifth and sixth year of secondary schooling.

7   SCHOOL LEAVER DESTINATIONS

From 1996, information on the early destinations of year 11 pupils in England has been collected via the Careers Service Activity Survey. This replaced the former School Leavers Destination Survey, which collected information on the destinations of year 11 pupils in England and Wales. It provides data about the choices of around half a million young people finishing compulsory education each year. In Scotland, data on destinations of leavers of all ages are collated by Careers Scotland. School leaver information is provided by the Department for Employment and Learning in Northern Ireland. Data for school leavers in Wales are now provided by Careers Wales Association Ltd, and although included in Table 5.1, are not classified as 'National Statistics'.

8   SCHOOLS STATISTICS

The Department for Education and Skills carries out an annual Census of schools in England on the third Thursday in January. Data are collected on the number of schools by type; number of pupils by age and sex; number of admissions; pupils' school meal arrangements; number of teaching and non-teaching staff; course of study followed by pupils aged 16 and over;

number of classes as taught and number of pupils with statements of special educational needs. Data collected in January 2003 were published the following October in the publication *Statistics of Education: Schools in England*. From January 2002 onwards, maintained primary, secondary and special schools, as well as CTCs, have reported data at an individual pupil level. In January 2003, the pupil level coverage expanded to include non-maintained special schools and academies.

Corresponding annual schools census counts are also carried out in January for pupils in Wales (at individual pupil level from 2003) and October for pupils in Northern Ireland. The annual schools census count for pupils in Scotland is carried out in September (excluding information on school meals, which is collected in a separate survey in January) - although the course of study followed by pupils aged 16 and over is not collected, but examination results for each subject are received in August.

9   GOVERNMENT SUPPORTED WORK-BASED LEARNING FOR YOUNG PEOPLE (WBLYP)

The main Government supported work-based learning programmes for **young people** (aged 15-24) are Advanced Modern Apprenticeships (AMA) (Modern Apprenticeships in Wales, and formerly in England), Foundation Modern Apprenticeships (FMA) (National Traineeships in Wales, and formerly in England), Life Skills/Skill Build, and Other Training for Young People. The Department for Education and Skills funds these programmes in England, and in Wales they are funded by the National Assembly for Wales.

Modern apprenticeships (MAs) prepare young people for an economy based on high level skills. MAs aim to radically increase the supply of skills at craft, supervisory and technician (intermediate) level within industry. They provide quality work-based learning for young people to achieve qualifications at FMA (national vocational qualification level 2) and AMA (national vocational qualification level 3) levels.

Since September 2002, young people who are not ready for apprenticeship have joined a new high quality programme, called 'Entry to Employment', which replaces Other Training. This will give them the help they need to enter modern apprenticeships or other employment.

Until 25 March 2001, WBLYP was delivered through the network of Training and Enterprise Councils (TECs), however, since 26 March 2001, work-based learning for young people has been delivered through the Learning and Skills Council (LSC) in England and the National Council for Education and Training for Wales (ELWa), in Wales.

Until 25 March 2001, the statistics came from three sources: aggregate management information returns provided by TECs, certificates that training providers completed for each individual joining a programme (starts certificates) and a postal questionnaire sent to each trainee[1] six months[2] after leaving the programme, asking for information on whether they completed their training, usefulness of the training, their current activity and what qualifications they gained. While the questionnaires have changed several times since their introduction, the core questions have remained consistent. From 26 March 2001, the statistics for England come from the LSC-maintained Individualised Learner Record.

Since 1 April 2001, work-based learning for **adults** in England has been delivered through the Employment Service (ES) as an integral part of provision for long term unemployed adults. ES is now part of the newly formed Department for Work and Pensions (DWP) and data for work-based learning for Adults are no longer shown in this Volume.

Further details of WBLYP can be obtained from the Statistical First Releases (SFRs) at the websites shown in section 1.2 of Annex B.

10   VOCATIONAL QUALIFICATIONS

Information on awards of National Vocational Qualifications (NVQs)/Scottish Vocational Qualifications (SVQs), General National Vocational Qualifications (GNVQs) (up to 1999/00)/Advanced Vocational Certificates of Education (VCEs)/General Scottish Vocational Qualifications (GSVQs), and non-accredited full vocational qualifications outside the National Framework (Other VQs), and, for the first time, on Vocationally Related Qualifications (VRQs) made by UK awarding bodies has been taken from the National Information System for Vocational Qualifications (NISVQ) held by DfES. GNVQ figures for 2000/01 and 2001/02, based on the Secondary School and College Performance Tables, are not included in Table 4.5. As part of the NISVQ project, the Qualifications and Curriculum Authority (QCA) provides annual totals (October-September) of NVQ awards by framework area and level. This is used for grossing up the more detailed NVQ award information, collected from the awarding bodies who participate in NISVQ, in order to produce UK NVQ estimates. QCA's totals are based on quarterly returns sent by all NVQ awarding bodies. UK NVQ/SVQ estimates are based on grossed-up numbers of NVQs plus all SVQs.

NISVQ receives detailed information on awards made by four of the largest awarding bodies: City and Guilds, Edexcel, OCR and SQA. However, in 2000/01 the SQA were only able to supply a small amount of information on their qualifications, which meant that it was excluded from any analysis by level.

---

1 Apart from those known to have ceased training as a result of serious injury, serious illness or death.

2 In the past, follow-up surveys have been carried out 3 months after leaving up to December 1990 leavers for Employment Training and up to September 1990 leavers for Youth Training.

More detailed statistical information on the awards of Vocational Qualifications is presented in the DfES Statistical Bulletin: Vocational Qualifications in the UK 2001/02, which can be found on the DfES Research and Statistics Gateway (www.dfes.gov.uk/rsgateway).

11 INTERNATIONAL COMPARISONS

The tables in Chapter 7, International Comparisons, are taken from the Organisation for Economic Co-operation and Development (OECD) 2003 edition of the publication *Education at a Glance*, the OECD PISA (Programme for International Student Assessment) 2000, and the UNESCO (United Nations Educational, Scientific and Cultural Organisation) Statistical Yearbook 1999. It is important to note, however, that international comparisons of education and training are very difficult and should therefore be treated with caution. In addition, some knowledge of the underlying systems in different countries is extremely useful in interpreting the data.

Annex B

UNITED KINGDOM EDUCATION AND TRAINING STATISTICS: OTHER REFERENCE MATERIAL

1 GENERAL

1.1 Various summaries of education and training statistics for all four parts of the United Kingdom are contained in the *Annual Abstract of Statistics*, *Regional Trends* and *Social Trends* publications prepared by the Office for National Statistics. Some education statistics also appear in the *Digest of Welsh Statistics*, *Scottish Social Statistics* and the *Annual Abstract of Statistics, Northern Ireland*.

1.2 Each of the home education departments also publishes statistics in a variety of press notices, bulletins and statistical volumes. The relevant websites are as follows:

England: http://www.dfes.gov.uk/rsgateway
Wales: http://www.wales.gov.uk/
Scotland: http://www.scotland.gov.uk
N. Ireland: http://www.deni.gov.uk
              http://www.delni.gov.uk

2 OFFICE FOR NATIONAL STATISTICS (ONS) PUBLICATIONS

Social Trends is produced annually, No 33 2003 (£39.50. ISBN 0 11 621571 2) being the current edition. This publication brings together some of the more significant statistical series relating to social polices and conditions and presents a series of articles, followed by tables and charts. One chapter concentrates on education and training.

Regional Trends is also published annually, however, the latest edition, No 37 2002 was issued on 24th October 2002 as a web-based publication only. The publication brings together detailed information highlighting regional variations in the United Kingdom and covers a wide range of social, demographic and economic topics. One chapter concentrates on education and training. The publication can be accessed at http://www.statistics.gov.uk. Regional Trends No 38 is due for publication, in both hard copy and electronic versions, in February 2004.

UK 2004 (£37.50. ISBN 0 11 621661 1), formerly known as The Britain Yearbook, is one of the best known and most respected reference works available on the UK. This 55th Edition provides a mix of statistics, maps, photographs, tables and text covering all aspects of life in the UK. One chapter concentrates on education and training.

Guide to Official Statistics 2000 Edition (£32.00. ISBN 0 11 621 161 X) is a comprehensive guide to UK statistics, listing all the statistical censuses, surveys, administrative systems, press releases, publications, databases, CD-ROMs, and other services, by industry sector. The information is also available on StatBase at: http://www.statistics.gov.uk.

Labour Market Trends (incorporating the *Employment Gazette*) is a monthly publication with over 70 pages of labour market statistical tables. It also contains regular analytical articles using Labour Force Survey data and every month includes an LFS Help Line feature, which presents information frequently requested by users of the LFS. The price per issue is £9.50 and it is available from The Stationery Office Bookshops.

The Office for National Statistics on behalf of The Government Statistical Service (GSS) has created StatBase® as an on-line access system for deposited official data. The data comes from a variety of individual sources throughout GSS. This can be accessed via the ONS website – the home page can be found at: http://www.statistics.gov.uk.

3. INTERNATIONAL STATISTICS

A number of publications providing comparative statistics and indicators on education and training in different countries are now available – some of the most important are listed below.

Education at a Glance: OECD Indicators 2003. Organisation for Economic Co-operation and Development. Stationery Office, 2003. £31.00. ISBN 92 64 10233 7.

Key Data on Vocational Training in the European Union: young people's. European Commission, Eurostat, CEDEFOP. Stationery Office, 2000. £13.25. ISBN 92 828 6215 1.

Key Data on Education in Europe 2002. Eurydice, Eurostat. Stationery Office, 2003. £12.00. ISBN 92 844635 8.

Education across the European Union: Statistics and Indicators 1999. European Commission, Eurostat. Stationery Office, 2000. £28.00. ISBN 92 827 9797 X.

UNESCO Statistical Yearbook 1999. United Nations Educational, Scientific and Cultural Organisation. UNESCO Publishing and Bernan Press. £65.00 + VAT. ISBN 92 3 003635 8.

INDEX (BY TABLE NUMBER)